BUT IF NOT

days 588 LIVING with **cancer**

Brenda Pue (WITH CARSON PUE)
FOREWORD BY J. JOHN AND KILLY JOHN

But If Not: 588 Days Living with Cancer
Copyright © 2016 Brenda Pue with Carson Pue and Quadrant Leadership
All rights reserved
Printed in Canada
International Standard Book Number: 978-1-927355-79-4

Published by:
Castle Quay Books
Tel: (416) 573-3249
E-mail: info@castlequaybooks.com
www.castlequaybooks.com

Cover design and book interior by Burst Impressions
Printed by Essence Printers
References to Jane's blog, Pix n Prose, made with permission.

Library and Archives Canada Cataloguing in Publication

Pue, Brenda, author
    But if not : 588 days living with cancer / Brenda Pue
; edited by Carson Pue.

ISBN 978-1-927355-79-4 (paperback)

    1. Pue, Brenda. 2. Pue, Brenda--Health. 3. Pue, Brenda--Death and burial. 4. Cancer--Patients--Canada--Biography.
I. Pue, Carson, 1955-, editor II. Title.

RC265.6.P84A3 2016   362.19699'40092   C2016-906802-1

TABLE OF CONTENTS

FOREWORD

Let us encourage you to read this book from our friend Brenda Pue. As you will have already appreciated, this book is, at one level, an account of one woman's battle with cancer. Yet at a much deeper, truer level, it is not about death or dying; it is about life and living. In this book "life in all its fullness"—the sort that Jesus promises in John 10:10—leaps and bounds off every page. We were privileged to know Brenda, and the word "vibrant" ("pulsing or throbbing with energy or activity" says one dictionary) could have been invented for her. This collection of blogs and reminiscences of her last year and a half conveys exactly that aspect of her character.

We want to encourage you to read it because we live in a time when a book like this is astonishingly relevant and helpful. The first (and possibly most harmful) lie we hear as children is "and they lived happily ever after." Our modern culture likes to pretend that living "happily ever after" is not just possible but also a right. The fact of our mortality is denied to the point that when, inevitably, we come face to face with death, we can find ourselves confused and dismayed. Of course, for the follower of Christ there is the certain hope of eternal life, but the fact is that our lives—like any book or film—must at some point have an ending. This failure to come to terms with death and dying means that we can find ourselves astonishingly ill-equipped to consider the prospect of the end of our days.

This book is a healthy antidote to the failure of our culture to acknowledge our finite lifespan. And indeed "healthy" is the word. All the things you might expect to read in an account of 18 months' worth of ups and downs with cancer are missing. So there is no mawkish sentimentality, no bitterness, no recriminations and no desperate bargaining with God for extra time. Yes, there are prayers for healing, but there is the acceptance that this is in the Lord's hands, and when healing doesn't come there is no raging against God, only a contented acceptance of his will. And equally, there is neither a naive trivialization of death nor any glib triumphalism. What one is most struck by in this account is how, in the face of the unpleasant realities, Brenda displays a sense of peace and joy and delight in God's good gifts of faith, family and friends. It is no cliché to say that this book is both life affirming and death defying.

Brenda was a remarkable woman, and it is not surprising that her account of her last days is equally remarkable. We want to suggest that this written legacy is a privilege, a blessing and a challenge.

First, this account is a privilege. We are, as it were, invited in to be alongside Brenda, her family and many friends as they struggle together with her illness. This is deeply helpful. It is easy to talk about suffering in the abstract, as a problem for philosophy and a challenge to theology. Yet we do not experience suffering as a theoretical element in some academic debate; we experience it as a painful, life-shaking event. Here, however, we are involved in the solid realities of a chronic illness: of encouraging and discouraging medical results; of the bittersweet nature of birthdays, holidays and family gatherings under the shadow of parting; and of the trials of busy lives thrown into disarray by illness. Here we read of real faith in the midst of the severest of trials.

Second, this account is a blessing. "Where, O death, is your victory? Where, O death, is your sting?" writes the apostle Paul in 1 Corinthians 15:55 (NIV). Yet for many people intimidated by the looming prospect of life's end, Paul's words can seem to be the ultimate example of whistling in the dark. For a lot of people, the prospect of dying overshadows the business of living. Every birthday, every obituary heard or read, comes as a menacing nudge that one day our time will come. Here, however, Brenda's faith allows her to rejoice deeply and genuinely; in the midst of it all, she enjoys life. For Brenda there is sunlight in the valley of the shadow of death. This book is not about dying with cancer; it is about living with it.

Third, this account is a challenge. Brenda writes, "I have chosen to live life with faith." It's a phrase well worth pondering on. Brenda's life was one well lived with God. In her life she was an enormous help and encouragement to many, and as her legacy this book extends that influence. This book challenges us to think about our own deaths. Would we—will we—face our end with such radiant hope? But oddly enough this account is also a challenge to how we live. In this book we see open, almost outrageous, happiness and delight in the pleasures of life. There is deep rejoicing in little things in family, friends and fellowship. There is, too, a rich joy and hope in the reading of Scripture. In her dying, Brenda seems more alive than many of us in our living.

You often hear it said that someone "lost the battle with cancer." To read this book is not to read of any lost battle. In fact, to read it is to learn of a victory. This account sounds a splendid and defiant note of triumph. In her life Brenda was a woman who inspired many. We have found this account of her last days on this earth no less inspiring. May it be so for you.

J. John and Killy John

PREFACE
By Carson Pue

This book is a journal written by the inspiring Brenda Pue throughout her living with cancer. It is filled with courage, faith, humour, love and specific requests for prayer in her time of illness. Her words have encouraged not only those closest to her but tens of thousands around the world.

Brenda is one of the authentic ones, the real thing. I only wish you could know and hear her voice so the tone of faith, love and laughter might be heard in her written words.

This is Brenda's book. You will find a few guest entries at the beginning as we share what led up to her starting to journal her journey. The book closes with a glimpse of her legacy as our children tell of "Mom's" journey from their perspective. Once in a while Brenda would ask family to do an update when she was simply unable.

Amongst Brenda's many talents she was an editor, having edited at least six published books that I know of. So I struggled with whether to edit her entries and decided to leave them untouched with the exception of obvious mistakes or a missing word or context. In these instances, we have used [square brackets] to indicate to you the reader that these have been added for clarification.

My role now is to share with you how this all started and give the backdrop to her writing, so let us begin what is a heartening, raise your spirits, uplifting story of life with cancer.

DAY
1
TO
11

DAY 1 TO DAY 11—THE BACKDROP
By Carson Pue

It was New Year's Day 2014. Brenda and I had gone to the airport to welcome an new associate pastor and his family arriving to begin their new life in Vancouver. Following this joyous welcome with a small group from the church, we went out with Darrell and Sharon Johnson (our senior pastor and his wife) for supper. We had a wonderful evening enjoying one another's company and talking about the start of a new year.

Over supper, Brenda was just Brenda—full of joy, wisdom and life. My how we loved that simple supper. We said goodbye and got into the car for the hour drive home.

While I drove Brenda retrieved a message on her cellphone and put it on speakerphone so we could both listen. She thought for sure it was one of our adult children leaving a message or perhaps, even more delightful, a call from one of the beloved grandkids.

Brenda approaches everything with an "all in" attitude. You will discover this as you keep reading her journal. She was "all in" to retrieving this voicemail—smiling as she pressed the buttons on her phone to get to the messages. Over the speaker came the recognizable voice of our family doctor, calmly stating he would like Brenda to come in to see him the next day. Her smile turned to her classic "what's that all about?" look as she asked me, "Why would Mitchell want me to come in tomorrow?"

Without recognizing the prophetic import I responded, "I don't know, but when your family physician calls you on New Year's Day, in the evening, it's probably not good news."

"Yeah, you're right, but I just don't know what it could be," she replied.

And with that the car became rather quiet for the rest of the drive. When we got home, Brenda asked if I would pray with her that she would have peace and be able to sleep well.

The next morning, January 2, Brenda hopped out of bed full of enthusiasm to face the day. She went about her daily routine of a quiet time, a healthy breakfast and dressing beautifully for work. She looked stunning.

Brenda worked at Arrow Leadership Ministries, a leadership development program for Christian leaders in the church, mission organizations and the marketplace (www.arrowleadership.org). No, let me correct that. She didn't just work at Arrow; she lived it. Brenda was the national founder of the ministry in Canada, starting it in 1995.

"Are you going to see Dr. Fagan before work?" I asked.

"No" she responded, "I'm going to go after work. All the staff are back today, and it's time to come together as a team and get refocused after the Christmas break. I can hardly wait to see everyone."

Brenda loved her work! She loved mentoring younger leaders, the mission of Arrow, Steve Brown, the president, and all the team members. It was contagious. Her joy overflowed whenever she spoke of Arrow.

Late that the afternoon Brenda called me, asking where I was on my commute home from downtown. I told her I was about a half hour away and asked what the doctor had been calling about.

"We will talk about it when you get home. See you soon, sweetie."

With her adding "sweetie" at the end of her call, I thought, *It can't be anything she is worried about.* There was not a hint of worry in her voice.

Arriving home, I walked in the door, and she came flying around the corner from the kitchen with a huge welcome-home smile and kiss. As she helped me take my coat off she asked if we could sit down and talk before we had supper. This was when I heard the whole story of her doctor's visit.

You see, in late December Brenda had gone to our doctor to get a referral to see a physiotherapist because she had a "knot" in her side. She thought she had twisted improperly, and it felt like a pulled muscle. She had been suffering for several years from a car accident, and she went for treatments like this frequently to relieve the pain. Our doctor was very familiar with this and would probably not think anything of her need for a new referral. However, this time he examined her and thought it might be good to get an X-ray to ensure it was not a broken rib causing this pain.

Brenda could not recall any action that would have caused a broken rib; however, it was pointed out that even a loving hug from one of her strong sons could do that. So the X-ray was done immediately at radiology. When Dr. Fagan got the report, there was no broken rib. However, in the background behind the rib cage, they noticed there was something else. It was a growth about the size of a golf ball in her lung, which had to be investigated.

"Mitchell could not look me in the eyes. He looked down at the floor." She teared up as she described our beloved doctor. I could see she was shaken, and amidst my own shock all I could do was respond by holding her quietly for minutes, until she handed me the phone and told me our doctor would talk to me about any questions I had.

I called right away and spoke to Dr. Fagan on speakerphone so Brenda could hear. He began to lay out the course of what would be taking place over the next two weeks. Tests, a biopsy and scans that would lead to a diagnosis of the growth being either cancer or non-cancerous. He spoke of how fortuitous it was that Brenda came in with a pulled muscle, for it led to the X-ray and hence the discovery of the growth. Without that, it may have remained there growing or spreading for a much longer period of time.

Inwardly, I felt better after talking with the doctor. It did not change the news in any positive way, but I felt his personal care, concern and love, as we have over many years. He is an incredibly intelligent and experienced physician, always sharing what he is learning from the latest medical research journals. He has always led our family well in medical matters, and we trust him.

Brenda was never a smoker, so I couldn't help but wonder how this could possibly be lung cancer. You begin to cling to anything that offers hope. One thing that was being explored was the possibility of a certain type of fungus that presents itself much like lung cancer in scans. Just in the past few years Brenda had visited parts of the world where this particular fungus exists, and any traveller there could pick this up in their lungs. The tests ahead would determine what was actually going on, but you can appreciate how we reached for hope and would take a fungus over cancer any day. *O Lord, let it be a fungus!*

The next ten days are a whirl in my memory, although my journal is filled with notes of all the appointments, scans, and specialists we experienced. Brenda quickly accumulated 12 doctors treating her, and every day there were more tests. This was exhausting, both physically and emotionally. We tried very hard not to run ahead in our thinking. We just wanted to get the facts in front of us.

On Day 11, Brenda's lung specialist, Dr. Whitman, asked to meet with us, as she had the test results. It was a Saturday, and that morning Brenda was the guest speaker at a fellowship breakfast at our church. Our three daughters (by marriage) joined us that morning, and we listened as Brenda/Mom, the gifted communicator, was once again remarkable in sharing spiritual wisdom— especially considering that no one there realized we were leaving right afterwards to receive her diagnosis.

The entire family came except for our little ones. We arrived and crammed into the small office. Brenda sat in a chair across the desk from the doctor, with her three sons standing behind her, creating what looked like an arc of protection over their mom. Looks of concern among our children were mixed with hope and stirred by disbelief that we were even in this setting. They all wanted to be there. In our family, we do things together and we face things together. They wanted to hear first-hand from the doctor and be able to ask questions.

Dr. Whitman began running us through all the test results by telling Brenda that she was a model patient. First was the bronchoscopy, and it went very well. She then continued, "I couldn't see anything abnormal on the inside, but I did get an answer, and it is cancer."

Can you imagine having her job? I can't. But she was very good in writing out notes for us to take home, knowing that things might get a little blurry for us from that point on. Her first note said that Brenda had non-small cell cancer, and she explained that there are many subtypes, but it was confirmed as being cancer. The doctor told us that samples were being sent to the lab to check for the fungus, but she didn't expect that the test would show anything.

Dr. Whitman continued, "When we talk about cancer we also talk about the stage of cancer, and this pertains to how advanced it is and where it has gone to. You at this point are stage four."

Brenda was shocked by this, knowing that stage four is the highest stage. This news had the impact of someone rolling a small scale nuclear device into the room. We may have all feared it being cancer, but we had not anticipated an advanced stage.

Dr. Whitman then reviewed the bone scan and the CT scan, both of which showed the spread of cancer to her lower back and also that cancer was present in her brain. She hinted that the bone image might be a little questionable and we would have to monitor it carefully. The brain scan, however, was conclusive and showed that the cancer was metastatic.

"If cancer starts in the lung and then goes somewhere outside the localized region, it is considered metastatic. Where lung cancer likes to spread to is bone, brain and adrenal glands."

The doctor continued sharing while she changed the images on the computer so we could see the images of the cancer in the brain. She continued to show the CT scan, showing a nodule where the cancer in her lung was growing into her chest wall. "Now what this means to you is that…[long pause] this is unlikely to be curable."

Boom!

This was the first of many occasions when we would hear the phrase "unlikely to be curable" over the days and weeks that followed.

The treatment Dr. Whitman would be offering depended on the particular subtype of cancer that Brenda had. Dr. Fagan had already anticipated this and ordered an MRI and referred Brenda to the cancer agency for special genetic testing of the cancer to determine the subtype, to see if she might have a mutation of cancer that they could target with a new medication.

"Brenda, what this also means to you is you are no longer able to drive."

Boom!

This was such a shock to Brenda. It's one thing to be told you have cancer, but the severity was driven home (pardon the pun) when she lost her license. Her life was now being dictated by others, and the implications began to flood her mind. *What about my work with leaders? How will I get to party days at preschool? Can I fly? Can we go to Kauai as we had planned and do each January?*

How long do we have? Anyone in this kind of situation cannot help but ask the question of how long they will live, and our entire family wanted an answer.

I feel deeply for doctors who are put in the position of having this question asked, but they must get it all the time. I could not help but think that, when asked, doctors have a miniature lawyer from the hospital on their shoulder guiding their next words legally, as they cannot really give a precise answer, and there might always be a possibility of litigation from making a promise they cannot keep. Doctors work off of their experience and reams of data when answering. So the answer is always an average. It could be longer; it could be shorter.

Dr. Whitman responded with a range, saying that probably Brenda would be dead by June, but then she added, "You definitely will probably not see another Christmas."

Boom!

Another shock wave went through the room, and all of us were stunned. Brenda then calmly and kindly responded, "You don't number our days." The doctor acknowledged this with admiration for Brenda's response.

Brenda was referencing the story of Job in the Bible where he acknowledged that his days were determined, and the number was with God. God has appointed limits that we cannot pass (Job 14:5).

Brenda knew her Bible well, having read through it every year for as long as I can remember. So I cannot help but think that Brenda was already reflecting on Psalm 90:12 where the psalmist instructs, "So teach us to number our days that we may get a heart of wisdom" (ESV).

So I invite you in to our numbering of days with Brenda and in doing so pray that you may get a heart of wisdom into how you might number your days with faith, relationships, prayer, and the fun of making precious memories.

Within one day our daughter-in-law Kristin set up a communication and support system using the wonderful tool of Caring Bridge online, helped by her dear friend and Arrow graduate Steph, whom we Pues lovingly refer to as "the other brother," along with Sharon, Kristin's mother. It's an online journal that allowed Brenda to communicate without our having to answer literally thousands of calls or messages.

What follows is that journal, starting on Day 12.

DAY
12
TO
50

DAY 12—THIS WEEK
By Kristin Pue—January 12, 2014 1:32 p.m.

This week Mom will be having some further X-rays and an MRI. An amazing community of people surrounds us, and we know how much each of you cares for our family. Mom and Dad do not have the capacity for personal phone calls and emails at this time, and we ask that you use our online Caring Bridge site and the update email address for all contacts. We will do our best to keep you updated as regularly as possible.

My mom, Sharon Paterson, has become the point person for contact during this time. This week we will be setting up the planner for meal preparation and any other ways that you can practically help during this time. For those of you that don't know, Mom's driver's license has been taken away, and so we will most likely need some help with driving—this will also become part of the planner section on this site.

Thank you for coming alongside of us in this journey. We covet your prayers and your support and know that God has surrounded us with all of you for such a time as this.

DAY 13—DEEPLY MOVED
By Brenda Pue—January 13, 2014 10:32 p.m.

I started reading posts in the guest book and am overwhelmed by the outpouring of love, concern and prayer. Lots of tears, lots of smiles. Thank you doesn't seem enough, but I thank you all from the bottom of my heart. Please know that even though we are still absorbing the impact of this news—it's only been two days—God is holding us close, giving us peace and moments of such tenderness and beauty in the midst of seeming chaos.

Three prayer requests:
1. Healing
2. Fast genetic testing, which will allow accurate treatment
3. Intimacy with God to overcome fear

DAY 14—MY FAMILY

By Brenda Pue—January 15, 2014 12:38 a.m.

I woke up this morning with Psalm 16:6 on my heart: "The boundary lines have fallen for me in pleasant places; surely I have a delightful inheritance" (NIV).

I first met Carson when we were 18 years old. I was drawn to him by his passion for God, which seemed to match mine. My, we've had a good life together…which does not equal easy…but oh so fulfilling. He has made me feel so special, so accepted, and so loved. He's challenged me when that was needed and helped me to be the person I am today. There is so much I love about him. Watching him navigate my cancer diagnosis, arguably the greatest challenge we have yet faced together, has been nothing short of inspiring. True to form, he has been wise, real, and faith-filled. How blessed I am to be married to him.

My three grown sons, Jason, Jeremy, and Jonathan, have blessed me beyond measure. I love who they've become by God's grace—men of faith, integrity and humility who bring large doses of love, laughter, and grace wherever they go. And my three daughters, Kristin, Shari, and Kirstie—wow! They are so lovely, beyond what I asked God for and beyond what I could even imagine. And my grandchildren…I can't quite find the words. Watching them all process the news of my cancer has been the greatest pain I have ever known. We are deeply committed to journeying this road together and figuring out how to do it well with God's help.

Three prayers on my heart today:

1. For my husband—more courage, faith, and wisdom as he leads me, our family, and others.
2. For my children—that God would draw them close, give them courage, and to find the wonders God has for us.
3. The kids gave us a family photo shoot for Christmas, and we've decided to do it sooner rather than later—pray that it will be a great day for us all, including the weather.

DAY 15—MEDICAL TESTS AND BLESSINGS

By Brenda Pue—January 15, 2014 11:43 p.m.

Today I visited the third different hospital in 10 days, this time for an MRI of a lesion spotted at the base of my brain. My doctors are 99 percent certain that the lesion has spread from the tumour that is in my lung. The lung cancer was confirmed just four days ago, and we learned about this brain lesion at the same time. As well there was a "spot" in one of the bones in my back.

I lost my driver's license that same night due to the risk of seizures and balance problems. It took me a few moments to process that loss, and then I quickly realized the blessing in it. People I love would be driving me to and from appointments, and we would be given the gift of time with each other. Right now, time feels so very precious to me. I have loved the quality time I am already getting, initially with Carson and my kids, but that circle will now widen as we get more clarity on the treatment phase.

We have another appointment with my specialist this Sunday afternoon to get the results from this week's X-rays and the MRI. As well my doctor will show us images of the brain and chest CT scans, X-rays, and bone scan. All of our boys are coming to that appointment, partly to get an understanding of what is going on and to ask questions. But Jason, our oldest son, said that the reason why he wants to see the images is so that he will know beyond any shadow of a doubt when a miracle happens.

Another thing that has deeply touched me was this: Our youngest kids, Jonathan and Kirstie, had been making tentative plans to move to another city in the spring, and they made the decision to stay here a few days ago. I cried big, fat tears of joy over that! I am so deeply blessed by all the prayers of friends around the globe. Today I beseeched the Lord to hear the prayers of his beloved everywhere...

Three specific prayer requests from today:
1. That God would shrivel the lesion in my brain, along with the mass in my lung and the spot in my bone.
2. To not be overtaken by dread and fear, but rather to focus on life and blessing.
3. For genetic coding (via biopsy) of lung mass to be scheduled quickly.

DAY 16—A NORMAL KIND OF DAY
By Brenda Pue—January 17, 2014 12:01 a.m.

No tests today! In fact, I went for a hair appointment. How normal is that? This is in preparation for our family photo shoot tomorrow. Our family is busy getting haircuts and flu shots (I know, not your average preparation for a photo shoot), and we are all pretty excited about it. Our family group chat has been hilarious, deciding what to wear (if you know our three sons, you will have no trouble imagining this at all). I also enjoyed time today with various friends.

There are so many things that are life-giving to me right now. One is this Caring Bridge website filled with encouraging messages, amazing prayers, and bits of comic relief too. Another thing is a practice that Carson and I have every morning, reading from the Psalms, then praying through our day and praying for people. We also share communion each morning, and that has been a rich way to start each day. As well, I have completely filled our large bathroom mirror with various Scripture verses, which bless us all day long. God is giving us peace and courage.

We have sad moments, but they pale in comparison to the feeling of being held tightly by our God. We feel so incredibly loved.

DAY 17—TODAY WAS A GIFT
By Brenda Pue—January 18, 2014 12:48 a.m.

Our family all convened at Williams Park with our talented photographer, Tawn DiMeglio, and dear friends Curt (videographer) and Char (babysitter and coat holder extraordinaire).

The photo session started, and it was one of those days in a person's lifetime that will stay etched in the mind forever. There were some teary moments for sure, against a backdrop of love, support and faith. A very special finale warmed our hearts. A sneak preview will be coming soon.

My heart is so full of gratitude tonight. I love my family!

DAY 18—TRIBUTE TO MY MOM
By Brenda Pue—January 18, 2014 9:41 p.m.

I have been working on a surprise party for my mom's 80th birthday since November. It was planned for today, January 18th. When we received the cancer diagnosis last Saturday, I somehow had the presence of mind to ask my doctor if I could still go to my mom's party. She said, "You *must* go." All week I have been pondering how to make this party honouring for her, even though I would be seeing my siblings, aunts, uncles, niece and nephew for the first time since this news.

So we got up at 5 this morning [and] drove to Vancouver Airport, and after a cancelled flight and a bit of fancy flight maneuvering by my clever husband, we at last arrived in Penticton. I'm so pleased to say that it was a wonderful celebration of my amazing mom. We created a memory book for her while we enjoyed lunch at a restaurant. I was *very* honoured to give a tribute about the godly influence she has had on four generations in our family line…there were no tears (on my part), just pure joy and gratitude for a life well lived.

By the way, we gave Mom an iPad for her 80th birthday. How cool is that?

DAY 19—FAMILY PHOTOS
By Kristin Pue—January 19, 2014 10:42 a.m.

On Friday we had the privilege of having family photos taken. It was a very emotionally draining time for all of us, but it was so, so special. We laughed, we cried, and we made some great memories. We ended the day by having Pue family night, with dinner and time spent filling up a tribute book for Brenda's mom's 80th birthday. A very close friend came to the photo shoot to capture it on film for us. We had no idea what a wonderful thing this would be, and in less than a day, he surprised us with this beautiful video, and we'd like to share it with you.

DAY 19—FAMILY MEETING WITH OUR SPECIALIST
By Brenda Pue—January 19, 2014 7:13 p.m.

Today all our boys and Kirstie came with us to meet my specialist who diagnosed my lung cancer. She's great. The family loved meeting her as well, even though the news was hard.

We learned today that there are other small lesions in the brain, and *that* is now the primary focus of concern, rather than lung cancer. My doctor is trying to move forward my appointment with the oncologist to this week, rather than next week. Please join us in praying that it would be so.

This new information, although concerning, does have an upside…I am fortunate that the new lesions have not affected my speech, memory, etc., thus far. I consider this a great mercy from God. I believe more than ever that I am in God's hands and am choosing to live in faith not fear. Your faith and prayers continue to be a lifeline. Thank you for your great kindness, love, support and prayer for me and for my family on this unexpected journey. You are blessing us more than you will know.

Carson shared an image with me today from sailing that I loved…when charting a course in a sailboat towards a destination, one also takes the time to identify alternate safe harbours along the way, where, if need be, one can tuck in if the weather suddenly changes. We were on a course, and the weather has changed. So now we are heading on a new course to seek shelter in a safe harbour. You are part of that safe shelter for us, and we are grateful to God for you.

DAY 20—A REALLY ENCOURAGING DAY!
By Brenda Pue—January 20, 2014 7:46 p.m.

After the news of yesterday, today dawned brighter. It began with our usual time reading the Psalms that was *so* uplifting for us. The rest of the day was filled with life-giving moments and prayers that have refocused the sadness and fear I was feeling into hope and faith today. We feel so "held."

I forgot to mention the good news that the spot on the bones from an earlier X-ray was *not* present in the follow-up X-rays. That feels so huge and hopeful to us. Another answer to prayer is that my first appointment at the cancer clinic was moved one week ahead to this Wednesday morning. Your earnest prayers, loving notes, Scriptures and meals are a breath of fresh air to us. And finally, we are looking forward to meeting with our church elders for prayer this Thursday at 5:15 p.m. We welcome your prayer support wherever you are, as you are able!

What a great day!

DAY 21—IT HAPPENED AT PANDORA, OF ALL PLACES…
By Brenda Pue—January 21, 2014 10:57 p.m.

Another rich start to the day in the Psalms!
Carson headed off to work this morning for the first time, and my heart was full that he could be about his ministry calling today, doing what he does so well— loving, leading, serving God and others with such grace and transparency. Carson handed off the "wife care" baton to my sweet friend. This arrangement is in place in case of a seizure event, and I might add that only a very sweet friend would sign

up for *that* job. But today is her birthday, and we had plans to celebrate together, as we have done for so many years. What fine memories we have!

She was given a Pandora bracelet for Christmas, and I really wanted to get her a charm from me for her birthday this year. So off we went to pick out the perfect one! We were having so much fun on this outing, and then it happened…I started weeping quietly right there at the counter. The bewildered salesperson, someone I'd never met, reached out and put her hand on top of mine. It took me a while to recover.

I have chosen to live life with faith, and I know that my emotions in this season are a good and vital part of this journey. I am learning much from the psalmist these days. And it is good. I love life. I love people. I love God. Passionately! The past 10 days have only refocused and deepened that love for me. I choose life. I choose blessing. I choose faith. And that is making all the difference right now!

DAY 22—UNEXPECTED…
By Brenda Pue—January 22, 2014 10:29 p.m.

We thought our day was nicely laid out and organized. We had a plan! We love planning. We would meet my new doctor (a radiology oncologist) at 8:15 a.m. at the cancer clinic for a "consult" and then would be on our way home by 10:30.

This is such a new, strange world to me. We learned much about my diagnosis today. I like my oncologist. He is quiet, gentle, knowledgeable, patient and skilled. Pretty much the kind of guy I want to have on board at a time like this. He spent almost two hours with us. I asked lots of questions, and he asked more. At the end of the appointment, he sent us to a different part of the building to watch a video about radiation therapy. We were ready to leave for the day and move forward with our "plan"—Carson heading into work, and me with a couple of appointments that we were looking forward to. That was not to be. Instead…

- my radiation therapy treatment started today
- a new blood panel was ordered and drawn
- a diagnostic mammogram [was] booked
- an appointment [was] booked with a chemotherapy oncologist
- the oncology team decided to move forward with a biopsy of the mass in the lung

That two-hour appointment turned into a seven-hour episode. A dear friend and mentor once told me that "confidence is a by-product of predictability." It is a wonderful truth. The problem is that there is nothing predictable about a cancer diagnosis. The target keeps moving. And God is meeting me even in the chaos and confusion of the unexpected.

DAY 23—MUCH NEEDED PEACE AND QUIET
By Brenda Pue—January 23, 2014 10:58 p.m.

Today started quietly for us, and I was grateful. I'm on an anti-inflammatory medication to control cranial swelling that wreaks havoc with sleep. So I've been doing a split-shift thing with sleep the past week…awake from 2:30 a.m. to 4:30 or 5:00, and sometimes I'm able to get a couple more hours before getting up for the day.

Now that radiation treatments have started, I am being weaned off that medication. I'm praying that the radiation will work quickly and efficiently so I can stay off. The net result of all this is that I'm pretty much done in shortly after dinnertime.

I had my second radiation treatment later this afternoon, and due to the timing of that appointment, we were not able to make our prayer time with our church elders. I was pretty disappointed about that. It is still a high priority for me, and so we will plan to reschedule. My thanks to all of you who prayed anyway. I am deeply moved by your care, kindness and faith. What an amazing gift you are giving to my family and me.

Tomorrow will be my third radiation treatment, and then I get a break for the weekend before starting again on Monday. I can't tell you how great it is in this season of weariness to be enjoying the most delicious meals without having to prepare them all myself. I love cooking…just not right now. :)

DAY 24—MEDICAL UPDATE AND SACRED MOMENTS
By Brenda Pue—January 24, 2014 5:32 p.m.

Here's a quick medical update from today. I had my third radiation treatment, and second daughter Shari came, bringing lots of love and joy along (third daughter Kirstie came yesterday, and first daughter Kris will join us on Monday).

When we arrived home today, we learned that the lung biopsy has been moved from February 17th to this Monday. This place sure moves fast, and we are grateful. My mom is going to come and stay with us, and I'm so excited.

Two days ago, I shared about our whirlwind day at the cancer agency on Wednesday. There is something from that day that I am still savouring. After seven hours of appointments, meetings, tests, and trying to absorb information "on the fly," we began our drive back to Langley. I think the word that best describes the tone of that drive home is "numb." We arrived home, where some of our family awaited.

We had slowly begun unpacking the day when the doorbell rang. A dear friend and soulmate, who was scheduled to bring a meal, stood there with smiling eyes and arms loaded with food, roses, and more treats. We went into the living room to talk. She ministered to me in her winsome way, telling me all the different ways she is praying for me. She had taken photos and written captions for each one. I'm including two of the photos here for you. The first one is an image of "Carson and Brenda" nestled in the Rock (Jesus), and the second one is an image of our whole family, all 12 of us nestled in the Rock. As I sat with her, I knew that somehow God was divinely present in those few moments we shared. Peace washed over me in gentle waves. I believe that life is full of sacred and divine moments—I seem to be noticing them more lately.

Photo credit: Kathy Bentall

DAY 25—PONDERING PAIN
By Brenda Pue—January 25, 2014 9:49 p.m.

It was good to have a break from radiation treatments today. We've been told that the radiation keeps working post treatments. I confess that this afternoon has been physically hard for me, so I'm pondering the difficult concept of pain and suffering. I've had a range of feelings about this. And this isn't my first time in the ring, staring pain down.

We all instinctively avoid pain. And yet it is unavoidable. So what do we do with it? Some run. Some self-soothe. Some get angry and frustrated. And every now and again, you come across a remarkable soul who embraces it. These ones, I believe, have learned profound truths about themselves, about the world, and about God in the very act of embracing. I'm aware that the crux of our struggle is marrying the idea of a good God with human suffering. They just don't seem to "couple" very well.

One of my favourite books on the subject is called *The Problem of Pain*, by C. S. Lewis. He tackles this unseemly marriage in this book. I commend it to you, if this is something you are wrestling with as a result of my circumstances or someone else's situation. This quote from the book resonates with me:

> We can ignore even pleasure. But pain insists upon being attended to. God whispers to us in our pleasures, speaks in our conscience, but shouts in our pains: it is his megaphone to rouse a deaf world.[1]

Thank you for your kind words and beautiful prayers for my family and me. Please know that we pray for you too!

DAY 26—ANCHOR
By Kristin Pue—January 26, 2014 3:58 p.m.

For those of you that don't know me, I am Kristin, Brenda's daughter-in-law (married to Jason).

As I was driving to church this morning I was struck by the fact that only a short four weeks ago, we were finishing up our family Christmas activities and settling in to enjoy the last part of our holidays. A week later we started on this journey with Mom that has changed everything. The last three weeks have felt

---

[1] C. S. Lewis, *The Problem of Pain* (London: The Centenary Press, 1940).

like months, but in this time I have grown to love my family more and more with each passing day.

I married into the Pue family almost 10 years ago. From the moment I met Brenda and Carson, they treated me like a daughter. Jer and Jon have always been my little brothers that I never had. And for the last 12 years, my parents and Jason's parents have been friends. That is something I will never take for granted. The love and care that our two families share is beyond anything I could have imagined.

For as long as I've known Brenda/Mom she has carried herself with such amazing grace and faith. She loves her boys beyond anything, and she has wisdom that is better than any book! She has often been the one I'll call in tears of frustration in raising my two boys, and she gladly and calmly talks me through each situation. And no matter what she has going on, her family is always put above it, and in this situation that she is now faced with—this has not changed.

Mom is leading us all through this with such strength. Her unwavering faith, her positive attitude, her strength and her character constantly amaze me. Now I'm not saying she hasn't had her moments, because we all have, and we all will, but she always comes out with a smile on her face because she is being held by the hand of God.

As a family, we are constantly encouraged by the amazing support that you all have shown us. We know without a shadow of a doubt that there is an *army* behind us, praying for Mom and believing for her healing. Thank you for doing that for us.

There have been days that have felt so low, so hopeless, but no matter what, God has given us all a peace that passes our own understanding. This song has been one that I've clung to these last few weeks:

ANCHOR
By Ben Fielding and Dean Ussher

I have this hope as an anchor for my soul
Through every storm, I will hold to You
With endless love, all my fear is swept away
In everything I will trust in You
There is hope in the promise of the cross
You gave everything to save the world You love
And this hope is an anchor for my soul
Our God will stand, unshakeable

Unchanging One, You who was and is to come
Your promise sure, You will not let go
There is hope in the promise of the cross
You gave everything to save the world You love
And this hope is an anchor for my soul
Our God will stand, unshakeable
Unchanging One, You who was and is to come
Your promise sure, You will not let go
Your Name is higher, Your Name is greater, all my hope is in You
Your word unfailing, Your promise unshaken, all my hope is in You[2]

Beyond all the fear, the unknown, we know that God is our anchor and we know that He has the ultimate plan. Thank you for being a part of this journey with us.

DAY 26—CALM BEFORE THE MEDICAL STORM
By Brenda Pue—January 26, 2014 10:39 p.m.

I was given the gift of a beautiful, calm day today. I treasured this day. I want to remember all the details of this day.

Wife-care duty started at 7:30 a.m. so that Carson could head into church for the first time since this all started two weeks ago. It was so good for him and for the church to see each other. Meanwhile, at home, my friend and I read the Psalms and talked and prayed. Then we went for a long walk together.

When Carson got home, I made us a nice lunch, and we talked about the day. And then we went out for dinner together. It was a sweet gift to us, because tomorrow begins another big medical week. I have my fourth radiation treatment first thing in the morning, followed by an appointment with my radiation oncologist and finally a biopsy of the tumour in my lung. On Tuesday my fifth and final radiation appointment for this round is scheduled. The remainder of the week will be more tests, more results, etc. No wonder I'm so tired. This is a full-time job!

Here are a few of my biggest prayer concerns as I head into this week:

1. Minimize the impact of the radiation to all the normal, healthy brain cells while destroying the cancer cells.

---

[2] Words and music by Ben Fielding and Dean Ussher, "Anchor," © 2012 Hillsong Music Publishing, CCLI: 6514121. Used with permission.

2. No complications with the lung mass biopsy and that they would get a sufficient sample the first time—they don't make more than three tries due to damage/complications to the lung.
3. That the genetic coding of the mass shows it is treatable.
4. I need a diagnostic mammogram appointment very soon.
5. That in the midst of all this we would not lose heart.

Those are the biggies—I know God will lead you to pray the long list of things that are not mentioned. Thank you for standing with me, and my precious family, in the greatest challenge we have ever faced. Your kindness/mercy towards us is a gift too rich for words.

DAY 27—FIRST@WORK
by Kristin Pue—January 27, 2014

On Mondays, Dad (Carson) typically writes an e-letter that goes out to business leaders at First Baptist Church. This week, in his absence, Darrell Johnson wrote it. Mom and Dad asked that I share it with you all to read.

First@work: A Framework for Prayer

I know that you, along with literally thousands of other believers, are praying for Brenda and Carson Pue as they, hand in hand with the Lord, continue the aggressive treatments for the cancer. I ache for them. And I am humbled by their faith.

And I know that you are praying for others in your life—in your family network and in your workplace—who also need God to do a miracle. You are, no doubt, praying for Him to work a miracle somewhere in your own life.

So I thought that I would share with you the framework, so to speak, in which I am praying. The gospel truths on which I depend as I pray.

The Living God knows. Everything that we are facing. Every dimension of everything we are facing. Everything we are thinking and feeling about what we are facing. He knows it all intimately.

The Living God hears. Everything we pray. The articulated prayers, and those we cannot articulate, that may only get expressed as "sighing" (of which the psalmist regularly speaks). He hears.

The Living God cares. About everything we are facing. About everything we are thinking and feeling. About our longings, about our fears, about our dreams and nightmares. He cares. Deeply. Non-judgmentally.

The Living God is able. To do something about everything we are facing. He is, after all, the Creator of the universe! He raised the Lord Jesus from the grave; He overcomes the greatest of all enemies. "Now to Him who is able to do exceeding abundantly above all that we ask or think" (Ephesians 3:20 NKJV).

He is able, more than able, to do what no one else can do or dream of doing. If this were not so we would be wasting our breath in praying.

The Living God invites us to share with Him our heart's desires. I often do not know whether what I am asking Him to do is what He wants to do. He tells us to not let that bother us. He invites us to simply express what we want Him to do—no holds barred. Just lay it out there. "This is my will, Lord. I do want Your will. But this is mine." He knows what we are wanting anyway, so just lay it out before Him in all our uncalculated desiring.

The Living God then asks us to trust Him. To trust Him to be at work in what we are facing, trusting Him to be good and work for the good (Romans 8:28). For more is going on than what we see, hear, think, feel, understand.

Four days before Christmas in 2000, our then 18-year-old son Alex, whom we had adopted from Russia six years earlier, was hiking with a group of friends in the mountains and fell off a 120-foot cliff. He sustained broken bones all over his body, as well as injury to eight different parts of his brain. He went into a coma. On the night before Christmas Eve, as I drove home after spending the day with Alex in ICU, I was feeling all alone. I then heard in my head the following words, to which I have clung in other crises.

"Things are not as they seem.
In your life.
In your son's life.
In the lives of other patients in ICU.
Things are not as they seem.

More is going on than meets the unaided senses.

There is a God.

A good God.

A faithful God.

A powerful God.

A reigning God.

An ever-present God.

There is never a time when this God is not good.

There is never a time when this God is not powerful.

There is never a time when the God of the Bible is not attentive.

There is never a time when this God is not on the throne.

There is never a time when the God who comes to us as Jesus is not present.

It is His promise: 'I will never leave you or forsake you.'"

Pour out your heart to Him, and trust Him to do what only He can do.

In Christ,

Darrell

DAY 27 EVENING—DAY IS DONE AND COMIC RELIEF
By Brenda Pue—January 27, 2014 8:57 p.m.

It is so good to crawl into bed tonight after a big day. Carson, Kristin and I headed to the cancer clinic first thing this morning. The first appointment for their day was my fourth radiation treatment.

It felt good to introduce another daughter to the radiation techs and to show her around the treatment area. The treatment itself is quick and painless, and the technicians are very nice. Our next appointment was with my radiation oncologist (loved it that Kris could meet him too). It was an opportunity to ask him lots more questions.

At the end of our time—this is the comic relief part—I informed him that the toll-free number on his business card was actually a number for an escort service and probably a little more. The look on his face was priceless! The funny thing is that he's had these cards for years and no one else has ever mentioned this until today. I don't know why I find this so funny…but I have always loved Gary Larson's *The Far Side* kind of humour.

My CT-guided lung mass biopsy was scheduled for 1 p.m. I checked in at noon and got prepped for it. I was intrigued to learn that they would not use conscious sedation, as I had been told, because they needed me awake for this procedure. So I ended up watching the entire procedure, and it was fascinating. Now I am home, in bed, and glad to have this day behind me. Thanks for the many prayers that got us through this day. It's so good to be home!

DAY 28—RADIATION GRADUATION
By Brenda Pue—January 28, 2014

Today was my final radiation treatment, so I guess it's a graduation of sorts. My son Jason and friend Kelly accompanied me today, and we had a great day together. The hospital has a Starbucks inside, so after the treatment we sat and talked, long and deep, just the three of us. I loved that moment.

This day has been filled with so many blessings, and I find myself just wanting to "park" there for a while…

- I discovered that the flower urns on my front porch are now filled with colourful primulas instead of the dried Christmas decorations that were there yesterday
- my house got cleaned today
- an iPod filled with worship songs arrived today
- a couple of beautiful letters from long-time friends came in the mail
- the most amazing in-laws ever
- a CD filled with more worship songs
- my sweet husband, who is so "there" for me
- more treasures from God's Word that are life-giving to me
- your prayers and encouragement, which keep my focus right where it needs to be

This all adds up to a wonderful Radiation Graduation day for me! I couldn't be more grateful! I'll give more of a medical/prayer update tomorrow—just really wanted to focus on and celebrate the goodness of this day!

DAY 29—MEDICAL UPDATE AND A FEW PRAYER THOUGHTS

By Brenda Pue—January 29, 2014 10:59 p.m.

I thought I would share what I am experiencing physically today, in order to help guide your prayers. I still have my hair…apparently not for long, I'm told…but my oncologist and radiology techs all seemed surprised by that. I'm okay with losing my hair, except for my grandkids. That's a bit of a gulp for me. Would you please pray for grace around that?

I'm feeling the effects of radiation today…mild headaches, mild brain swelling/pressure, and mild nausea. I've learned that the effects of the radiation treatments will continue for two to three months…I'm hopeful that I won't feel like this the whole time. That's another area for prayer.

The lung biopsy went well, and I've had no complications at all. Also, in spite of the nausea, I have been able to keep eating and therefore I am able to keep my weight up. In fact I've gained two pounds and am feeling pleased about that.

A dear friend and mentor who has faced a cancer battle three times said to me that the hardest part of a cancer journey is what it does to the mind: fear, despair, hopelessness, etc., almost more so than what is happening to the body. As I look around the waiting room, at least in the radiation section of the clinic, that's exactly what I see on the faces of everyone there. What a sad place! Lord, have mercy. And I confess momentary struggles in my own mind. Much prayer is needed to overcome the impact that cancer has on the mind…not just for me but for so many. How blessed I am to be able to find relief, guidance and hope in Scripture and in your prayers.

Tomorrow evening we get to meet with our church elders for prayer. I'm feeling much in need of prayer and am so grateful to our church leadership for making this happen.

DAY 31—BLESSED BY OUR CHURCH

By Brenda Pue—January 31, 2014 7:58 a.m.

We (Jason, Kristin, Carson and I) had the joy of meeting with the leadership of our church for prayer. The Bible says, in James 5:14, "Is anyone among you sick? Let them call the elders of the church to pray over them and anoint them with oil in the name of the Lord" (NIV). So it's been in my mind and heart to do this since we received the cancer diagnosis earlier this month.

We walked into the room of our pastor's (Darrell Johnson) home, where all the leadership were gathered. Darrell led us through Scriptures, prayers and anointing with oil. The main Scripture that Darrell choose, Luke 18:35–43, was the same one that came to me two nights earlier in the darkness as I was lying awake. Profound. I will long remember this night…the faces of those amazing people, the prayers, the tears, the smiles and the incredible love in that room.

Our church has been one of the greatest blessings and expressions of care we have ever experienced. It just doesn't get any better than this. All four of us were deeply blessed by our church. I had been thinking I might feel a bit tired after this momentous evening, but the opposite happened: I was buoyed up with energy and joy! So, we ended up having a wonderful, spontaneous double date with our kids downtown. I didn't expect that. The whole evening felt magical to me!

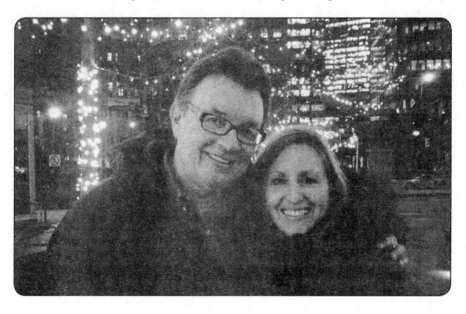

DAY 31—QUICK NOTE AND MORE TOMORROW
By Brenda Pue—February 1, 2014 12:17 a.m.

The top blessings of today came through family and a wonderful ministry friend. Today my mom and sister from Penticton arrived! My mom is moving in for a while, and my sister is here for her first instalment visit :) There is something about their presence that is "home" for me. More on that later....

And then there was the visit with our friend from Kuwait. He came in and we visited…deep, deep, deep. Then we went for a long walk together. The day was beautiful, and the conversation continued. We came back home, and he got down on his knees and prayed for us. It seems that people who minister in difficult settings seem to understand things about prayer.

DAY 32—REPRIEVE
By Brenda Pue—February 1, 2014 11:41 p.m.

I have a week off before a few tests and meeting with two different oncologists the following week: another radiation oncologist for follow-up and a chemotherapy oncologist (I think to discuss results from the lung biopsy and a treatment plan).

Here is one specific prayer for this week. My doctor has been gradually weaning me off an anti-inflammatory medication that reduces cranial swelling but has some nasty side effects like diabetes and sleep deprivation. Today was my last dose, and I'm praying that I will respond well enough to stay off that medication. I'm hoping for some much needed rest this week.

So the gift of reprieve this week is precious to me. It's good for me to be with my mom and sister right now. That wonderful place of knowing and being known, and being loved. That is family at its best, a place of honesty and grace. True home. I wish you could have seen my kitchen today. They decided to clean my pantry for me. I can honestly say, it has never looked that organized.

I think this is going to be a great week!

DAY 33—ISRAEL TRIP
By Brenda Pue—February 2, 2014 7:58 a.m.

Today is the day that Carson and I were to leave for Israel. We were to be part of the leadership team for a tour from our church. With my cancer diagnosis on January 11th, that door was firmly closed. For some reason, this loss felt big to me, even bigger than losing my driver's license.

So you may be able to imagine the significance of some very precious "gifts from Israel" that were given to me over the past two weeks. The first one came from our in-laws: a beautiful bottle of anointing oil from Israel. Carson uses it to pray over me every night before we go to sleep.

Three more gifts came from our long-time friend (from Toronto) who recently visited Israel and on the return flight home from the Holy Land changed his flight to Vancouver to hand deliver these gifts. The first of the three actually came via technology: a photo of my friend praying for me at the Wailing Wall. Not sure why, but I can't look at that photo without crying. The next two gifts were hand delivered: one is a little box made of olive wood and filled with eight little wooden communion cups, one for each adult in our family; and the second is called a mezuzah. It is made of Jerusalem stone with a tiny scroll embedded into the base of it. It is to be placed at the door of a home and is a Jewish blessing for all who enter or leave.

I'm overwhelmed by generosity and kindness. Needless to say, I'm excited about following the adventures of our FBC Israel study tour!

DAY 34—GOOD DAY
By Brenda Pue—February 3, 2014 11:21 p.m.

Today was wonderful—for lots of reasons. I slept well and a lot! That just feels so good right now. I feel like I'm catching up on the past few weeks of very little sleep. Headaches (and pressure) were minimal today. I keep a medical log every day, and today's is my best log entry. That gives me hope.

It was a beautiful sunny day, and we were able to go for a couple of long walks, both morning and afternoon. My sister cooked up a storm today, and since I happen to love eating…

The best part about today is celebrating my mom's 80th birthday. What a gift she has been and is to me. Selfless, humble, fun, energetic, godly, woman of prayer, wise, sensible, quiet, steady and faith-filled, just to name a few of her attributes. She has blessed me enough for two lifetimes. Although we formally celebrated this milestone birthday a couple of weeks ago, it is a joy to have her be the focus today. I almost had to wrestle her to the ground to keep her from cleaning the kitchen after dinner tonight! That's just who she is, and I love her for it.

Definitely a good day!

DAY 35—LEGACY

By Brenda Pue—February 4, 2014 10:11 p.m.

I have legacy on my mind a lot these days. Actually this isn't a new thing for me, because, thanks to the influence of Arrow Leadership over the past 19 years, legacy is a priority for me and a part of how I order my life. My husband, my kids, my grandkids, my family of origin, and my extended family have an important place in my life.

It might have been easy with a full and satisfying ministry career to relax my legacy standards. And sometimes it was a struggle to find a sense of rhythm with all the demands on my time. But I always had a sense that this was really important, and so I muddled through the best way I knew how. I can honestly say I've worked at being intentional about legacy. It just feels like there is a bit more urgency to my sense of legacy since my cancer diagnosis on January 11th. So today, I began working on a memory book for my grandchildren. It was a ton of fun! It is going to take a lot of time and effort to finish it, but I'm committed to it. I'm including a photo of the memory book with this journal entry. It's never too late to act on leaving a legacy!

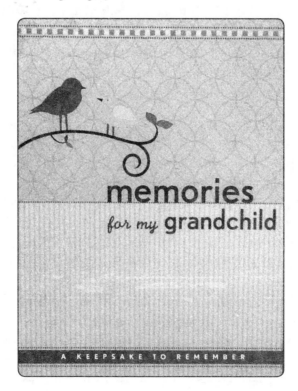

DAY 36—NAVIGATING TIREDNESS AND OTHER CANCER REALITIES
By Brenda Pue—February 5, 2014 10:01 p.m.

Last week when I met with my radiation oncologist, I told him that I struggling with my lack of energy as I have always been a high energy kind of gal. He looked me right in the eye and said, "That was before. This is your new normal. Listen to your body. Let your body lead you now."

I really needed to hear that. He was giving me permission to embrace this journey I am on, rather than fear it. I've noticed that Carson (and other family members too) is also struggling with various levels of tiredness. Carson read that great emotional sadness is the equivalent to eight hours of digging ditches by hand. However subjective that statement may be, it seems to be our reality right now.

Another reality is that my hair started falling out today. So I'm wrestling with the realities of what I am experiencing physically—low energy, hair loss, mild headaches and nausea—and what I am experiencing spiritually—peace of God when life isn't going the way I imagined or assumed it would. Which brings me to another thought. I've been through all kinds of ups and downs throughout my life, and I have found Him to be completely trustworthy and loving through it all. I can't help but feel that He was working hard at proving Himself to me so that I would be at peace and ready to trust Him for this very place I am in…a place where the faith of a lifetime meets tremendous need.

DAY 37—PACKING UP
By Brenda Pue—February 6, 2014 11:21 p.m.

Tonight I started packing for our family weekend at Barnabas retreat centre on Keats Island. Tomorrow, our whole family—yes, all 12 of us—will convene at the government dock at Horseshoe Bay. We will catch a water taxi to Keats Island and are looking forward to four glorious (though a little on the cold side) days at Barnabas.

The Irish have a wonderful expression for sacred spaces (rare locales where the distance between heaven and earth collapses). They call it a "thin place." It seems like certain areas are closer and more accessible to God. Barnabas is a "thin place" for me. Whenever I am there, God meets me in lovely ways. I'm praying that I will feel as good for the next four days as I have felt today!

I am excited! One suitcase is solely devoted to stuff for grandkids. Need I say more?

DAY 38—THE FINE ART OF WELCOME
By Brenda Pue—February 8, 2014 1:18 a.m.

We departed [from] the government wharf, adjacent to the Horseshoe Bay Ferry Terminal, under a clear blue sky. The sun was shining brightly. The seas were calm and sparkling. The grandkids were buzzing with excitement. It was a great crossing to Keats Island.

When we arrived at Barnabas, all the staff were there to greet us with lingering hugs, warm smiles and a few tears. It felt so good to be back at Barnabas once again. We hauled our 18 bags (and yes, we are only away for four days) to Applegate [our favourite cabin on the property]. What a sight met our eyes when we entered! There were fresh flowers everywhere (heartfelt thanks to my Soul Stream class for this beautiful and thoughtful gift) and delicious fresh baking, and the kitchen was loaded with amazing snacks. It will simply *not* be possible to lose weight this weekend. This will make my oncologist very happy! Our dinner was an exquisite Barnabas gourmet creation, for which they are so well known.

As I write this, I realize that I am completely overwhelmed by the warm welcome that has embraced our entire family. Having been a recipient of many warm Barnabas welcomes for many years, I now place high value on the art of welcome…the art of making people feel special. Our lives are often so hurried and rushed that *welcome* isn't always practiced the way that it could be. At least that is my experience. After today's welcome from our dear friends at Barnabas, I am inspired.

I also realize that this experience feels familiar to my soul. Simply put, I have felt welcomed by God my whole life.

For me, God is the ultimate *welcome,* and Barnabas is a close second.

DAY 39—AMAZING DAY
By Brenda Pue—February 9, 2014 12:13 a.m.

Today dawned beautiful and sunny. It officially began with a wonderful Barnabas breakfast served at Applegate. We set up a movie for all the kids, so the adults could read a psalm and share communion together, as has been our regular practice. It was lovely to experience this as a family.

Afterwards Landon and I made bracelets for some of the family. Then we all got dressed in our winter gear and walked down to the beach to throw stones in the ocean. Other activities of the morning included time in the pirate ship playground and playing ice hockey on the frozen pond. Lunch was served in the dining room and was typical Barnabas amazing.

Although this entire day felt sacred…eating, playing, music, Scripture, talking, reading, resting, laughter, delighting in the children and the sheer beauty of the day…God had more for us. After lunch we put the kids down for a quiet time, and the Barnabas staff team came over to Applegate to share with our family about some of the healing moments that have occurred over the past few years in this "thin place." Next they gathered around our family and prayed for us all. It was hugely encouraging for us.

After a little quiet time, we enjoyed more outdoor time with the kids. Jason, Landon, Liam and I played tennis in our winter coats, toques and gloves. This was Canadian winter tennis at its best. It was a ton of fun. And, wonder of wonders, suddenly it was time for another beautiful Barnabas gourmet dinner. After we got all the kids settled into bed, Carson led us through a sharing time as a family. This, too, was lovely—honest, hopeful, helpful sharing as a family.

Wow—what an amazing day!

P.S. I should tell you that I am now sporting a short haircut, compliments of my second daughter, Shari, who has been trained [as a] hairdresser. I will post photos from this weekend as soon as I get home.

DAY 40—REST
By Brenda Pue—February 9, 2014 4:06 p.m.

After the excitement and beauty of yesterday came…rest. It was a gift. I wish I had taken photos of everyone sleeping after breakfast, but I was sleeping too! A few of us went to play ball hockey and winter tennis after our morning nap.

Rest is one of the good gifts that God gives us. It is built into all of creation, including you and me. I have never been one to rest during the day, until recently. I think I felt like I would be wasting time. Now rest has become a necessity for me. I have relinquished this seeming "wasted" time to God, along with a long list of many other things that I have relinquished since this cancer journey began. Things like my energy, my physical body, my independence, my waking and sleeping hours. I have handed all these things over to God, and it hasn't been as difficult as I thought it would be.

God knows that I have a few projects and dreams that are on my heart. Would you join me in praying that the rest I am given will provide the time and energy to realize those dreams in due season?

DAY 41—MAKING MEMORIES
By Brenda Pue—February 10, 2014 9:44 p.m.

We arrived home from our Barnabas weekend with full hearts. Yesterday when Landon and I were out walking, he said, "Grammy, wouldn't it be great if we could all just live here in this big house together, forever? I love it here." I agree that it was a truly wonderful time for all of us. A fun project that Landon and I did together this weekend was making custom bracelets for the whole family.

It's good to be home, though.

Now begins a new week, and here is what I'm facing: I am back into doctor appointments and more tests this week. The main appointment is another brain MRI on Thursday. This will be to determine what is happening with the cancerous lesions in my brain. I hope to get the results from the MRI the following week. I am experiencing fewer and less extreme headaches. I'm not entirely pain free but grateful to be feeling better than I was. I've noticed whenever I have a test or scan that my mind fills with questions. And the one thing the human brain doesn't like is an unanswered question. So this will be a week of waiting until I get some answers. Since patience is not my strong suit, I will be leaning in to God a little more this week.

Enjoy a few photos from our weekend.

DAY 42—TSUNAMI AND HOPE

By Brenda Pue—February 11, 2014 8:43 p.m.

We received a card today with a drawing of a great wave on the front, and inside the card it talked about this experience being a personal tsunami. I closed my eyes for a moment to fully absorb the impact of that word picture. That is an apt descriptor of how this journey has felt for us. And like a tsunami, with little warning and little time to prepare, the results are unpredictable as far as how each day after unfolds.

And in all this uncertainty God shows up in hundreds of ways to bring hope. Every card, every meal, every flower, every Scripture, every gift, every act of kindness, every song, every message, every prayer brings *hope* to our overwhelmed souls.

As we were leaving Barnabas yesterday, my dear friend Kathy, who heaped blessing upon blessing on our family throughout the entire weekend, handed me a Christmas children's book and said, "This is to read to your grandchildren next Christmas." I haven't read the book yet, because every time I look at it the tears come. Not tears of sadness, but tears of hope.

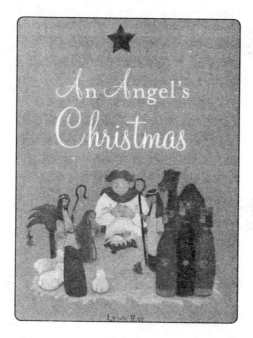

DAY 43—ECLECTIC DAY
By Brenda Pue—February 12, 2014 9:05 p.m.

My day began with a friend recording a short video greeting for Arrow Leadership alumni, before my first medical appointment of the day.

Sharon (Kristin's mom) and my mom accompanied me to a radiation follow-up appointment to track what I have been experiencing this past week since my brain radiation treatments. I reported that, generally, I have fewer and less intense headaches and that I am off all medications. Gale, my radiation therapy nurse, asked lots of specific questions and at the end of our time said, "You are doing *really* well." And, with the exception of a couple of rough days, I do feel so much better than I have felt in a couple of months, in terms of head pain.

My second appointment of the day was more medical imaging, and I will share results, hopefully next week.

Now for the fun part. I took Sharon and my mom to the cosmology department at the cancer agency. It is full of wigs, hats, toques and scarves. Because I am losing my hair at an alarming rate the past few days, and since Carson is liking my new short hair look, I asked if I could buy a short-haired wig. Brianna, who was overseeing this department today, said, "You can *have* any one wig and two hats you like." I was so astonished at such generosity that there was a notable loss of oxygen in the room for a few moments when I inhaled. :) So Sharon and Mom helped me choose a short wig and a scarf today.

The wig, while fun, is a visible reminder of the storm that rages around me. Despite the storm, I feel peace, joy and contentment in my heart and soul... remarkable gifts from my Heavenly Father...that are indescribable but so real to me.

DAY 44—LIVING A DIFFERENT STORY
By Brenda Pue—February 13, 2014 9:31 p.m.

I read an article today by J. I. Packer drawn from his latest book *Weakness Is the Way*. I share it with you because it is a very real part of my journey over the past month. Packer was born in 1926 and writes from personal experience of one who has navigated 88 years of life in this world. He says, "The Christian way of life and service is a walk of weakness, as human strength gives out and only divine strength can sustain and enable."[3]

I simply cannot function the way I always have. I have loved being strong and, yes, even powerful. But I am not that right now. I am learning to find contentment in Christ being my strength. He is so much better at this than I ever was. As Packer says, "We all crave to be admired for strength in something."[4] This was my story.

Now I'm living a different story. I am learning to lean in to 2 Corinthians 12:9: "My grace is sufficient for you, for my power is made perfect in weakness" (NIV). By leaning in, I mean that I am not panicking about pain, weariness, hair

[3] J. I. Packer, *Weakness Is the Way* (Illinois: Crossway, 2013), 22.
[4] Packer, *Weakness Is the Way*, 50.

loss, etc. Even though what I am experiencing is strange and uncomfortable, I am putting my hand in His and trusting God to lead the way. It's actually a relief to not have to manage all this. So, no panic...just lots of grace and peace.

And while I'm on the topic of grace, I was delighted to learn that I didn't have to have the MRI after all! A mistake was made in scheduling—they forgot to cancel the original appointment after it was moved forward a month. I was on the phone with my doctor (real time), who suggested, "Perhaps the person who made the scheduling could use your MRI slot." LOL :).

So instead I enjoyed lunch with my friend, my mom and my third daughter, Kirstie. That's *way* better than having an MRI of my brain.

DAY 45—A WORD ABOUT MY MAN TODAY
By Brenda Pue—February 14, 2014 3:39 p.m.

The first words Carson spoke to me this morning were "We've celebrated 38 Valentine's Days together." He loves any opportunity to celebrate the two of us, not just on Valentine's Day. He has loved me so well all these years. So many times I have thanked God for Carson and have wondered what I ever did to deserve him. In the end I've decided he is God's gift to me. God knew I would need someone just like him.

I know if Carson was writing this, he would probably say the same thing about me. We've been married long enough to finish each other's thoughts and sentences. But somehow I feel like I got so much more.

I've often pondered the secret of a great marriage. My best thought on this is mutual humility. I became a follower of Jesus when I was 12 years old. That was my first profound act of humility. That was when I first admitted my pride and my selfishness to both myself and God. This first moment of humility has made all the other moments of humility possible. And there have been many. This has not been one-sided. Carson became a follower of Jesus when he was 17 years old. This was his first humbling moment with God. Having experienced humility to the depths has allowed both of us to long for forgiveness, which has built great trust between us. It's worked so well for us for almost 37-plus years...

Another benefit of mutual humility is that it has produced authenticity in our marriage and in our family. I am grateful for a loving, godly and trustworthy husband, who is a ton of fun, very wise, full of adventure, and who loves laughter, loves others and just generally loves life.

DAY 46—THE LIST OF THINGS ON MY MIND
By Brenda Pue—February 15, 2014 4:17 p.m.

There are a number of things that I find myself thinking about these days. So I thought I would download my list. Yes, I am one of those "list" types. The reason is that I have been influenced by a story that I heard years ago and have put it into practice for years in both my ministry context and the home context.

I wish I could remember all the specifics, but here is how I remember the story. A US company hired the president of another successful enterprise as a consultant. What did the company want? They asked the consultant for the number-one business practice to which he would credit the success of his company. They offered to pay him a large sum of money for his help.

So the president agreed to meet with them as a consultant. His idea? Have each person on the leadership team make a list every day of the top ten things to be accomplished and prioritize each item. Tackle the critical must-dos first, working through the list. Any unfinished items simply move to the next day. The business that hired the consultant agreed to try it. It worked so well that they ended up paying the consultant double the agreed-on amount.

When I first heard this story, I decided to try it, and it has been a helpful practice over the years. However, the list that is swirling around in my mind doesn't lend itself to being an action checklist per se. But here's a list of what is most on my mind and heart lately:

- the impact that my cancer diagnosis has on my immediate family
- the impact on my parents, siblings, friends, and relatives
- the impact on younger ones
- the impact on Arrow Leadership with my sudden, unanticipated departure
- time for legacy matters
- time for research and pro-active health
- the unknowns of the impact of treatment
- the uncertainty around energy and my tiredness
- our meeting on Monday morning with my new chemotherapy oncologist re lung biopsy results and possible new treatment plan
- wisdom to prioritize my limited energy
- my whole scalp soreness from radiation
- my desire to live in the present while giving attention to some future matters
- living in hope and faith

This is my list. These are the things that wander through my mind and heart that I find myself praying about. If you are a praying person, I invite you to join in. Thanks for every prayer and every encouragement along the way. I know that God is hearing. I sense that He is up to something. I have no idea what, because I'm not Him. And I'm deeply humbled and blessed to have you along on this journey…

DAY 47—GRANDCHILDREN

By Brenda Pue—February 16, 2014 9:41 p.m.

Today is my second oldest grandson's birthday. The whole family was there to celebrate. What an incredible privilege it is to be a part of a grandchild's life. I love experiencing life through a child's eyes. How refreshing is a child's sense of wonder at the world! It's so good for us busy and overwhelmed adults to be with children (and I would add dogs too). Children and dogs have no idea how to be anything other than who they are. There is something so wonderful about that. We all *need* children in our lives.

Photo credit: Tania Di Meglio, RedHanded Photography

I also believe [in] investing in following generations as a great trust as well. I want to pass along my love, values and faith to the next generation and the next. It's my joy and my responsibility. It requires time and effort to invest in children and grandchildren, but it pays huge dividends—I would say eternal dividends. If I am given more time on this earth, this is how I want to invest my life…serving generations that follow and serving my God wholeheartedly.

For Christmas, our kids gave us a gift of a family photo shoot. We had planned to do the photos [in] late spring or early summer. When we received the news of my cancer diagnosis we decided to do the photos right away. Enjoy this photo of my beautiful grandkids.

DAY 48—MEDICAL UPDATE AND FAITH WORDS
By Brenda Pue—February 17, 2014 7:19 p.m.

Carson and I met with my new oncologist this morning at 9 a.m. She is a chemotherapy oncologist. My last oncologist specialized in radiation. We learned that my last lung biopsy was inconclusive in terms of a chemotherapy treatment plan. This was the last thing we expected to hear today, even though this is not unusual. So we made the decision to move forward with one more lung biopsy. This will be my third and last biopsy. So I'm hopeful that this procedure will be conclusive. A request has been made for the biopsy to be done in a week. Then waiting for results. Then sorting out a treatment plan. And so we wait…

In the meantime, I have been pondering a verse in the Bible: "Man shall not live on bread alone, but on every word that comes from the mouth of God" (Matthew 4:4 NIV).

What this means for me as I walk this road is that there is so much more to my life than my physical, material being. If that is all I have as I travel along, I'm pretty much doomed. The hope part of my journey is that I live on every word that comes from the mouth of God.

As I think on that, I realize that I need to read and digest God's words and His perspective on *everything*, including cancer.

I received an affirmation of this today. I read a true story about a woman who was given three weeks to live. She took to heart the story in the Bible from John 2:1–12 where Jesus' mother said to some servants, "Do whatever he tells you" (NIV). Twenty-two years later, this lovely woman still lives by "Do whatever God tells you." In other words, she has taken the time to absorb God's Word daily for 22 years.

I've found [that] God's words have been profound all my life. Now, I feel like God's words are life itself. This is the kind of bread I want to eat every day!

Our day ended better than it started. We met with our kids tonight to talk through our disappointment and to pray together. How I love doing this journey with our family…they are amazing. Total blessing!

DAY 49—HOW OR WHEN?
By Brenda Pue—February 18, 2014 10:16 p.m.

I'm not sure how it happened or even when it happened. But somewhere in my life journey I got the idea that I would live to a certain age. In my mind I had it all sorted out. I even decided the perfect way for me to pass from this life into the next. Of course it would be painless. And the best part is that it would be what I wanted and how I imagined it. These are just two of a very long list of assumptions that I've made about my life and myself.

My cancer journey has challenged every preconceived notion I ever made about life and myself. I am asking myself hard, uncomfortable questions. God is opening my eyes to see more than I've ever seen before. Why am I entitled to anything? It's an easy answer. I'm not. I don't deserve anything at all. Why should I deserve more or better treatment than any other person? It pains me to see others who have been given such a heavy load to bear in this life. So many people endure far greater suffering than I will ever know.

It feels like God has stretched my heart and mind wide open to see outside of the box. I'm seeing life, God and myself differently. I'm feeling things I've never felt before, and I'm praying differently. Marriage, and family, is richer. Every night Carson and I share our top three blessings of the day. There have been so many. Amazing! I no longer feel the need or desire to control my destiny. I feel more strongly than ever that God's got this at so many levels.

P.S. I learned today that my lung biopsy is scheduled for this coming Monday (more on that later this week). I am grateful that it is moving forward quickly and that wheels are set in motion for treatments as well.

DAY 50—THE PEOPLE CLOSE IN
By Brenda Pue—February 19, 2014 9:21 p.m.

My mom moved in with us a few weeks ago. What an incredible gift that is to us. I know she is deeply missed by her family, church and friends back home—thank you all for understanding that we need to be together now. I appreciate sharing these precious days with her. What an amazing gift she is.

Since I am not able to be on my own due to the possibility of seizures (to my knowledge, I haven't had one), I can't think of anyone better to hang out with. She "gets" me. God definitely cut us out of the same piece of cloth. So it is easy and comforting to be together in this season of unknowns.

Mom is also a gift to Carson. He has been able to be back at work without worrying about me. That is huge, as he has lots going on at so many levels. I pray for him the most, knowing that it is such a helpless feeling for a spouse. So much of our lives has changed the past five-plus weeks. Just having my licence taken away has been a game changer for us. I'm not able to support him in that way anymore, which has added a degree of difficulty to our lives.

I feel that these ones who are "close in" need some extra prayer these days. They absorb the day-to-day realities with me and need extra prayer covering. I am grateful for all the extra help we are getting, with driving, meals, prayer, practical care and your encouraging cards and posts. My heart is full. Thank you!

DAY
51
TO
100

DAY 51—A LETTER FROM THE FAMILY
By Kristin Pue—February 20, 2014 7:14 p.m.

Since January, when we received Mom's diagnosis, our lives have changed. We have been completely blessed by the outpouring of messages, prayers and love from our "village" or community. We want to take a quick moment to thank you for your support. Even just logging on to the website and seeing the nearly 20,000 visitors is so encouraging. Because this has been a difficult journey that we have embarked on, it's almost unimaginable how we could ever do this without all of your love and support. Honestly, we have a hard time communicating just how much your support has meant to our mom and the rest of our family.

We as a family have always lived fast-paced, action-packed lives. We fit a lot into everyday life, and one of the things that we have noticed is that we no longer have the same capacity day to day that we used to have. It has become normal for all of us to experience exhaustion. Our time and energy are very precious to us right now. One thing that we are seeing in our mom is her desire to accomplish some important priorities each day. We are learning that in order for her to be able to accomplish these priorities each day we need to be better stewards with her time and energy. As her family we are doing everything that we can to help her make each day count.

One thing that we have noticed is our mom's heart to connect with each and every person who has reached out to her in this time. However, the reality of her situation is that this simply is just not possible. We hope that you can help us remove a bit of pressure from her life by simply understanding that she may not be able to respond to all of her phone calls, text messages and emails as quickly as she normally would. I know for many of you this would go without saying, but we just want to say it on her behalf so that she knows you will understand.

We also understand that many of you would like to have some time with Mom, so we would like to set up a few guidelines to help steward our mom's time so that she can use her energy doing what she both loves and needs to do, including time with family and friends, without having to worry about scheduling and appointments. So we are asking that you call Sharon Paterson to schedule an appropriate time. We also ask that you keep the visits to 20 minutes, so that she is able to thoroughly enjoy the time with you without feeling the stress of wanting to stay engaged when she doesn't have the energy to do so. Thanks for understanding our circumstances and needs. Thank you again for loving and supporting her in so many beautiful ways.

We have also added grocery shopping to the planner section, as this is another way that help can be provided. Right now the grocery shopping has been added to Thursdays. *Thank you!*

Jason and Kristin

On behalf of Jeremy and Shari and Jon and Kirstie too!

DAY 52—THE STRANGER IN THE MIRROR
By Brenda Pue—February 21, 2014 9:56 p.m.

When I get up in the morning and look at myself in the mirror, a stranger looks back at me. While I sleep I forget everything that has happened these past weeks, and the stranger looking back at me reminds me that this cancer journey isn't just a bad dream after all. So each day, the stark reality of my health looks me squarely in the eye. I need God more than I know.

There have been other times throughout my life when I've faced down a stranger in me. Mostly when I've seen things in myself that I didn't like seeing. Things that made me uncomfortable with me. God has faithfully led me through those moments too.

So these days I wake up early. After my mirror moment, I need to reorient myself as God's beloved daughter by reading the Bible, reading a few devotionals, and spending time in prayer (this is a long-time practice that has allowed me to climb outside of me to see myself and the world from a wiser perspective). This is one of the places where God meets me. There are many other meetings between us each day. I have no idea how I could manage this journey without my Father above.

At the end of every day, the person who looks back at me in the mirror isn't a stranger anymore. I've come to terms with her throughout the day. I have a new perspective. I am filled with gratitude and blessing. There is so very much I am thankful for.

DAY 53—BLESSING OF FRIENDSHIPS
By Brenda Pue—February 22, 2014 9:07 p.m.

Someone once said that friends double our joy and halve our sorrow. I have always felt that to be mostly true in my life. There is something so wonderful about sharing all of life with friends.

Carson and I have amazing friends. We love what friends bring to the table of life. Things like laughter, understanding, kindness, challenge, prayer, wisdom, adventure, caring and loyalty, just to name a few. Our lives are so rich because of friends whom we love and who love us. So I believe that adage to be, as I said, mostly true. Until recently, that is.

Since this year began, and my diagnosis, I've likely cried more over…with…because of…friends (and I include my family here) than anything else because I am so deeply blessed by friends. I feel more deeply than I have ever felt before about this treasure of friendship. And honestly, I've come unglued a few times over it. So I want to take a few moments to say thank you to all of you who have invested your lives [in] mine (and ours). Some of you, for 20 or 30 years or more. Some of you are Arrow friends, and we've gone deep. And others of you we haven't known as long, but your impact and influence on our lives are profound. All of you have made a difference. You have brought much joy as you've journeyed with me (and us) in this storm. Thank you!

DAY 54—ONE PERCENT PERSPECTIVE
By Brenda Pue—February 23, 2014 6:26 p.m.

A highlight from today was attending our granddaughter's baby dedication along with her parents, Jeremy and Shari. She is the first girl in our family. Need I say more? It was so wonderful to witness this precious one being dedicated to God. I've included a photo of four generations (Great Granny—my mom, Grammy—me, Mommy—Shari, and, of course, Ellie).

As I head into my lung biopsy tomorrow morning, I have lots of emotions and feelings. Earlier this week I mentioned that my earlier biopsies were inconclusive and so we made the decision to try one more time. One repercussion of this procedure is that I am not able to do anything for a period of time and [am] literally grounded until the lung heals fully. Knowing that fact caused me to pause when making the decision.

The motivation for moving forward with this decision has to do with the course of chemo treatment that is recommended. One chemo option is clearly better in terms of side effects than the other. Here is why. Only 10 percent of people with lung cancer are "never smokers." I am a never smoker...well... except for a couple of puffs when I was in grade eight (it didn't go well, and thus ended my short-lived smoking habit). I digress. Of those 10 percent, 40 percent have a mutated version of the cancer. If the cancer I have tests positive for a mutation, the chemo treatment is in pill form and has fewer side effects. If I am in the 60 percent category, the chemo treatment suggested is much more troubling. Most medical people pause long and hard over that treatment. It might be my vivid imagination, but it seemed that my oncologist wanted to avoid discussion when I asked her what she would do if she was in my place. She advised that we take it one step at a time. And that is why we made the decision to go with another biopsy, knowing that each test and procedure forces another decision.

I have been much in prayer this week as we head towards this procedure. It is my desire, in this, and always, to thoroughly discuss everything with my Father. As I pray, I am fully aware that my perspective represents a 1 percent perspective and that God has the other 99 percent. Therefore, I trust Him with the outcome of the results of this biopsy. He's got this, in ways I may never fully understand. And so I step into tomorrow, and the days to follow, way more confident in God's ability than in my own ability.

DAY 55—THANKFUL

By Brenda Pue—February 24, 2014 8:19 p.m.

We left for the hospital early, due to the falling snow. "We" meaning my lovely entourage and me. Five of us in total. I think the hospital is catching on to me by now...I only come to appointments with my "village," for the most part.

This was a CT-guided biopsy, which means every step of the procedure is monitored by a CT scan. I was awake for the biopsy, so after numerous scans for the setup, the doctor told me I could close my eyes for the actual biopsy. I said, "Why would I do that? I don't want to miss anything!" He said, "You are one courageous woman. Most people really don't like this sort of thing." Just between us, I never said I liked it…but it is kind of interesting.

I'm thankful that he secured four different samples, instead of the usual three, to help ensure that there would be enough tissue for diagnosis.

I'm thankful that I didn't have a partial pneumothorax (where a small portion of the lung collapses) like I did last time. I was able to leave an hour after the biopsy. Last time I was there for a few hours with regular X-rays to monitor progress.

I'm thankful for a great medical team today. My doctor was skilled and caring.

I'm thankful that I feel good physically and that the peace of God fills me.

I'm thankful for all the prayer and love that surrounds me. I have much to be thankful for.

I'm thankful that God is leading me every step of this journey. Here is the word from God for me today: "But as for me, how good it is it be near God! I have made the Sovereign LORD my shelter, and I will tell everyone about the wonderful things you do" (Psalm 73:28 NLT).

DAY 56—PADDLING QUIETLY
By Brenda Pue—February 25, 2014 7:24 p.m.

A long-time and dear friend, who has also lived with cancer, gave me a little book of meditations and prayers recently called *Facing the Storm*. I want to share with you the following story that brings peace to my soul. Perhaps it will do the same for you.

It was cold down at the nature reserve. The sky was steel grey, clouds torn by an almost gale-force wind. It ripped through the trees, scattering the last leaves. The water was grey and ruffled. A great armada of Canadian geese was in the water. They all floated there, facing the storm.

Their environment had suddenly become hostile, threatening. They didn't protest, or run for cover. They didn't use up precious energy flying into it or fighting it. They faced into the wind, paddling quietly. They didn't try to make headway, but paddled just enough to keep their direction and position in the water.

Maybe we can learn from the birds. Jesus thought so. They tell us of God's concern, he said, and remind us that we achieve little by worrying.

When the going gets tough, the tough get going, says the cliché. I'm not sure that's always the best way. We're not all as aggressive as that suggests. Another way is just to face the storm, and keep position. Not scream and shout, not protest and ask what have I done to deserve this, but just hold onto faith and wait for the wind to blow itself out. It will, because the creator of the winds is stronger than the wind.

It may take time, but it works, and I don't remember ever seeing a Canada goose with acute depression.[5]

Paddling quietly and trusting much,
Brenda

DAY 57—SOUL FRIENDS
By Brenda Pue—February 26, 2014 8:11 p.m.

For about 17 years, I have been a part of a close-knit group of women. What first brought us together was our kids—who all needed prayer desperately. So way back when our kids were young, we met together and started praying (our husbands get air time as well).

I'm not sure which one of us suggested an annual retreat weekend, and we did that for some years. I'm pretty sure that I was the one who suggested a week-long retreat in a warm place! That would be something I would concoct. And it didn't take much convincing of the other five. :) I'm not sure how many years we've been going away for week-long retreats together, but it is one of the most treasured weeks of my year. I only missed one year when a certain blond son's car was hit and almost totalled by a young mom. I needed to stay home that year and fight (with mountains of paperwork) to keep that car for him. It

---

[5] Eddie Askew, *Facing the Storm: Meditations and Prayers*, ed. by Donna Bowers (South Carolina: Leprosy Mission International, 1989). Inspired by Matthew 6:25–27, this story was written by artist and author Eddie Askew, who has given years of service to leprosy sufferers along with his wife Barbara, through The Leprosy Mission International.

was so important to him and seemed like the right decision at the time. Love that boy!

The focus of the week is prayer, rest, hearing from God, learning from each other and *lots* of laughter and joy in the midst. What a remarkable journey it has been for all of us...lowest lows and highest highs. And the best part has been watching God at work...not always when we wanted or how we thought it should happen. But God used it all to open us to His good plans for our families. Our journals are filled with stories of God's surprises.

All our kids are grown now and have started having kids of their own. We continue to pray for all our kids, and now we have the joy of praying for the next generation.

Today my prayer group (minus two) brought lunch, and we did, once again, what we do best: share life, eat well and pray deep. It was wonderful. I wish that everyone had something like this in their lives. What a difference it makes. I am grateful for these ones who embraced me so many years ago and who suffer and hope with me now in this season of great need.

DAY 58—A PATHWAY NO ONE KNEW
By Brenda Pue—February 27, 2014 10:53 p.m.

I was going through my medical file today. Just over one month of testing and diagnosis, etc., has generated a lot of paperwork for this girl. Paperwork is overwhelming to me at the best of times. I'm not a detail person, so it's not my thing. In fact, my sweet friend Sharon (we also share two grandchildren), who is much better than I am at this sort of thing, was over today, helping me to strategize the management of household affairs. Usually, paperwork has little impact on me at an emotional level. But my medical paperwork has weightiness to it. I wasn't able to get through it. I literally needed to walk away.

Then I remembered words that I read early this morning. The psalmist, recounting God's greatness, says, "Your road led through the sea, your pathway through the mighty waters—a pathway no one knew was there! You led your people along that road like a flock of sheep" (Psalm 77:19–20 NLT).

The original story about this historical event (found in Exodus) is awesome. I feel like my medical situation is like a personal version of the Israelites' escape from Egypt, in that when they got to the end of the road, in a seemingly impossible scenario, God made a way, or road, through the Red Sea. No one but God could have come up with solution like that. I am reminded that the God I love found a pathway no one knew was there. I don't know what my pathway is, but I know He is great at making paths for all of us. That is a great comfort for me, and I hope it is for you too.

DAY 59—COLOURED TEARS
By Brenda Pue—February 28, 2014 6:55 p.m.

Friday night is family night. All 12 of us get together every Friday (this week Great Granny joined us) over a fantastic meal to get caught up with each other, to enjoy each other and to play with all the kids, and once the kids are bedded down for the night, the adults play a game together. Then we talk and pray together.

This week our whole family is in waiting mode. We are waiting for results from Monday's lung biopsy, which usually [takes] two weeks. So we talked about this place of waiting. Some of us are glad for a season of lower intensity. Some are finding it to be emotionally hard work. Some of us are trying hard to live one day at a time.

Jon captured it well. He said, "Generally I feel peaceful and hopeful, but occasionally it's really hard—often I feel exhausted." We all still have our tearful moments. As we talked about the kind of tears we are experiencing from time to time, I found myself wishing we all had coloured tears…a different colour for every feeling. I think that God sees our tears that way. He knows exactly what kind of tears we cry. We don't have to explain it to Him. He just knows.

It's just good to be able to go deep with family. We closed our evening in prayer and offered all our emotions and tears to the One who knows us better than we know ourselves. It was the perfect end to a good day.

Today I came across the following quote that has much truth: "The art of living lies less in eliminating our troubles than in growing with them."[6]

DAY 60—IT FEELS STRANGE
By Brenda Pue—March 1, 2014 7:02 p.m.

Spring is just around the corner in our part of the world. Usually, at this time of year, I start making plans…all kinds of plans. Spring cleaning plans, gardening plans, repairing plans, travel plans, St. Patrick's Day plans, Easter plans, etc. It's always an exciting time of year for me.

I realized today, though, that I'm not making my usual plans. My focus is completely altered this year. All of my energy and focus, physically, mentally, emotionally and spiritually, is headed in a different direction. I can honestly say this is a first for me. It feels so strange.

But God is calling me to something new. I now realize that He does this. As I read about great heroes of the faith, God always called them to new unknowns. It must've felt strange and frightening for them too. As I ponder why God does this, I believe it has lots to do with trust.

I read Proverbs 3:5–6 today:

Trust in the LORD with all your heart, And lean not on your own understanding; In all your ways acknowledge Him, And He shall direct your paths. (NKJV)

This cancer journey is my new unknown. I fully admit that I am way out of my depth on understanding this new, and sometimes frightening, place. I am praying for greater faith and more trust. Is there any better place to find it than God?

---

[6] Bernard M. Baruch.

DAY 61—OUTRAGEOUS GENEROSITY
By Brenda Pue—March 2, 2014 4:11 p.m.

I've been on the receiving end of generosity for about seven weeks now. The generosity comes in all shapes and sizes, from individuals, families and groups. Here are some examples:

> Handwritten cards and letters
> Music
> Hats and scarves
> Books
> Food
> Juice, teas and coffee
> Candles
> Financial help
> A family retreat
> Jewellery
> Quilt and throw
> Bible verses
> Prayers
> Flowers
> Skin care products
> Bed

What has been most amazing about the list is how deeply personal it all is. Everything has been meaningful. So much care, thought and intentionality has gone into loving and encouraging me. I am completely blessed. I now keep a basket beside the fireplace for all the cards and letters that I've received. It's full. That basket is a treasure to me.

Generosity is transforming. I had the privilege of travelling to Bolivia three summers ago with World Vision Canada. There I saw the impact of generosity on kids, families and communities. The children were bright-eyed, healthy and happy. The parents and grandparents wept tears of joy for our visit. They hugged us and kissed us because they had experienced the "before and after." But a highlight for me was visiting a young, destitute family where the Area Development Project was just starting. All the food they owned was on one tiny shelf of their cooking hut. And yet, when our group of six arrived, the mom had cooked a bowl of potatoes and presented it to us. Such generosity. I stumbled back to the car, barely able to see through my tears.

Generosity is a game changer; unmerited, unexpected generosity turns the world upside down. Generosity has been extended to me over and over throughout my life, and God has used it to shape me. My experience of God Himself has been generous and outrageous. A person could debate that all of God's attributes stem from His generosity. It's an interesting thought. Whatever the case may be, I know that I will never be the same after my profound experiences of generosity.

Proverbs 11:25 says, "A generous person will prosper; whoever refreshes others will be refreshed" (NIV).

DAY 62—BREATHING
By Brenda Pue—March 3, 2014 8:45 p.m.

We all take breathing for granted, for the most part. It just happens. Except when it doesn't operate properly. Last night at bedtime, I noticed that my breathing wasn't quite right…a bit laboured and shallow. So this morning, I contacted my doctor to let him know and was shortly on my way to get more X-rays. We are waiting to find out if I've developed a pneumothorax as a result of the lung biopsy last week.

This has caused me to think about some of the most basic things that sustain life. Like breathing. The past couple of years I've been paying more attention to my breathing. I notice when it speeds up, indicating that I am anxious or concerned, and I notice when it is slowed, indicating that I am relaxed and at peace. Breathing can be a good barometer for what is going on inside.

I now ask myself deeper questions, prayerful questions, around these "noticings." I think God is always encouraging us all to be more aware…more aware of Him…more aware of others…more aware of ourselves. For much of my life, I've just ignored my "awarenesses" and powered through. I'm not wanting to ignore the things that God is pointing out to me anymore. I don't want to miss the good stuff that He has for me in this journey.

"Let everything that breathes sing praises to the LORD!" (Psalm 150:6 NLT).

P.S. You may notice a unique word here and there as I write. That is because they are unique. If I can't find just the right word, I make it up. My family and friends know this about me. :)

DAY 63—THROUGH THE BACK DOOR!
By Brenda Pue—March 4, 2014 9:06 p.m.

Today, I received results of the lung X-ray that I had yesterday. I learned that there is no infection, no lung collapse and no pneumothorax. But the best news that I've had in a very long time came in the back door via my breathing concern. Six small words from my doctor: "The tumour is the same size." This means that the tumour has not grown since the first X-ray taken on December 30th. That's nine weeks. I have no way to know if this is medically remarkable, but it feels very remarkable to me.

The physical impact of chest/lung pain and laboured breathing was troubling me as I went to bed last night and still this morning when I awakened. So to hear these words was like a balm to my soul. I am still dealing with the physical facts, but the difference is hope that came in the back door. God knew that Carson and I were in need of some encouragement. Here's the verse that is touching me today: "Be joyful in hope, patient in affliction, faithful in prayer" (Romans 12:12 NIV).

DAY 64—PUZZLING LANGUAGE
By Brenda Pue—March 5, 2014 9:27 p.m.

Carson and I have been trying to come up with better language around my cancer diagnosis because it does have its awkward moments. :) To speak of the actual diagnosis to a person for the first time is so shocking that most people simply don't know how to respond, and it can be difficult to have a conversation.

Occasionally, however, it goes well…as it did with a grocery clerk today. My sister and I took our few items to the counter, and my sister wanted to pay for one item, so she set it aside. I gave her a hug and said to the clerk, "That's my seester!" Then for some unknown reason, I joked, "I know it's hard to tell that we're sisters, because she has hair and I don't." The clerk's response surprised us: "The great thing about hair is that it will grow back. And you look beautiful in your hat. Not everyone looks so good in a hat." The lovely conversation continued, and when we got back in the car, we both commented on how encouraging those few moments were for us.

Sometimes it doesn't go quite so well. The question that always stops me is "How are you?" It's such a broad question, and how does anyone who is suffering answer a question like that? I prefer "It's good to see you."

So, with much grace and understanding of life's uncomfortable moments, Carson and I prefer to think of cancer as a puzzle. In fact, cancer is puzzling. The pieces of the puzzle are emotions, information, tests, results, appointments, pain, hair loss, exhaustion, etc. They are scattered everywhere in disarray. We can't see the whole picture, because it unfolds slowly, with lots of careful pondering (and prayer), one piece at a time.

We think this language is more helpful than much of the militaristic language that we have heard and read about.

Eventually all the pieces of the puzzle come together, with God's help.

Be kind to one another, tenderhearted, forgiving one another, as God in Christ forgave you. (Ephesians 4:32 ESV)

DAY 65—CHILDLIKE
By Brenda Pue—March 6, 2014 7:47 p.m.

This cancer journey is a first for me. Like [with] so many childhood firsts, there is no way to gauge a response. That's the beautiful thing about kids— the response just happens. It's authentic. Some firsts are wondrous, and others feel threatening. Strangely, this journey is a little bit of both, so I am wide open to all that God has for me, and I will keep running towards Him, as I always have when I am unsure of myself.

Carson, my mom and I attended a two-hour chemo class today. Lots of questions are bouncing around in my mind. There's much to process! On the upside, during that session, I noticed that my breathing improved, and it has been mostly normal today.

Today, I read a devotional about being childlike that has stayed with me all day. I think this a sign that I should share it. It's from a little book entitled *What Cancer Cannot Do* by Phyllis Ten Elshof.

Our souls...remain relatively childlike. Even though outwardly we look mature and in control, inwardly we still react like we have never grown up. We still smart like a kid at a public reprimand, still sting when someone passes us up for someone else, still hope for something wildly wonderful when unwrapping a gift or opening the mailbox. Like little kids, we're still tempted to eat what we shouldn't, spend what we don't have, and try to weasel our way out of the consequences of our wrongdoing. We still lie, cheat, steal, covet, and break all of God's commandments, even after a life of asking forgiveness for sin and committing our lives to Christ Jesus.

Thankfully, we're still capable of childlike trust, as well. Though our bodies are frail and beaten down, our souls still cling like newborns to the promise of salvation through Jesus Christ. Time after time we stumble in our brokenness to the Savior, begging to be made whole again.

And, wonder of wonders, the Master does not turn us away. Rather, he gathers us into his arms and assures us, "Let the little children come to me, and do not hinder them, for the kingdom of heaven belongs to such as these" (Matthew 19:14 NIV).[7]

DAY 66—THANK YOU FOR PRAYING
By Brenda Pue—March 7, 2014 6:42 p.m.

Have you ever wondered whether a scientific study has ever been done on prayer?

I read about one today that was fascinating to me. Published by Dr. Randolph C. Byrd in the July 1988 *Southern Medical Journal*, it's entitled "Positive Therapeutic Effects of Intercessory Prayer in a Coronary Care Unit Population." Dr. Byrd took 393 patients from the San Francisco General Hospital Coronary Care Unit and put their names into a computer. The computer randomly divided the patients into two groups. One group, the "prayer group," was prayed for by a home group of Christians. The patients in the control group did not receive prayer. This was a double-blind study, which is when neither the patients nor physicians are aware of which patients are receiving the treatment (in this case, prayer) and which are not. The study adhered to the same stringent guidelines that all pharmaceutical studies have to abide by to be considered valid.

The results showed that prayer was a significant therapeutic agent. Not one patient from the prayer [group] required an artificial airway and ventilator, whereas 12 from the control group did. In addition, prayer group patients were

[7] Phyllis Ten Elshof and Sarah M. Hupp, authors and compilers, "Trusting Like a Child," in *What Cancer Cannot Do: Stories of Hope and Encouragement* (Grand Rapids: Zondervan, 2006), 98.

five times less likely to require antibiotics and three times less likely to develop complications than their control group counterparts.

These findings are amazing to me, especially as I consider these two things:

1. The many people who are praying for my family and me.
2. The good news that I received earlier this week—that the tumour has not grown in nine weeks.

Prayer is a mystery. So, you may ask, why bother? I bother because prayer changes me and I learn much about God. I have been the recipient of both yeses and nos when it comes to prayer. Often God's mercies have been mine… undeserved, but lovingly given. The fact remains, there is power in prayer, as indicated in the scientific study…and that is always humbling and wonderful to me. I continue to be grateful for your constant and faith-filled prayers. Thank you!

Answer me when I call to you, O God who declares me innocent. Free me from my troubles. Have mercy on me and hear my prayer. (Psalm 4:1 NLT)

DAY 67—PUSH THE PAUSE BUTTON
By Brenda Pue—March 8, 2014 9:50 p.m.

Today, Carson was speaking at a breakfast meeting at our church. I would normally go with him for something like this, as I love being with him and listening to him teach. One thing that I am struggling with since being diagnosed with cancer is that we have always done things together. Not so much anymore. I haven't been to church in two months, and that is another thing that feels strange to me. Since this whole thing began, I think I miss these kinds of shared times with my husband the most. I didn't expect this at all.

When life doesn't seem to work the way that we hoped for or expected, there is often something more just beyond our reach. If we can push the pause button on our disappointment, God often shows us something new.

So I've been reflecting on how to manage my disappointment. We have established some lovely rhythms every morning and evening that are life-giving for both of us. After pausing, I realize that I have been given a rare treasure of time for reflection, research, writing and prayer. This is how I am choosing to adjust to my new normal. What a gift, for however long it lasts. Once medical appointments resume, my life will change yet again.

I am truly grateful for the time I am getting to sort things out.

Let the words of my mouth and the meditation of my heart be acceptable in your sight, O LORD, my rock and my redeemer. (Psalm 19:14 ESV)

DAY 68—SMALL THINGS CAN BE BIG
By Brenda Pue—March 9, 2014 10:29 p.m.

I have not been able to sneeze, hiccup, cough or take a deep breath since mid-December due to pain in my chest wall. This is the pain that originally drove me to make a doctor's appointment, thinking I had a pulled muscle that wasn't healing. That seemingly innocuous appointment, that seemed so small at the time, started the avalanche, which now seems big.

Now back to the inability to sneeze and cough. What usually happens is that every day I get the intense urge to sneeze or cough, but as it is building up, my brain takes over and says, "I don't think we're going to do that right now." But yesterday I actually sneezed. It was so tiny that most people wouldn't have been able to identify the muffled sound that came out. But it happened! It felt like another win for me. Something so small brought big hope.

It often seems to be the small, almost unnoticed actions or words of encouragement that end up being so big in life. Sometimes it's a squeeze of the hand or a hug at just the right time that can change a person's perspective. One of my favourites came from one of our medical team, during the chaos of appointments, results and fast decisions when we were feeling overwhelmed and scared. Carson said, "I need to know who's in charge here. Who's driving this thing?" Long pause. "Well…God is driving this thing." It was exactly what we needed to hear. It was like a breath of fresh air. That message was sent from heaven, through a medical doctor, to our hearts. Six small words that have made such a big difference for us!

"We have here only five loaves of bread and two fish," they answered. "Bring them here to me," he said. And he directed the people to sit down on the grass. Taking the five loaves and the two fish and looking up to heaven, he gave thanks and broke the loaves. Then he gave them to the disciples, and

the disciples gave them to the people. They all ate and were satisfied, and the disciples picked up twelve basketfuls of broken pieces that were left over. The number of those who ate was about five thousand men, besides women and children. (Matthew 14:17–21 NIV)

DAY 69—TEACH ME
By Brenda Pue—March 10, 2014 11:58 p.m.

I've been thinking about how to make the most of my time. I get a little overwhelmed when there is too much to do—especially when all of it is good. So I've been a little back and forth on where best to put my limited energy.

I recently received an email from a friend who was given a cancer diagnosis that, like mine, seemed hopeless. She was given one year to live. It is four years later, and she is well. She shared with me the priorities and practices that she put in place to make it through that year. She gave herself permission to focus on her health. This was life-giving to me.

She shared that the medical profession only references statistics. She wrote, "The entire medical world measures everything by 'statistics.' But what they don't know…is what support is like, or faith, or heart, or family and love, or lifestyle habits or any of the fine details that nurture a sick person to living as well and stress-free as possible with amazing tools of family, friends, faith, love, care and tenderness. How can you measure those in a field of statistics?" And so I am giving myself permission to focus on things that God has put before me during this season of my life.

During the past two weeks of waiting, I have been reading and researching. Most of my reading has been inspiring, though some has been very hard. Just when I started feeling anxious, I received a short message that a close friend felt led to send. It only said, "Exodus 14:14, 'The Lord will fight for you; you need only to be still' (NIV)."

As I try to make the most of my time, I know I am in need of much wisdom along the way.

Teach us to realize the brevity of life, so that we may grow in wisdom…
Satisfy us each morning with your unfailing love, so we may sing for joy to the end of our lives. (Psalm 90:12–14 NLT)

DAY 70—BEING WELCOMED
By Brenda Pue—March 11, 2014 11:06 p.m.

It was two months ago today that we were given my cancer diagnosis: stage four non-small cell cancer, which had metastasized to the brain and the bone. The fallout of this diagnosis was sobering to say the least. Any medical person who hears about this is quiet and sad. Just two months ago…

As I reflect on the past two months, it's interesting to me where I first turned for comfort: God, Carson, our kids, our in-laws and families. And this one surprised me the most…thoughts of our dog.

We had a Wheaton terrier named Connor for 13 years. He died a few years ago. For some reason, I wanted that dog back. No other dog would do. The past few weeks I've wondered what it was about Connor that elicited such a strong longing in me. Some fine memories have come to me as I've walked down memory lane.

When we first got that little puppy, I was determined that he would be crate trained. So our first night, he was downstairs in the laundry room, all cozy and comfy in his little crate. Well…he cried and whimpered for a long time, and I ended up comforting him all night long in the laundry room. The next night, I brought the crate upstairs beside my bed, but the crying continued. I ended up sleeping on the floor, with my hand inside the crate, resting on our new puppy. It only took a week until he felt safe in his crate. I think that was when we bonded. :)

And then, life with a dog just unfolded. He was supposed to be the boys' dog in terms of caregiving, but somehow that didn't quite work out. I got up before dawn every morning to walk and run with Connor. Every now and again, he would get away from me and run like he hadn't a care in the world. I was *not* happy whenever he ran away. When I finally retrieved him, I would stomp towards home, with him in tow, still mad at the effort it took. During one such scene, I think I heard God say, "Your dog is a lot like you. You run off, in different directions, distracted with the latest thing, too!"

Hmmm. There are so many other life lessons from living with that dog. I could never stay mad at him for long. Even though he was a substantial dog, he was a cuddler. It never took long to forgive and forget (even so, I became an avid fan of the Dog Whisperer during that season of my life, in an effort to get him to be more obedient). The fact remains that few could equal the welcome that Connor gave when any of our family walked through the door.

I think that was what my heart longed for when we first got this news. There's nothing quite like a dog welcome…that dog had a way of making me feel like I was the most important human in the world.

Yet here's another interesting thing…God has more than filled this longing in hundreds of ways that I could never have imagined through my caring family, church, and this amazing praying community. My heart is grateful.

Put on then, as God's chosen ones, holy and beloved, compassionate hearts, kindness, humility, meekness, and patience. (Colossians 3:12 ESV)

DAY 71—ON WAITING
By Brenda Pue—March 12, 2014 7:54 p.m.

I am waiting for the results of my lung biopsy from February 24th, which was just over two weeks ago. I'm not a good waiter at the best of times. And even though I feel like much hinges on this next appointment with my medical oncologist, I am keenly aware that there are many who wait months and years for something or someone. It's a hard place to be.

Second only to suffering, waiting may be the greatest teacher and trainer in godliness, maturity, and genuine spirituality most of us ever encounter.[8]

I remember a time in my early twenties, when I waited for six years to hear the words from my doctor, "You're going to have a baby." There were lots of tears and prayers during those years of waiting. I now know that God was shaping and forming my character. Here are a few things that began to emerge during that season of waiting:
- The world didn't and doesn't revolve around me.
- Instant gratification is not necessarily a good thing.
- Patience (still not my strong suit).
- Joy is possible, even when I'm not happy.
- Compassion for others who are suffering and waiting.
- God still cares for me, even when I don't get my way.

This last one I know to be true from being a parent. My kids didn't always get what they wanted, yet I still cared deeply for them. I know that God cares for me that way…it's always a little harder to apply to myself, though.

---

[8] Richard Hendrix, *Leadership*, vol. 7, no. 3.

While I have been waiting for lung biopsy results, I've focused on other things, like reading, going for daily walks and working on a few projects…things I may not be able to do in the coming weeks. This is healthy self-soothing. There are unhealthy ways to self-soothe. So it's important to figure out the difference.

Be still in the presence of the LORD, and wait patiently for him to act. Don't worry about evil people who prosper or fret about their wicked schemes. (Psalm 37:7 NLT)

DAY 72—GOD LOVES THE IMPOSSIBLE
By Brenda Pue—March 13, 2014 10:13 p.m.

There are moments every day when I read or hear something that reminds me that the cancer diagnosis I received is an impossible situation. When I am confronted with this, I ask God how He sees my situation. I picture Him smiling and saying, "I love impossible…"

Scene after scene, beginning to end, the Bible is filled with stories of the impossible. Here are just a few:

The nation of Israel was wandering in the desert with no water anywhere in sight. God told Moses to tap the rock, and a torrent of water burst out of the rock to sustain the thousands of people and their herds. It happened twice (see Exodus 17:7 and Numbers 20:11).

Israel was at war, under Joshua's leadership, and needed more time. The sun and moon stood still for about a day (see Joshua 10:13–14).

Jesus healed a man who was lame for 38 years. After 38 years, the man actually walked (see John 5:2–11).

Jesus raised his good friend Lazarus from the dead, after *four* days. In other words, a person couldn't be more dead. But at Jesus' word, Lazarus walked out of that grave, larger than life (see John 11).

And I continue to read and hear about impossible, wonderful stories today. Almost every night, Carson and I read an "impossible" story. It's a great way to end a day, with a sense of peace. I'm grateful that He loves the impossible.

Jesus looked at them intently and said, "Humanly speaking, it is impossible. But with God everything is possible." (Matthew 19:26 NLT)

DAY 73—BLESSING WELL
By Brenda Pue—March 14, 2014 10:06 p.m.

Today could have been a difficult day. I planned to clean out my Arrow office. [This year] was the beginning of my 19th year with Arrow Leadership. Last June, we began talking about hiring a new enrolment person for Arrow and began formulating a new role for me. Then the month of January opened a new direction for me: namely, my health. With chemo starting in the near future, I felt it was important to continue with the original plan, which was to get my office cleaned out and ready for the next person.

Even though this was "the plan" all along, there was still lots of potential for difficulty today for me and others. But it ended up to be much better than I imagined, thanks to the team at Arrow.

And this is something I appreciate about Arrow Leadership: they know how to bless well. We walked into the Arrow office to happy smiles and warm greetings. When I looked into my office, there on my desk was a beautiful potted plant and a gift. Not just any gift, but a puzzle of our family photo from the photo shoot in January. Amazing!

They set a tone for this time, knowing that it could have been hard. They anticipated. They blessed. They cared. Long before we ever arrived today.

This ended up being a lovely and positive day. Thank you, Arrow, for making this day a truly blessed one. I continue to learn from Arrow, as I have for so long.

P.S. We started making the Pue family puzzle as soon as we got home today. Enjoy the photo.

Therefore comfort each other and edify one another, just as you also are doing. (1 Thessalonians 5:11 NKJV)

DAY 74—CHOOSING WORDS
By Brenda Pue—March 15, 2014 10:03 p.m.

Back in January, when we were meeting with our radiation oncologist, part of the conversation was the probable side effects of full brain radiation. Radiation impacts healthy cells as well as cancerous cells, but the healthy cells make a bit of a comeback, and the cancerous cells hopefully won't.

The oncologist said that I would be very tired—check. He also said that many of my normal processes would slow—check. I walk, talk, think and move a little bit slower than I did before. Usually my family is very understanding, but there are moments that they thoroughly enjoy at my expense, especially around word retrieval. This has never been my strong suit, but it is definitely more pronounced now.

For example, I was trying to explain to Jason and Kristin how blessed I felt that the cancer hadn't caused any "peech spathology." Those of you who know Jason would understand that this was too rich a moment to pass by.

Another time, I asked Carson if he would like me to make a shake for breakfast. He nodded affirmation, and we went on to talk for a few minutes. I got up to leave and said, "So you want a 'snake' for breakfast."

My family just rolls with this, which is what I love about them. We are having some wonderful laughs over it all.

Words are so important. They have power for good or for evil. Winston Churchill is said to have agonized over a broadcast speech that he knew President Roosevelt would be listening to. He knew that his choice of words would influence whether the United Sates would join the war or not. His words changed the course of history.

Every person who speaks publicly knows the importance of words. Words can have eternal impact. And how very critical it is for every parent to choose words well over the course of a child's lifetime. Words help to form every person's character.

In my mind, there isn't anyone who knew the power of words better than Jesus. His words, His questions, His conversations are beyond insightful. No words were wasted. At least, none that were recorded for us. I can assure you that my wasted words far exceed my words that matter. I would dearly love to change that about myself in the future.

Let no corrupting talk come out of your mouths, but only such as is good for building up, as fits the occasion, that it may give grace to those who hear. (Ephesians 4:29 ESV)

DAY 75—MEMORY LANE
By Brenda Pue—March 16, 2014 9:18 p.m.

As I continue [to] work on my grandparent's book, I've relived a lifetime of memories from my own birth on. It's been wonderful having my mom available as I work on this project. She is a wonderful resource, and we've enjoyed some fun stories and great laughs.

So far, I've covered my heritage and birth, my parents and grandparents, my childhood and teenage years, my school years, love and marriage, and parenthood and family life (I'm just over halfway, with four more chapters to go). What has struck me thus far is God's faithfulness to me, even when I had no idea He was being faithful. Now as I look back on the landscape of my life, I can see His activity more clearly. There are strategic places where He intervened that have made a difference in the overall scheme of my life. Could I add that it is never too late to take notice of God?

When I think of the span of one person's lifetime, all the ups and downs, the joys and the fears, the embarrassing moments and the noble moments, I am stretched to imagine God's capacity to oversee the span of *one* person's life. When I try to add more people to the equation, I can't. I'm not able to do that kind of math. Yet I know from meeting hundreds and hundreds of people over my lifetime, and from reading numerous books, that God is intimately involved with others' lives as well; across the earth, not one person gets missed. Every human is a treasured creation. Psalm 139 puts it this way:

> *O Lord, you have examined my heart and know everything about me. You know when I sit or stand. When far away you know my every thought. You chart the path ahead of me and tell me where to stop and rest. Every moment you know where I am. You know what I am going to say before I even say it. You both precede and follow me and place your hand of blessing on my head.*
>
> *This is too glorious, too wonderful to believe! I can never be lost to your Spirit! I can never get away from my God! If I go up to heaven, you are there; if I go down to the place of the dead, you are there. If I ride the morning winds to the farthest oceans, even there your hand will guide me, your strength will support me. If I try to hide in the darkness, the night becomes light around me. For even darkness cannot hide from God; to you the night shines as bright as day. Darkness and light are both alike to you.*

You made all the delicate, inner parts of my body and knit them together in my mother's womb. Thank you for making me so wonderfully complex! It is amazing to think about. Your workmanship is marvelous—and how well I know it. You were there while I was being formed in utter seclusion! You saw me before I was born and scheduled each day of my life before I began to breathe. Every day was recorded in your book!

How precious it is, Lord, to realize that you are thinking about me constantly! I can't even count how many times a day your thoughts turn toward me. And when I waken in the morning, you are still thinking of me! (Psalm 139:1–18 TLB)

DAY 76—CELEBRATING AND PRAYER UPDATE
By Brenda Pue—March 17, 2014 10:12 p.m.

It's St. Patrick's Day. This is an occasion we celebrate annually as a family. When our boys were young, we arranged with their teachers [for them] to have the day off school. We started the day with an Ulster fry. There's so much cholesterol in this meal, I calculate that 15 more such celebrations should effectively kill off our line of the Pue clan.

While most people get into green beer and leprechauns, we focus in on the historical St. Patrick. As a teenager, he was a slave in Ireland. After he escaped, he was called back there as a missionary. He is credited with planting 200 churches and saw over 100,000 people convert to Christianity.

We have tucked away some great family memories celebrating St. Patrick's Day. Really, any excuse for a celebration will do. It's all about celebrating people and life. This happens in big and small ways, and laughter is usually a big part. We have a picture of *The Laughing Christ*. I often picture Jesus enjoying people and life to the full. If laughter is a magnet, it helps to explain why people were so drawn to Him (I'm sure curiosity was a factor as well).

Here's to some laughter and celebrating something special in your near future.

Prayer Update:

We received a call from the cancer clinic for the following appointments this week:

- Blood work in preparation for chemotherapy.
- Receiving news about the genetic coding of the lung mass.

- Meeting with the medical oncologist Tuesday afternoon.
- Meeting with radiation oncologist on Thursday afternoon.

I am experiencing head discomfort and am not sure what's going on.

This feels like a big week for us, at every level, and we feel in the need of prayer. Thank you for continuing to hold us close in prayer.

You lead me in the path of life; I experience absolute joy in your presence; you always give me sheer delight. (Psalm 16:11 NET)

DAY 77—CAUSE FOR JOY
By Brenda Pue—March 18, 2014 9:14 p.m.

Tonight our family is rejoicing with the news that I have a mutated form of lung cancer. When our oncologist told us, I cried tears of joy. Here's why:

1. My timeline has been extended from months to years (two or three or maybe more).
2. The treatment is in pill form rather than IV chemo form. This means I've been spared trips to the hospital every three weeks, as long as the cancer doesn't build up antibodies to the treatment.
3. Waaaaaay less side effects…three pages versus eight pages.
4. I get to go to church as soon as I feel well enough. I'm trying a new anti-nausea drug that will hopefully help with this.

I know that in the big scheme of things, this is a small thing. Yet I am grateful that God cares about small things.

When I was 20, I moved into my first apartment. My first week there, a friend was visiting town and asked if she could stay with me. I said of course, even though I didn't even have dishes, pots and pans, etc. We had a wonderful time, she at her conference and me at work each day. We said our goodbyes the night before she was to leave, since she would be long gone by the time I arrived home from work. The sight that met my eyes when I walked in the door that evening was almost too much to comprehend: my kitchen was filled with everything a kitchen should have—dishes, glasses, cutlery, pots, etc. The bathroom now had a shower curtain, floor mats, accessories, towels, etc. All these are small things, yet I felt Someone cared and provided through my generous friend.

That captures how I feel tonight about this news. That God really cares.

Cast all your anxiety on him because he cares for you. (1 Peter 5:7 NIV)

EASY 78—MORE ROOM
By Brenda Pue—March 19, 2014 9:31 p.m.

I feel like I've won a cancer lottery, of sorts…except the payout is time, not money. Now that my timeline has been medically extended, I'm rethinking what that means for me and for my family. Thank you for celebrating this "win" with us.

Before the cancer diagnosis, my focus might have been a 90 degree angle. For the past two months my focus narrowed to about 10 degrees, namely God, my health, my family and friends. I have many treasured memories from the past two months. After yesterday, I feel [like] my focus expanded to 25 degrees. What I've noticed is that there has been a release of pressure. I now have more room, so to speak. The intensity has been lifted. This seems healthier to me. I'm still largely focused on the same things, with one or two add-ons, but with less stress. I didn't realize that I was even carrying such high a degree of stress until it was removed. I prefer to evaluate stress during quieter times, not in the thick of high stress.

In my reading and research about causes of cancer, there is a fair bit of discussion around compromised immune systems arising from poor nutrition, environmental problems and stress. In other words, taking care of the immune system is the best way to fight cancer.

It is a wonderful gift to have been given more room to navigate life. I still desire to be purposeful with time, yet how good it feels to breathe and to catch the nuances of life with God. Part of this is forced, since I am still managing nausea, headaches and chest wall pain (where the tumour has attached). These three things continue to be hindrances to functioning well. I'm praying that the oral chemo treatments, which I started today, will make a difference. Would you join us [in] praying?

> *"O LORD, make me know my end and what is the measure of my days; let me know how fleeting I am! Behold, you have made my days a few handbreadths, and my lifetime is as nothing before you. Surely all mankind stands as a mere breath!"* (Psalm 39:4–5 ESV)

DAY 79—GRATITUDE

By Brenda Pue—March 20, 2014 9:39 p.m.

I am grateful for many things. My heart is full today. I need to pause and thank God and give Him credit for His grace and mercy towards me and my family.

How amazing to know a God who listens and hears when we pray. That's a remarkable thought if we pause. The God of the universe actually hears and cares.

For thousands of prayers on my behalf—I am grateful. For the kindness, generosity, and especially faith, when my faith was flagging.

I am humbled and amazed by such love…Truly, I am overwhelmed. That's how God prefers it, I think. He loves to overwhelm His children with His outrageous love and care.

As I've navigated the past few weeks with a sense of gradual decline physically, I was reminded of a wonderful word picture by a dear friend. As crocuses push their buds above the ground, there has [already] been much activity in the absence of the flower. Seeing the flower isn't the only evidence of activity. Armed with that truth, it became important for me to acknowledge that God is always working, even I am experiencing little evidence of this. And so I rejoice. This psalm says it so well:

> Let all that I am praise the LORD; with my whole heart, I will praise his holy name. Let all that I am praise the LORD; may I never forget the good things he does for me. He forgives all my sins and heals all my diseases, He redeems me from death and crowns me with love and tender mercies. He fills my life with good things. My youth is renewed like the eagle's! (Psalm 103:1–5 NLT)

DAY 80—WHAT CANCER FEELS LIKE

By Brenda Pue—March 21, 2014 9:07 p.m.

In an effort to describe cancer for people, I've come [up] with a water metaphor. This past summer, we joined our friends on their boat for a week of cruising up the BC coastline. A few times that trip, when we had anchored, we donned our bathing suits and jumped into the ocean for an afternoon or morning swim.

The Pacific Ocean was *cold*. So the first moments of warm bodies meeting with cold water were met with lots of screaming, laughter, splashing and thrashing. Eventually, we started swimming. It was delightful and invigorating.

With my cancer diagnosis, everything slowed physically and mentally, as if [I was] swimming in slow motion, like treading water, and somehow it didn't feel invigorating anymore. As the weeks of waiting, biopsies and tests results took its toll, I seemed to move into just floating and just keeping my head above water. There was little energy for even treading water.

As I progressed towards a treatment plan and began to experience symptoms like brain pressure, shortness of breath, nausea, headaches, visual problems and varying degrees of pain, it felt like I was slowly slipping below the waterline. Another way to describe it is feeling quite sick, yet knowing that your body will fight for you. Cancer is so unpredictable. Feeling well one day does not mean the next day will be better. It's back and forth and up and down. When a person with cancer reaches this stage, there is no confidence that the body will, or even can, fight. It feels so powerless.

This is the point at which a person knows that their destiny is fully in God's hands. God intervenes, medically or miraculously. I consider both to be miracles. When, if and how God intervenes is His plan—and this comforts me. There is a plan, even if I don't know the details. In the meantime I step forward, trusting. "You saw me before I was born. Every day of my life was recorded in your book. Every moment was laid out before a single day had passed" (Psalm 139:16 NLT).

I am grateful for God's intervention this week. Family night is a wonderful way to celebrate!

DAY 81—THE POWER OF A SMILE
By Brenda Pue—March 22, 2014 11:43 p.m.

Since starting at the cancer agency, I've had five doctors, two radiation oncologists, two lung biopsy specialists, and one medical oncologist. The newest one I met on Thursday. It was a great 30-minute appointment.

As we were leaving, I said, "He is my favourite doctor."

Carson asked, "What is it that set him apart from everyone else?"

"He smiled," I responded.

I've had the least amount of interaction with this doctor compared to the others, so it didn't make sense. But a smile in a cancer clinic is indeed a powerful thing.

It's made me realize that a smile accomplishes much in the heart of the recipient. Power and fear can't get there the way a smile can. Children are drawn to a smile and will trust it until experience tells them otherwise. That tells me something. Smiles have power that we seldom realize.

I will not forget the smiles and kindness shown by that doctor. It makes me want to be that for other people.

A cheerful look brings joy to the heart; good news makes for good health. (Proverbs 15:30 NLT)

DAY 82—A CHURCH CHEERING
By Carson Pue—March 24, 2014 1:55 a.m.

Carson here. Brenda is tired this evening (one side effect of the new medication), and she asked if I would share with you today.

I realize that not all of Brenda's readers necessarily have a context for this, so let me share. I was on staff, and we are both members, of First Baptist Church, located in the downtown of our great city. It is a very busy place where ministry programs happen every day and night right in the heart of this very densely populated part of the city. First Baptist is over 127 years old, and the building looks a lot like a castle. But the building is not the church. The church is actually the people who gather there.

Today, Sunday, I shared the good news we received this week about Brenda's mutation, in both services. I did so during the time when I usually stand to share matters concerning our community life together. Today this also included the birth of a baby girl and the death of "Shadow," a man who came off the streets in our Shelter Program and who volunteered with Shelter and also our church security team.

When I thanked our community for their prayers and told them God had listened and acted by extending Brenda's life two to three more years, they burst into applause at both services. Some cried with joy, others with smiles from ear to ear. It was an incredible expression of love, and my heart was deeply touched.

Our church (the people) have been absolutely incredible in walking alongside us in this cancer journey—and they continue to be committed to pray. I am so touched that Brenda has received thoughtful and helpful gifts, beautiful cards, handwritten notes of encouragement and the many written comments on Caring Bridge. I smile each time I see the beautiful handmade cards from a grade 2 class in our Family Ministries who write to Brenda expressing their love and prayers—

what a church family. One young gal wrote, "We love you Brenda! Our family prays for you every day."

At the cancer center during intake you are asked if you have a spiritual community that you belong to. They are trying to discern if you have a support network around you, because they know how hard this journey is going to be. It is hard for us to imagine how someone goes through a life challenge like this outside of a caring community like our church.

So today we cheered—and there is really nothing quite like a church celebrating. I have attended football and hockey games where there were times of revelry that came with winning a championship game. But that is nothing compared with a worship service when the Spirit of God is moving, heaven comes down, and glory and hope fill the souls of the saints. Now that is a celebration!

DAY 83—GLIMPSES OF GLORY
By Brenda Pue—March 24, 2014 10:12 p.m.

Today I received a lovely handwritten card from a precious friend. It was so beautiful! Perhaps what made it so poignant is that I know she is going through deep waters as well. And yet, here she is, reaching out to us. This made me cry.

She reminded me of one of my favourite stories in Scripture, where Moses asked God to show His glory. And God said, "When my glory passes by, I will put you in a cleft in the rock and cover you with my hand" (Exodus 33:22 NIV). Maybe the cleft in the rock looked something like this photo my friend included with her card.

Over the past two months I have been given glimpses of God's glory. These glimpses have increased my faith on some dark days. They occurred at night, except for once during an MRI brain scan. Those events will always remain with me—there is nothing in this world that comes close to a glimpse of God's glory.

She commented that "God is up to something really good!" and I couldn't agree more. When we feel that life is dark, remember that in the darkness—in the darkness of the cleft—is exactly the place where God wants to give us a glimpse of Himself.

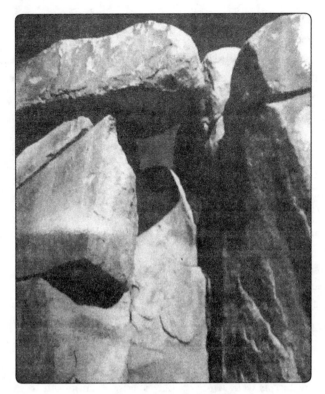

Photo credit: Kathy Bentall

DAY 84—WHEN LIGHT COMES BURSTING IN
By Brenda Pue—March 25, 2014 7:48 p.m.

My first experience of light happened when I was 12 years old. My mom took me to a Leighton Ford crusade. God's light came crashing through the darkness of my soul. I have never looked back. Without any doubt, it is full-on the best decision I've ever made.

There have been other experiences of God's light throughout my life. The most recent experience was one week ago when we were given the news that my life had been extended from months to years. This was such a clear affirmation that God still has plans for me this side of heaven. God's light came bursting through the wonderings about my future.

> *Praise the LORD! How joyful are those who fear [reverence] the LORD and delight in obeying his commands…Light shines in darkness for the godly.*
> (Psalm 112:1–4 NLT)

DAY 85—INVITING GOD IN
By Brenda Pue—March 26, 2014 10:06 p.m.

Today I had a contrast dye CT scan of my chest, to establish a baseline of the lung tumour. Then I had a second CT scan of my brain to try to get a read on some new headaches, mild nausea and dizziness.

I have had numerous CT scans since the beginning of January. It should've been a case of "same old, same old," but for reasons unknown to me, I could feel anxiety rising. It may have been my receiving little forewarning of the appointment. But off we went to the hospital, the whole thing feeling rather routine. But when I got on the bed, it stopped feeling routine. So I started praying. I invited God into the space. I welcomed Him to take ownership of the time. I began to thank Him for all the answered prayers. I felt calm and at peace.

I can't think of a better way to deal with anxiety. Although I always have lots of questions for God—who, what, why, when, where and how—I'm learning that if the "who" question gets settled first, the others seem to fall into place better. This has served me well when anxiety comes knocking at the door.

Be anxious for nothing, but in everything by prayer and supplication, with thanksgiving, let your requests be made known to God. (Philippians 4:6 NKJV)

DAY 86—TUGGING AT THE HEART
By Brenda Pue—March 27, 2014 8:44 p.m.

My heart has been tugging at me all week. A group of leaders is meeting at the Muskoka Woods Leadership Studio. It is the second of three Arrow Leadership residential seminars…an amazing and transformational week.

For 19 years, this has been my ministry rhythm. Normally I would have been there. So no wonder my heart has been pointed that direction. I wish that everyone could experience how God uses Arrow to impact leaders, churches and communities. Or at least experience an Arrow leader in action.

I am grateful to have invested in a fine organization like Arrow Leadership. Arrow helped me to care about legacy. I want to leave,

1. A godly legacy.
2. A legacy of a healthy marriage.

3. A strong family legacy.

4. A great legacy for my grandchildren.

Love the LORD your God with all your heart and with all your soul and with all your strength. These commandments that I give you today are to be on your hearts. Impress them on your children. Talk about them when you sit at home and when you walk along the road, when you lie down and when you get up. (Deuteronomy 6:5–7 NIV)

DAY 87—ONE PHONE CALL
By Brenda Pue—March 28, 2014 9:30 p.m.

Have you ever had the experience of being evaluated? I have, many times. The strange thing is that I can have 39 perfect evaluations and one negative (often constructive) evaluation and the only one I can remember is the one. Maybe I'm not alone in this.

Today, I received a phone call from the Langley Home Care Nursing folks (a.k.a. palliative care) telling me that I have officially been registered. Even though I am experiencing gradual improvement of symptoms since starting chemo treatments, this phone call stopped me cold. I started praying—in a stunned sort of way. What else could I do?

One minute I'm looking forward to family night, and the next minute I'm sitting on the steps with my chin in my hands and my head spinning. Funny how one phone call can alter the course of a day.

Then I remembered that God is driving this thing, not the palliative care unit. I was reminded of one of my favourite psalms, which has seen me through other discouraging times.

I lift up my eyes to the mountains—where does my help come from? My help comes from the LORD, the Maker of heaven and earth. He will not let your foot slip—he who watches over you will not slumber; indeed, he who watches over Israel will neither slumber nor sleep. The LORD watches over you—the LORD is your shade at your right hand; the sun will not harm you by day, nor the moon by night. The LORD will keep you from all harm—he will watch over your life; the LORD will watch over your coming and going both now and forevermore. (Psalm 121 NIV)

DAY 88—HE KNEW

By Brenda Pue—March 29, 2014 9:22 p.m.

If God truly knows everything…and I believe He does…then it follows that my surprise phone call yesterday was not a surprise to Him at all. If it wasn't a surprise to God, I surmise that there is something God wants me to learn.

Here are a few thoughts since yesterday:

• "They" aren't the enemy but rather here to bless and help.
• Rather than panic, I need to embrace.
• Pray and pray some more.
• Beware of pity.

All of these are important, but my long-time prayer mentors often warned me about the danger of pity. The context was around judgment being clouded by feeling sorry for someone. But self-pity also counts. It can short-circuit what God is trying to say. And if I'm honest, God is often trying to speak to me. Yet my fear and self-pity cause spiritual deafness.

Is it resolved? No. That would mean perfection. But God has my attention!

Give thanks in all circumstances; for this is God's will for you in Christ Jesus.
(1 Thessalonians 5:18 NIV)

DAY 89—QUIETNESS

By Brenda Pue—March 30, 2014 7:00 p.m.

It's been a day of quietness. Sundays are not usually like that for me. It actually started last night at 8:30 when we darkened our house inside and out for Earth Hour: Turn off the lights—save the planet.

It felt like the peacefulness after a power outage. The quietness continued into today. Sometimes this can be an amazing gift. My life, for the most part, has been fairly high octane up until recently. I imagine that most of our lives are hurried and distracted much of the time, so that slowing down feels strange and counterintuitive. And yet, it's something we are all desperate for.

I came across a quote by Etty Hillesum that puts it so well:

Ultimately, we have just one moral duty: to reclaim large areas of peace in ourselves, more and more peace, and reflect it toward others. And the more peace there is in us, the more peace there will also be in our troubled world.[9]

"Come to me, all you who are weary and burdened, and I will give you rest." (Matthew 11:28 NIV)

DAY 90—COMMONALITIES
By Brenda Pue—March 31, 2014 11:23 p.m.

I am reading two books about well-known people who have received a cancer diagnosis. The first is David Watson, who learned that the he had colon cancer on January 7, 1983. The second is David Jeremiah, who received a cancer diagnosis on September 26, 1994.

There are commonalities in their stories and in my story. Indeed, I'm convinced that the early hours and days following a cancer diagnosis have some universal emotions.

First—pure disbelief. Should anything be said in case the doctors made a mistake?

Second—how to engage those closest, such as family and friends.

Third—how to manage future plans. Can this be happening?

Fourth—the whirlwind of appointments. How then shall I move forward?

Every time I read someone's else's story, all the feelings come flooding back. I realize that every story is unique. But it seems to me that the early days of diagnosis have glaring similarities. The treatment phase is where the variations occur.

The thing that encouraged me in both cases was the role of faith, prayer, the Bible and the people who rallied around. Again, this is our experience. There are many verses that bring such strength.

God is our refuge and strength, a very present help in trouble. (Psalm 46:1 NKJV)

---

[9] Etty Hillesum, *Etty: The Letters and Diaries of Etty Hillesum,* 1941–43 (Grand Rapids: William B. Eerdmans Publishing Company, 2002).

DAY 91—LAUGHTER AND WELL-BEING
By Brenda Pue—April 1, 2014 10:19 p.m.

Much has been written about the importance of laughter in a person's life and how laughter impacts a person's well-being. I am always drawn towards the person with a smile on his or her face.

My mom and I took advantage of the beautiful spring weather this afternoon to go for a walk. While we walked, we discussed how we had read in two separate books about the life-giving nature of laughter and joy. On two occasions, cancer patients were known to check out of the hospital and watch everything they could from all the great old comedians. Good, clean fun. Both men literally laughed their way to healing and health, from very serious cancer diagnoses.

I am not saying that laughter heals cancer. What I am saying is that laughter helps with a person's general outlook or attitude on life. There's a real shortage of laughter in the world anyway. I am grateful that God has given me a family and good friends where there is no shortage of laughter. I hope you can get a good belly laugh in soon.

A cheerful heart is good medicine, but a broken spirit saps a person's strength.
(Proverbs 17:22 NLT)

DAY 92—WHAT IS IT LIKE BEING WITH BRENDA?
By Carson Pue—April 2, 2014 11:01 p.m.

Carson here, as I am letting my dear one have a rest. This means I get to write whatever I want even if it embarrasses her when she reads it.

Last week I took some shirts into the local dry cleaners. The manager is a woman from Asia, and English is not her mother tongue. When I walked in the door she jumped up from her sewing machine and excitedly asked how my wife was (as she looked out the window to see if Brenda was in the car). She acts like Brenda is her best friend, and maybe she is!

Brenda heard that these new immigrants were opening a laundromat in our neighbourhood, and she had it on her heart that we needed to support her. For the first few months mine seemed to be the only shirts on the rack for pickup. This week Brenda smiled when I told her the rack was filled to capacity and about the greeting I get when I enter the shop. Brenda's purpose in supporting her is not just to provide shirts to launder but also to build a relationship, a friendship, with this dear woman. That is our Brenda. So, when we as a family read your comments about our wife/mom—we are deeply touched by how she has obviously connected with you too.

A husband asked me, "What is it like being with Brenda going through this?"

"In many ways," I responded, "it is consistent with our 37 years of marriage—filled with love, deep talks, trust, faith, creativity and an ability to still laugh." I adore this woman I am married to, and this season of challenge only amplifies these feelings within me. Oh, and have I told you she is stunningly beautiful? (That's the embarrassing part.)

So how does someone face a life-threatening cancer diagnosis with this much grace and courage? Brenda does it with God's help: "When you pass through the waters, I [God] will be with you; and when you pass through the rivers, they will not sweep over you. When you walk through the fire, you will not be burned; the flames will not set you ablaze" (NIV). Brenda reads a text like this from Isaiah 43:2, and she imparts it as truth in her life, as a promise, because she actually has a relationship with God, and she trusts Him.

So maybe that verse is for you too? What difficult situation are you facing today? Do you trust that God will protect you?

On behalf of our entire clan, thank you for loving us through this journey.—Carson

P.S. I asked our kids what adjective they would use to describe their mom. I'm collecting all the answers. What single word would you pick out to describe Brenda? Here are some of the responses from Caring Bridge friends.

- Courageous
- Pure joy
- Gentle
- Loving
- Vibrant
- Precious
- Legit, real, light
- Serene
- Resplendent
- Selfless
- Joyful
- Faith-filled
- Intentional
- Celebration
- Glowing
- Caring
- Light
- Connected
- Radiant
- Inspiring
- Fun
- Loyal

- A blessing
- Encouraging
- Forthright
- Inclusive
- Thoughtful
- Kind
- Listener
- Treasure
- Comfortable
- Nurturing
- Full of grace
- Giving
- Pure
- Engaging
- Positive
- Genuine
- Fabulous
- Extraordinary
- Love
- Compassionate
- Loverly
- Beautiful
- Authentic

DAY 93—SPRING CLEANING
By Brenda Pue—April 3, 2014 10:42 p.m.

Well, we are getting to that season of the year when we think about "stuff" that needs to get done on the home front, inside and outside. How does a person get it all done and still embrace the eternal?

I think the answer is that there is no separation. I love working in my garden, even weeding! There is something about getting the hands dirty. Though I confess that the fingernails take a beating. One of these days, I hope to feel well enough to putter around in the garden.

And then there is endless paperwork, bill paying, and the like. Again, perhaps there is no separation. It's the stuff of life, and nobody knows that better than God. But it can get a little lopsided sometimes. That's the difficult part. For myself, I have probably tended to pick up more of these kinds of activities because I enjoy them. When both people are working outside the home, it can get unbalanced.

I'm an advocate of shared ventures in order that everyone finds time for the sacred and for little pleasures. You will see from the following story that even Jesus clearly knew his way around a beach.

At dawn the disciples saw Jesus standing on the beach, but they couldn't see who He was. He called out to them, "Friends have you caught any fish?" "No," they said. "Throw your net on the right hand side for the boat and you'll get plenty of fish." So they did, and they couldn't draw in the net because there were so many fish in it. The disciple whom Jesus loved said, "It's the Lord!" When they got there, a charcoal fire was burning and fish were frying over it, and there was bread. "Bring some of the fish you've just caught. Now come have breakfast," Jesus said. Then Jesus served them some bread and fish. (See John 21:4–14.)

DAY 94—WHAT TO DO? WHAT TO DO?
By Brenda Pue—April 4, 2014 10:59 p.m.

Last week at family night, the discussion rolled around to our kids trying to sort out their holiday plans for the spring. So that is the big topic for family night tonight.

I lean towards making plans and trusting that the plans will work themselves out. It is a little challenging though. And far be it from me to have everyone's plans revolve around me.

Proverbs says,

> To humans belong the plans of the heart, but from the LORD comes the proper answer of the tongue. All a person's ways seem pure to them, but motives are weighed by the LORD. Commit to the LORD whatever you do, and he will establish your plans. (Proverbs 16:1–3 NIV)

I like the part about committing to the Lord whatever hopes and dreams we may have for the immediate future, in my case and in my family's case. There has been a lot of pressure the past three months for our family. We are looking forward to another family weekend up at Barnabas next weekend. Also, it's my heart's desire that my kids will not feel any anxiety about getting away for short breaks next month. Will you join me [in] praying it will be so?

DAY 95—PUTTING LIFE IN PERSPECTIVE
By Brenda Pue—April 5, 2014 8:36 p.m.

It's been almost three months since that day our family sat in stunned silence, digesting the news of the cancer diagnosis. It took a few minutes to actually formulate thoughts, words and questions. Eventually, we got there. But it all felt a little half-hearted.

Now, three months later, I sense that all of our family has found beauty in the midst of agony. And, yes, I would call the early days agonizing. Since those days, each of us in our own way has tried to make sense of something that really only God can make sense of. Here are some beautiful things that I've captured:

Seeing people differently: If I took anyone for granted, and I know I did, there is a new depth that wasn't there before. There are things I love more about the man I married. I won't publicly embarrass him though. All my children are even more amazing than I knew them to be. And I could sit and watch the grandchildren endlessly.

And God is amazing to me. We've always enjoyed a rich, honest relationship, through no effort on my part at all. Yet somehow it is even better.

In my reading, I came across this wonderful comment in a newspaper article by a radiation oncologist in New Zealand, and it expresses so well the upside of a cancer journey:

> Cancer makes people start thinking about the quality of their lives. Everything they do has a keener edge on it, and they get more out of life. In fact, some people never become complete human beings and really start living until they get cancer. We all know we are going to die sometime, but cancer makes people face up to it...They are going to go on living with a lot of extra enjoyment, just because they have faced the fear of death. Cancer patients aren't dying. They're living. I have never seen a suicide because of cancer.[10]

The steadfast love of the LORD never ceases; his mercies never come to an end; they are new every morning; great is your faithfulness. (Lamentations 3:22–23 ESV)

DAY 96—LIFE IS GOOD
By Brenda Pue—April 6, 2014 11:43 p.m.

Carson and I were reflecting with our good friends tonight about our upcoming family weekend at Barnabas on Keats Island this Friday. For our grandkids, and their parents, there will be no sleep prior to [it] because of their excitement. Do you remember that wonderful feeling? It is a very special place for us all.

---

[10] Frank Mihalic, "Death Faced," in *The Next 500 Stories* (Manila: Logos Publications Inc., Manila, 1993), 145.

This past week Jason was putting his youngest (Liam) to bed. The conversation went like this:

Dad: "I love you, son."

Liam: "I love you more."

Dad: "No you don't!"

Liam: "I love you all the way to Australia."

Dad: "Well, I love you all the way to the moon and back."

Liam: "Well, I love you all the way to Disneyland."

Dad: "Well, I love you more than hockey."

Liam: "Well, I love you to Barnabas and back!"

Dad:...pause..."Okay, you got me."

In five more sleeps, we will be there. I can't help thinking how incredibly blessed we are to have this time together as a family to talk, play, pray and plan.

Back to our conversation with our sweet friends...They asked, "Can you imagine what it would be like if your kids lived around the world at a time like this, or there was unresolved strife?" When I think of my many blessings, family ranks very high for me. Just being able to carve out the gift of time together in the midst of everyone's full lives is a true gift.

I love the image of this word picture from the Psalms:

How joyful are those who fear the LORD—all who follow his ways! You will enjoy the fruit of your labor. How joyful and prosperous you will be! How rich your life! Your wife will be like a fruitful vine, flourishing within your home. Your children will be like vigorous young olive trees as they sit around your table. (Psalm 128:1–3 NLT)

DAY 97—SIMPLE JOYS

By Brenda Pue—April 7, 2014 9:07 p.m.

I'm working away on my grandparent book. Only 14 pages left, not including photos. One of the questions asked me to describe a perfect day. There are so many directions a person could go with a question like that, such as a wonderful holiday.

In the end, I decided to roll with my limitations and describe a perfect day filled with simple joys. It included a day much like today. A lovely, healthy breakfast with my family, discussing the day to come. Carson off to work, and Mom and I catching up on correspondence and talking quietly. I love visiting with my mom. She is a wealth of information, now that she is sporting her new iPad. :) It also included a lovely prayer time, reading a great book that is bringing me joy. Add to that a lovely walk this afternoon on a perfect day weather-wise, 20 degrees Celsius or 68 degrees Fahrenheit. And an hour pondering the state of my garden.

Simple joys.

If there was anything that caused consternation, it was wearing a hat in warm weather. I toyed with the idea of going hatless for about 30 seconds until I recalled that my husband is really the only person who *loves* my "streamlined" look. So I am definitely going to have to figure that out.

I believe I have a lot to learn about simplicity; apparently two-thirds of a lifetime hasn't been quite enough time for me to get this important life secret secured in my soul. Enjoy the little things in life, for one day you will look back and realize they were the big things.

Ecclesiastes 5:18 says, "Here is what I have seen to be good and fitting: to eat, to drink and enjoy oneself in all one's labor in which he toils under the sun during the few years of his life which God has given him; for this is his reward" (NASB).

DAY 98—HARDEST WORD IN THE DICTIONARY— WELL, MAYBE THE SECOND HARDEST

By Brenda Pue—April 8, 2014 8:54 p.m.

I've been thinking about some of the hardest parts of dealing with cancer over the past few months. For me it is waiting. There is a complete loss of control when we are required to wait...for almost anything. Even benign things like a meal in a restaurant.

I recall one time when Carson and I went out for dinner in another city. It seemed to take a long time—about 35 minutes to place our order. Dinner arrived at the 90-minute mark. The meal arrived with a flourish and included the chef, who came and sat down with us to explain why our pizza had taken so long. "Nothing but the best and the freshest ingredients will do," he said with flair. Fresh baked crust, topped with homemade tomato sauce, made from fresh Roma tomatoes. I could go on and on. Suffice it to say, it was far and away the best pizza we have ever had. We also had such an enjoyable time with this chef, and it changed how we felt about the long wait—it was an experience!

Prior to the meal's arrival, we were getting a little antsy and had even discussed the possibility of leaving for some fast food. We like being in control. But I wouldn't have missed this experience for anything. It is one of those fine memories that I have tucked away and came oh-so-close to missing.

That is why there is such genius in waiting. God knows this about me and you. It is such a helpless feeling to have to wait—for even the smallest thing. But it is a wonderful thing for parents to encourage children to wait as much as possible. It prepares them for the bigger waits that are to come. Such great character development comes with loss of control. And how badly we all need this. In fact, I am certain that few of us really know much. Yet God knows, and He will meet us right in this very place.

P.S. Maybe the hardest word is "forgiveness."

I waited patiently for the LORD; he turned to me and heard my cry. (Psalm 40:1 NIV)

DAY 99—HOPE IN THE FACE OF MORE RESULTS
By Brenda Pue—April 9, 2014 9:40 p.m.

Yesterday, Carson and I were discussing our thoughts and feelings about my upcoming appointment with my medical oncologist this week. Tomorrow is another "results day" at the cancer clinic. I should receive the results from the CT contrast chest scan and also the CT brain scan that I had two weeks ago.

So how do I feel? Part of me wants to fully embrace the good news from our visit almost a month ago. I would welcome another bit of good news. The purpose of the chest scan was to set a baseline for the tumour in the lung. So that is the scan I am mostly curious about. It's the brain scan that is unnerving for me. The one thing I know about a cancer journey is that it is one day at a time…physically, emotionally and spiritually. And so, every day I start fresh… with myself…with the Lord…with my marriage…with everything.

I came across a great quote in a book I am reading that has been so helpful and true for me. Ben Patterson, in his book called *Waiting*, says, "You cannot hope in God until you have ceased to hope in yourself."[11] I believe that I may have come to this place, although God might challenge me on this.

---

[11] Ben Patterson, *Waiting: Finding Hope When God Seems Silent* (Downers Grove: InterVarsity Press, 1989).

And so, I head into tomorrow's appointments, knowing that God has been my help each step of this journey thus far and that He is the one constant day and night for me. I know I may walk into a little "heat" tomorrow, but I won't fear, as the following verse says.

"But blessed is the one who trusts in the LORD, whose confidence is in him. They will be like a tree planted by the water that sends out its roots by the stream. It does not fear when heat comes; its leaves are always green. It has no worries in a year of drought and never fails to bear fruit." (Jeremiah 17:7–8 NIV)

DAY 100—CELEBRATING WITH CHINESE FOOD
By Brenda Pue—April 10, 2014 9:47 p.m.

Carson and I made our way to the cancer clinic this afternoon. There is always blood work to be done one hour prior to meeting with my medical oncologist. The idea is that prior to me meeting with the oncologist, she will receive the results of my red blood cell count and my white blood cell count and results on my liver function.

It's a very efficient system. All my blood work checks out, and the results on liver function will be received early next week. That would be an item for prayer since the particular drug I am on can have fairly serious side effects to the liver. This will be closely monitored every two weeks, we learned today.

Now for results of the chest and brain CT scans. Both scans show no growth or changes in either area. The tumour in the lung has not grown since January. We are grateful. There are still six lesions in the brain, which have not changed except that there is no swelling this time around. I still have some pain and nausea—perhaps once or twice per day. That would be my second item for prayer. I asked my oncologist what she makes of this. She gave us a big smile, shrugged and said, "Let's take it!"

So the bottom line is that this is good news for us. In one book, I read that an X-ray was shown of a man with lung cancer, showing the man's tumour. Another oncologist showed an X-ray of a shrivelled tumour, indicating that the cancer had been eradicated even though this man had died. However, the first individual was fully alive, years after prognosis, even though the tumour was still there. They call it "living with cancer." Those were my exact words to

Carson as we were leaving the agency today. God has His ways, and they are far beyond mine. I'm learning to roll with His ways, I think…or at least I'm being stretched.

Regardless, we felt it was worth a Chinese food moment! <Big Smile>

"For my thoughts are not your thoughts, neither are your ways my ways," declares the LORD. "As the heavens are higher than the earth, so are my ways higher than your ways and my thoughts than your thoughts." (Isaiah 55:8–9 NIV)

DAY
101
TO
150

DAY 101—ONE HUNDRED DAYS AGO
By Brenda Pue—April 11, 2014 10:25 a.m.

One hundred days ago, on January 1st, we as a family received the first news of the lung cancer diagnosis. And yesterday we arrived at beautiful Barnabas once again—our entire family. So much has happened that we almost can't absorb it, so last night after the grandkids were in bed, we took the evening for a 100-day conversation. Here are some of our reflections:

- We've all changed for the good, but it's been hard.
- Lots of prayers have been prayed—impossible to put a number on it.
- There have been lots of answers—some we know and lots we hope to learn.
- The intensity of the past 100 days has caused a feeling of compression at times.
- There is a sense of optimism.
- We all have more confidence in God.
- Good news is backfilling doubts.

I believe that 100 days ago, God started a conversation, with me, with Carson, with our immediate family, with my family of origin and with the wider community. I feel like 100 days ago, God wanted to get our attention in order to begin a significant conversation…not an easy one, but a worthy one.

We are learning, growing and loving. It's been quite the 100 days.

P.S. It has been restoring to be with family. Little people have a way of giving love without even trying.

Whether you turn to the right or to the left, your ears will hear a voice behind you, saying, "This is the way; walk in it." (Isaiah 30:21 NIV)

DAY 102—A SURPRISED DONKEY
By Brenda Pue—April 12, 2014 8:14 p.m.

As I have been pondering Palm Sunday and Easter week this year, I came across a prayer that fits me well. It is based on Luke 19:28–38 and is my prayer as I enter the coming week:

Lord, the donkey must have been surprised.

It wasn't used to all that noise.

It wasn't used to people riding on its back.

The flash of clothes thrown down before its feet
was disconcerting.
Palm branches near its eyes,
off-putting.
The shouting of the crowd
incomprehensible.
And yet it seemed content to carry you.
I've seen no record of it rearing up, or kicking.
It didn't seem to be shy, or back away.
Just plodded on,
the weight of God light on its back.
I'm not like that.
I'll join the crowd,
cry blessings on you, Lord.
But then, like them,
my welcome is conditional.
I like the thought of your disturbing other people's lives.
I'm with you, Lord,
in pointing out their faults,
and making your demands on them.
It's when you look at me that I begin to get uncomfortable.
For, suddenly,
you take the tables of my life and tip them all upside down.
And all the things I hold so dear
go rolling down the aisles of my hypocrisy.
Scattered and lost,
shown up for what they are,
or aren't.
And I stand before you, empty.
All I can ask, Lord,
is that you'll put into my life
the same willingness the donkey had.
That bearing you will be no heavy weight,
your burden light,
your yoke an easy fit.[12]

[12] Eddie Askew, *Facing the Storm* (South Carolina: The Leprosy Mission, 1989). Used with permission.

DAY 104—A MARATHON, NOT A SPRINT
By Brenda Pue—April 14, 2014 10:12 p.m.

We ended up enjoying a wonderful family weekend away at Barnabas, made all the sweeter with two of my life friends offering to cook for our whole family, since the Barnabas kitchen staff were away this past weekend.

The weekend started a little slow for me, as I was navigating some side effects of my chemo treatments. This, by God's mercy, turned around partway through the weekend, and I was able to corral enough energy to play with the grandkids for the remainder of the weekend. So, it finished strong for me.

There were so many great moments: feeling-level conversations, board games, so many good laughs, amazing meals and prayer times. I couldn't have asked for more. I am including a photo of Landon from our boat ride back to the mainland, which says it all.

One night, we talked about how some of the great news we've received has been a bit of a game changer for us concerning the intensity of family times. As Carson says, this is no longer a sprint but rather a marathon. This started a discussion about a different rhythm for our family nights and for Caring Bridge posts. We haven't yet fully defined what this will look like but feel like it's time to explore new possibilities.

So even though I may not post every night, I do want to invite continued prayers. I am in need of prayer…always. Here is what I am facing this coming week:

1. An appointment with a cancer dietician to help me sort out how I can maintain my weight.
2. An appointment at the cancer clinic for another month's supply of my treatment (technically called molecular-targeted treatment) if the blood test for liver function checks out (you may recall that [problems with] this is one of the [possible] side effects of this treatment plan).

I will stay in touch, and I am incredibly grateful for your encouragement and prayer support. I have no idea where I would be today without it, since God chooses, at times, to allow our prayers to influence Him. I thank you for standing "in the prayer gap" with me and my family.

"I looked for someone who might rebuild the wall of righteousness that guards the land. I searched for someone to stand in the gap in the wall." (Ezekiel 22:30 NLT)

DAY 106—ENCOURAGEMENT CAME MY WAY
By Brenda Pue—April 16, 2014 9:54 p.m.

At Barnabas I had been navigating a few side effects of my cancer treatment plan at the beginning of this past weekend and was struggling physically. So a group of us decided to pray together on Saturday. Encouragement came in answered prayer within the hour. I was so grateful and relieved.

The next day, I was able to get lots of playtime with the grandchildren. We played Frisbee, navigated the giant playground pirate ship, and attempted hockey and tennis. I also brought bubble wands for the kids. The gift of watching little ones navigate life and play always makes me smile. I received this gift as more encouragement to my soul.

On Monday afternoon, we arrived home to my mom and sister Jenny, who had enjoyed weekend adventures of their own. Encouragement came in the form of smiles, adventures and stories shared as we reconnected. Wonderful.

Also on Monday, I received a card from our cousin. She had great news about the treatment plan I am on through a friend who has headed up the cancer clinic where she lived. When I read this, I closed my eyes and quietly whispered, "Thank You."

On Tuesday, encouragement came through conversations and phone calls. It was really helpful to talk with my sister, an RN, about my treatment, especially as she has had lots of experience in pediatric oncology. I felt lighter in my spirit after that conversation. Following that, I had a long conversation with a cancer dietician, who was so helpful and practical with ideas for helping me regain and maintain my weight.

The next phone call was with Langley Home Care (think: palliative care), who has been calling me regularly. Although I've tried to explain numerous times that my radiation oncologist says I wouldn't qualify because I am too high functioning, the message had not gotten through. But yesterday was different. I finally spoke with someone who *heard* me. When I explained the scenario, she said, "So you are not needing home care, correct?" I said, "That's correct." She responded, "That is such wonderful news! I'm so happy for you." I can't tell you how wonderful it felt.

My last call was with my brother Dave. He and my nephew Jonas are driving out from Alberta this weekend to see me (and the family). I can hardly wait to see them.

And today, I was back at the cancer clinic to get my next round of treatment pills, being grateful that my liver function test results came back normal.

After the previous week of managing discouraging side effects of my treatment plan, God knew that I would need encouragement in all shapes, sizes and packaging. I just had to share all this goodness!

> *The eyes of all look to you, and you give them their food in due season. You open your hand; you satisfy the desire of every living thing. The LORD is righteous in all his ways and kind in all his works. The LORD is near to all who call on him, to all who call on him in truth. He fulfills the desire of those who fear him; he also hears their cry and saves them. (Psalm 145:15–19 ESV)*

DAY 108—OH MY!

By Brenda Pue—April 18, 2014 8:08 p.m.

Today is Good Friday. I've always puzzled over that title. How could it possibly be good that Jesus was killed? It took me many years to understand—and

I'm not convinced that any human can fully understand such a selfless act of grace.

We all have many noble moments throughout our lives. Those times when we most reflect the image of God. We were created for goodness, kindness, love, patience, peace, joy, grace and mercy. But we also have many "other" moments... let's call them ignoble moments.

What makes Good Friday so very *good* is that our ignoble moments are fully dealt with by Christ's death on the cross, allowing us all the gift of being able to live life the way that God desires and intends, reflecting His peace, goodness and grace. Really, it doesn't get any better in this life. Nothing comes close to living in a forgiven state.

My young grandson has an expression whenever he sees or experiences something that wows him. He says, "Oh my!" Of all the events historically, the world over, Good Friday truly deserves an "Oh my!"

For his unfailing love toward those who fear him is as great as the height of the heavens above the earth. He has removed our sins as far from us as the east is from the west. The LORD is like a father to his children, tender and compassionate to those who fear him. (Psalm 103:11–13 NLT)

DAY 110—ONE THING I AM LEARNING
By Brenda Pue—April 20, 2014 11:56 p.m.

Easter Sunday, our church was full for both services. This was my first time back since the diagnosis—three months plus ago. How wonderful to see everyone's smiling faces. We have been so well loved by our church. My family and I attended the second service, and I was given an opportunity to say a few words of greeting. That it was Easter Sunday was a bonus.

I want to elaborate with you here [on] what I shared very briefly with the congregation.

One thing I have distilled from the ups and downs of the past three months is that God has good intentions. It's so easy when the road of life suddenly gets washed out to assume that God's intention towards me, or others, is malevolent. Although I've had difficult—even desperate—moments, everything that I have read in Scripture and experienced personally tells me that God's intentions towards me (and towards you) are so very good.

I can't tell you how healing it is for me to know this. Even though God hasn't revealed the details to me, He gives me enough to trust Him with all of me. I have found Him faithful, reliable, kind, wise, merciful, loving and grace-filled.

This is one thing I am seeing more clearly about God as a result of the cancer diagnosis a few months ago. He is the God of good intentions.

"For I know the plans I have for you," declares the LORD, "plans to prosper you and not to harm you, plans to give you hope and a future." (Jeremiah 29:11 NIV)

DAY 112—OUT OF CHAOS
By Brenda Pue—April 22, 2014 6:40 p.m.

One of my favourite life quotes comes from Bruce Waltke. "Without intentionality, life will always tend towards chaos." Indeed!

The first words in the Bible tell me that "In the beginning God created the heavens and the earth. Now the earth was formless and empty, darkness was over the surface of the deep, and the Spirit of God was hovering over the waters" (Genesis 1:1–2 NIV). The verses that follow describe how order, peace and beauty came to be out of this chaos.

This past January, I was told that my physical body was in chaos. When our bodies function according to their intended design, it is remarkable. When everything in our bodies, minds and souls reflects God's order and harmony, it is nothing short of amazing.

Years ago Dr. Leonard Hayflick discovered that most cells in our bodies age and die after approximately 50 divisions. This programmed cell division is uniquely genetically predetermined for different parts of the human body. This means that different cells for facial features stop growing when they should, for example. One exception is cells related to procreation and birth, which are considered immortal.

Unfortunately, cancer cells are also considered immortal. They have the ability to reinvent themselves and to resist treatment, giving these cells an "immortal" quality. At a physical level, this is chaos. God wants to bring order to my physical body, but He doesn't want to stop there. He desires my mind and spirit to have order and peace as well. Redeeming what is in chaos is God's very nature.

What I know to be true of God is that He loves to bring order out of chaos. Knowing this about God brings great peace to me. The God of the universe has a good design for my life. He is for me, not against me. He is for you too!

What shall we say about such wonderful things as these? If God is for us, who can ever be against us? (Romans 8:31 NLT)

DAY 116—CELEBRATIONS AND DISCOURAGEMENTS
By Brenda Pue—April 26, 2014 10:31 p.m.

This was a big weekend for our family. Our youngest daughter by marriage, Kirstie, graduated with her nursing degree. It was the culmination of lots of hard work and dedication for many years. The celebrations covered the past two days, and I am so honoured to have been able to experience it all and to encourage and support this precious daughter in a wonderful milestone in her life.

Now for the discouragements. Last week, for a few days, I was wrestling with some side effects of my chemo treatment. Part of the problem is that it is so unpredictable. The main things causing concern:

Lack of sleep—sometimes I sleep well, but those times are few and far between. So I'm putting some prayer and thought into that. I also notice that sleep doesn't always resolve tiredness.

Losing desire to eat some foods—one day it's delicious and the next day the same thing tastes like cardboard to me, and unfortunately my memory is very unforgiving in this matter.

Rash on my body and face—I am able to manage this without using the prescription cream, which has side effects of its own with long-term usage.

Challenges with my digestive system—after consulting with my oncologist and my dietician, I feel like I may be on a good trend line. Time will tell.

Please don't feel sorry for me. All this helps keep me dependant on God, and I like that (most of the time). I'm still enjoying food and daily walks. Pain is minimal much of the time. I'm grateful for energy. I'm grateful that I could attend Kirstie's graduation festivities. I'm aware that there is great suffering all around me—and us—and I'm deeply thankful for all the goodness that God has given me. A friend of mine taught me the value of listing my top three blessings at the end of every day. What a wonderful, life-giving practice!

To conclude, one thing that I gleaned from a daily devotional book by Anne Buchanan is the idea that sometimes my physical realities take over (think: chemo treatment side effects). This has caused me a few overwhelming moments. It's easy to let physical realities cloud over the fact that there are also spiritual realities. God cares and is at work. I wish my eyes were more attuned to the spiritual dimension. It's so easy for me to stay stuck in the physical dimension.

He gives power to the weak and strength to the powerless. Even youths will become weak and tired, and young men will fall in exhaustion. But those who trust in the LORD will find new strength. (Isaiah 40:29–31 NLT)

DAY 118—HOPE HORIZONS
By Brenda Pue—April 28, 2014 10:26 p.m.

I've been reflecting on a speech given by Kevin Jenkins, who received an honorary doctorate from Trinity Western University during Kirstie's convocation. Kevin is the president of World Vision International, working with the world's most vulnerable children in poverty. He shared a wonderful story that resonated with me and I know many others in the audience.

He told the story of personally meeting a 14-year-old girl who was a third generation beggar in India. World Vision worked with her and her family, to encourage her to get an education. She eventually did graduate, and when asked about the difference between her life before and since her graduation she said, "My life before was measured by a day. I hoped that I wouldn't get hurt and that I'd get a meal each day. Since receiving an education, I have hope for the future." In other words, her hope horizon went from one day to years.

It seems to me, as I've pondered this idea of a hope horizon, that a reversal of this happens when a person receives a critical illness diagnosis. It seems that the hope horizon goes from years to months.

When the hope horizon narrows in our lives, it can have as serious implications as a physical diagnosis. Hopelessness, or giving up, impacts our physical well-being in unimaginable ways. Over the past months, I have read many true stories that went both ways.

God, the source of all hope, has significantly grown my hope horizon since January.

Now faith is the assurance of things hoped for, the conviction of things not seen. (Hebrews 11:1 ESV)

DAY 119—A DIVINE APPOINTMENT
By Brenda Pue—April 29, 2014 10:24 p.m.

Today is my sister Kerry's last full day with us, so my mom and I decided to take her out for lunch. While Kerry and I were waiting at the counter, a woman came up beside me and asked if I was going through chemo treatment (my hat motif seems to tip people off). I replied affirmatively. She told me that she was diagnosed with stage four cancer two years ago and was given two to three weeks to live.

Next she asked if I was a person of faith, and I said yes. She said, "I am standing here talking with you today because of the healing power of prayer. May I pray for you?" I nodded. She asked me my name and right there in the restaurant began to pray for my healing. Then she reached out and touched Kerry and said, "It's hard on everyone."

I am typically a very friendly, talkative person, but I had no words over this encounter.

This unplanned moment felt very planned by God to both Kerry and me. It felt like a divine appointment. Kerry and I looked at each other, to confirm that the conversation really happened. We were speechless and moist-eyed. I turned to get the woman's name, but she was no longer there. In hindsight, it's not important. Heaven came down and enveloped us for a few precious moments.

Do not forget to show hospitality to strangers, for by so doing some people have shown hospitality to angels without knowing it. (Hebrews 13:2 NIV)

DAY 121—LAUGHTER AND PRAYER
By Brenda Pue—May 1, 2014 9:53 p.m.

My prayer group brought lunch over today. We have shared life at the deepest level for many years, although none of us can remember exactly how long we've been connecting. Regardless, it has been one of the sweetest and most worthwhile pursuits of my life.

When people pray together, souls are laid bare, and there is such peace in knowing that I can share personally and deeply with these trusted friends, and somehow they still like me! The truth is, they *love* me even more because of my willingness to "let them in," our mutual willingness to be transparent with one another.

Because we have shared a lot of life together, we highly trust and value one another. Trust is a key ingredient, as is humility. God has enriched our lives as a result. I honestly can't imagine my life without these incredible women.

So today was a gift. Great food, laughter and joy paved the way for yet another prayer time together. I am blessed beyond measure to have these praying, faithful friends in my life. I highly recommend making this a priority in one's life.

A friend loves at all times, and is born, as is a brother [sister], for adversity.
(Proverbs 17:17 AMPC)

DAY 123—GIFT OF ENERGY
By Brenda Pue—May 3, 2014 10:00 p.m.

I've enjoyed a remarkable week, energy-wise. There were graduation events, birthday celebrations, a visit from my sister, plus other shorter visits and family night. Also, moments with my darling grandchildren. I feel grateful to have *felt* like participating, as that has not been the case over the past months. I simply lacked the energy to want to participate.

So last week, it was exciting for me to take a few tentative steps towards renewed energy, even in spite of unpredictability with chemo treatment side effects, which I was able to navigate around.

Having said that, today has been a quieter day for me. I think perhaps a recovery day. :) So I look forward to evaluating the next couple of days to begin to understand the lingering impact of a full week of activity and people on my health and energy.

I am thanking God for giving me the gift of a great week and the energy needed to enjoy every moment.

> *Wait for the LORD; Be strong and let your heart take courage; Yes, wait for the LORD.* (Psalm 27:14 NASB)

DAY 125—I BELIEVE

By Brenda Pue—May 5, 2014 9:22 p.m.

The other night our family was listening to a beautiful song based on the Apostles' Creed, so called because it briefly summarizes what the apostles believed. After the song was finished I recalled that I memorized and recited the Apostles' Creed at church when I was six years old. Perhaps that is why it has a special place in my heart.

The Apostles' Creed
I believe in God the Father Almighty, Maker of heaven and earth; and in Jesus Christ, His only begotten Son, our Lord, who was conceived by the Holy Ghost, born of the Virgin Mary, suffered under Pontius Pilate, was crucified, dead and buried; He descended into hell. The third day He rose again from the dead; He ascended into heaven, and sits at the right hand of God the Father Almighty; from thence he shall come to judge the quick and the dead. I believe in the Holy Ghost, the holy catholic church, the communion of saints, the forgiveness of sins, the resurrection of the body, and the life everlasting. Amen.

One thing that has become clearer to me since my cancer journey began is the importance of who I believe. Having a personal relationship with God, nurtured over time in countless ways (reading my Bible regularly, experiencing answered prayer, going to church, journeying heavenward with other amazing people, etc.), has allowed me to wrestle with my big life questions and to learn about God's character. Not that I have all my big questions all sewn up. Rather, I am at peace with the faith work I have done. At the end of the day, when faced with my greatest life challenge to date, I am ready to trust God.

Who and what I believe has always been important to me, even more so since the cancer diagnosis. I suppose who and what we believe should matter regardless, since none of us knows when our time here on earth will draw to a close.

And this same God who takes care of me will supply all your needs from his glorious riches, which have been given to us in Christ Jesus. (Philippians 4:19 NLT)

DAY 127—DADS AND SONS
By Brenda Pue—May 7, 2014 10:40 p.m.

Today I am celebrating both my dad's and my son's birthdays. Two different and important relationships in my life. In the one, I was dependant, and in the other, I was depended upon. The parent-child relationship requires sacrifice, maturity, patience and love. Daunting—especially for those of us who lean a little on the self-centred side of the human equation.

When I was growing up, I had no idea how difficult parenting was. When I became a parent, my eyes were opened to the challenges of parenting. It's hard work! And so rewarding, when done well. I wouldn't trade it for anything.

My dad and my son come at this cancer diagnosis from vastly differing perspectives. I just got off the phone, wishing my dad a happy birthday. At one point he said, "I'm 80 today. I've lived my life. I wish I could trade places with you."

My son Jonathan views it differently. He is still young and newly married. From his perspective, there is still a lot of life to be lived. We've shared so much of life together, and there is so much more yet to come.

God sees this panorama, the early decades of life and the latter ones. He knows the unique pain at either end of life's continuum and everything in between. God longs to bring comfort. That is the nature of a loving father. In fact, God is the essence of the perfect father.

> *Blessed be the God and Father of our Lord Jesus Christ, the Father of mercies and God of all comfort, who comforts us in all our affliction, so that we may be able to comfort those who are in any affliction, with the comfort with which we ourselves are comforted by God.* (2 Corinthians 1:3–4 ESV)

DAY 129—GOD HELPS
By Brenda Pue—May 9, 2014 9:44 p.m.

I've heard it said, "God helps those who help themselves." Many think this phrase comes from the Bible, but it is nowhere in Scripture. In years past, those very words have escaped my lips. Now I see that God often helps those who cannot help themselves. When we can't help ourselves, great faith is required.

When I received the cancer diagnosis back in January, I couldn't "fix" myself. I quickly figured out that God is my help. Leaning on God and my praying "village" comes out on top. Here's how I lean on God: I talk with Him every day, I read about Him, and I hang out with people who will help me walk in the right direction. It's a great way to live, even for someone with cancer, or perhaps I should say for anyone who struggles. These three simple practices will nurture the health of a person's soul.

Dallas Willard says it so well: "If your soul is healthy, no external circumstance can destroy your life. If your soul is unhealthy, no external circumstance can redeem your life."[13]

There's so much more to me, to all of us, than the physical realm…I've always had a profound sense of that. Almost four months after a life-altering diagnosis, I know this quote to be true experientially.

> *For God has said, "I will never fail you. I will never abandon you." So we can say with confidence, "The LORD is my helper, so I will have no fear."* (Hebrews 13:5–6 NLT)

---

[13] Indirect quotation of Dallas Willard, in John Ortberg, *Soul Keeping* (Grand Rapids: Zondervan, 2014).

DAY 129—IMPACT OF A GOOD MOM
By Brenda Pue—May 11, 2014 8:18 p.m.

The impact of a godly mother can't be overstated. She is humble. She puts the welfare of others before her own wants or needs. She listens to the heart, not just the words. She prays for her children—everyday concerns (nothing is too small) and eternal matters—because she knows that prayer changes things. She works diligently to help provide for her family. She nurtures the soul, not just the body. She is dependable and trustworthy when few others in life can be leaned on. She knows that eternity is a part of every human heart, and she partners with God in it. I am blessed enough to be writing about my mom.

We phoned her a few hours after receiving the diagnosis. All of us kids phone Mom first. Upon hearing our shocking news, she didn't come unglued. It pained me to make that call. I can't imagine what it would be like to hear news like that from one's child. She was the first one to wish she could trade places with me. She was deeply concerned, yet steady. She stayed peaceful, positive and faith-filled. It was just what I needed and hoped for.

In just over a week, she arrived. She has been cooking, cleaning, organizing, doing laundry, driving me to appointments and praying continuously for us for almost four months now, I can't imagine how we could have navigated the days, weeks and months without my mom. This Mother's Day has new depth for me and our whole family. To be the recipients of such sacrificial love is almost more than I can bear. And Mom would simply say, "To God be the glory."

Charm is deceptive, and beauty is fleeting; but a woman who fears the LORD is to be praised. Honor her for all that her hands have done, and let her works bring her praise at the city gate. (Proverbs 31:30–31 NIV)

DAY 133—FEELING THE LOVE
By Brenda Pue—May 13, 2014 7:41 p.m.

On Sunday afternoon we enjoyed a picnic with our kids and grandkids at Derby Reach Park. It was a beautiful sunny day, and all of us sat around eating, talking and playing with the kids. It was perfectly relaxing, especially since the boys did all the work. Then…

Last night my three sons contrived to take me out for a continuation of Mother's Day. They booked a reservation at my favourite restaurant in Fort

Langley. Jonathan came and picked me up, and we all met at the restaurant. The evening was a wonderful mix of great food, good conversation, great memories and lots of laughter.

I couldn't have planned a better evening. Although I've pulled off some good gatherings with great food, complete with a planned itinerary, it was so good to let the guys lead our time together. It was peaceful and restoring, and I enjoyed the moments we shared.

My life has been fairly structured, and I believe I am learning a new way of being since receiving the cancer diagnosis in January. Since then, life has been a bit of a free fall for me, in a good way. I'm not saying there is no structure. Rather, structure with more internal flexibility. Most of what I am describing is an attitude of my heart. My soul is calming.

This has been a long time coming for me. The cancer diagnosis, the support of my family and the outpouring of love and prayer from my Caring Bridge and global "village" have been used by God in profound ways in my soul.

Definitely feeling the love!

No, despite all these things, overwhelming victory is ours through Christ, who loved us. And I am convinced that nothing can ever separate us from God's love.

Neither death nor life, neither angels nor demons, neither our fears for today nor our worries about tomorrow—not even the powers of hell can separate us from God's love. No power in the sky above or in the earth below—indeed, nothing in all creation will ever be able to separate us from the love of God that is revealed in Christ Jesus our Lord. (Romans 8:37–39 NLT)

DAY 137—ALL THINGS IN MODERATION
By Brenda Pue—May 17, 2014 3:26 p.m.

We had a first this week. Carson was speaking at a retreat and was away from home for four nights. One good thing about this is that both of us felt like it was doable. My energy and capacity are bit by bit improving, which allowed both of us to feel good about him being away.

So I had a little extra time to think about people and activities that are restoring. As I focus on my health this year (and as my energy capacity will allow), I am beginning to add in a few more activities. I am giving careful thought to things that sustain and things that drain.

Some things that nourish and sustain me are people, gardening, good food, reading and nature. As much as I enjoy all these good things, for the past several months I haven't had the capacity to engage them fully. Yet all these things that restore me will only do so if they aren't overdone.

All things in moderation—even good things. For example, too much good food = weight gain = other problems. Too much time reading = other necessities don't get accomplished. Too many people = exhaustion, even for extroverts. Too much gardening = well, all analogies break down somewhere. But I'm sure there is something wrong with excess in that area too.

So I'm thinking differently about balance in life these days, partly because I need to and partly because it's a wise approach for the immune system and the soul. I feel like God is nudging me to pay better attention to balancing work that needs to get done and finding rhythms of restoration in my life. Excess either way is not good.

Almost everything I read agrees that keeping one's immune system healthy is the best prevention for cancer. I'm not sure how I got here, but I now know that a multi-faceted approach to immune system health is essential: physical, emotional, and spiritual. I am experiencing this truth in my body and my soul as I live out the ups and downs of a cancer journey.

Thank you for continued prayers. I'm not sure where I'd be today without the undergirding power of prayer.

Look to the LORD and his strength; seek his face always. (1 Chronicles 16:11 NIV)

DAY 139—A FAMILY MILESTONE
By Brenda Pue—May 19, 2014 10:21 p.m.

This morning we hosted World Famous Pancakes for the kids and grandkids— at our house. The last time we enjoyed this family tradition together was over four and a half months ago. That was the Saturday before eight days of intense appointments and tests that confirmed the early diagnosis of stage four non-small cell lung cancer.

Perhaps the hardest thing I have ever done was to dispense the news that day to my family of what my doctor suspected. The children were playing in the other room. I looked into the eyes of each of my sons and daughters and laid it out as carefully and sensitively as possible. There is just no good way to share that kind of news. I will long remember the scene that day around the table…

Shock. Disbelief. Tears. Questions. Such deep pain.

How do we respond when the unthinkable happens in life? In my case, I tried to absorb the information the best that I could. I gathered facts. I didn't cry at first. I hoped it was a bad mistake. I turned to God for comfort and for wisdom. He had been faithful and trustworthy all my life, and I knew that He would show me the way somehow.

The scene and the mood around the table today were very different from ones four months ago.

Joy. Hope. Laughter. Peace.

So today we ate our breakfast together with four high-octane kids loving every bite, with the adults visiting and laughing and just enjoying it all thoroughly. It felt so normal. At least, as normal as having a meal with a bald lady can be. :) There were even presents to open. That isn't our normal routine, but all of our kids celebrate their anniversaries this month, so we made an event out of it.

All of this to say that God has answered prayers and continues to show me (and us) the way forward. Hope has paved the way for this family milestone.

Know therefore that the LORD your God is God, the faithful God who keeps covenant and steadfast love with those who love him and keep his commandments, to a thousand generations. (Deuteronomy 7:9 ESV)

DAY 141—A NATURAL MOMENT

By Brenda Pue—May 21, 2014 10:38 p.m.

I was given a beautiful orchid. It came as a gift from our daughter Shari's parents. The distinguishing thing about this plant is [the addition of] a little hummingbird made of feathers. I am so taken with this orchid that I brought it upstairs to my bedroom so that I can gaze at it.

This past February, only a month or so after the diagnosis, I was feeling low, so I thought I would sit on my front porch. It was a warm, beautiful, sunny day. As I came out a friend of mine was coming up the walkway. He hadn't heard about the diagnosis yet, so I took a deep breath and shared it with him. He responded quietly and seemed a little shaken by the news.

As we were standing there, me on the front porch and him down a few steps on the sidewalk, a little hummingbird flew right up to me and hovered about one foot from my face. It stayed hovering there for about a minute (which is like an eternity for a hummingbird), then darted off to the side and then came back and hovered in front of my face once again. Then it finally flew away.

Both of us breathed again, as we had stopped momentarily. My friend, who is a long-time landscaper, said, "I've never seen a hummingbird behave like that. That was amazing." It was one of life's precious moments.

After my friend left I sat down and pondered what had just happened. I felt that God had given me a much-needed gift of encouragement. The message? "I see you. I haven't forgotten about you. I'll keep coming to you."

Hummingbirds have a special place for me now. Every time I look at my little orchid, I am reminded that God has me in mind.

She gave this name to the LORD who spoke to her: "You are the God who sees me," for she said, "I have now seen the One who sees me." (Genesis 16:13 NIV)

DAY 145—THERE IS NO WAY TO GET NORMAL OUT OF THIS
By Brenda Pue—May 25, 2014 10:01 p.m.

Carson and I got away for a mini retreat this weekend, courtesy of the generosity of a number of people. It's the first time that we've been away, just the two of us, since the onset of this cancer journey.

It was very relaxing and restoring. We talked and read and relaxed. During one of our conversations, we reminisced about the many ways our lives have changed this year. At one point Carson said, "I wish life could just be normal again." I let out a sigh of agreement and said, "There is no way to get normal out of this."

For now, this is our new normal. And our greatest challenge and delight is discovering God in the midst of the new normal. Every minute of each day requires intentional focus to see God in the ups and downs—especially the downs.

When I am facing daily side effects of the chemo treatments, plus oncology appointments, blood work, brain and chest scans, and all the questions that surface, I am learning that this is my "normal" for now. This means that my new normal has me looking heavenward more than I ever have before.

And that's a good thing…a very good thing!

The LORD will guide you continually, and satisfy your needs in parched places, and make your bones strong; and you shall be like a watered garden, like a spring of water, whose waters never fail. (Isaiah 58:11 NRSV)

DAY 148—WHAT'S IN A WORD?
By Brenda Pue—May 28, 2014 10:50 p.m.

Last week my mom and I were reading through my medical documents and reports. The words were so bereft of hope that neither of us could finish reading them. I noticed how deeply I was affected for the remainder of the day. According to those reports, I should have one foot in the grave right now.

So that evening I decided to read different words. Words filled with hope, love and grace. Ultimately, God has the final word on everything, so I decided to hear His words on the medical reports. I opened my Bible and began reading for His perspective. I read wonderful stories of healing that filled me with hope and blessing again.

I've shared before that each night Carson and I count our blessings from the day. We each share our top three, though I sometimes need a few more. :) Then we thank God. My prayer that night started with "God, I thank You that I'm still here."

Words have great power—for good or for evil. I'm not even sure that there are neutral words. So as I live out the days, weeks, months and years that God has numbered for me, I choose to focus on His words of life, blessing and wisdom.

My son, give attention to my words; incline your ear to my sayings. Do not let them depart from your eyes; keep them in the midst of your heart; for they are life to those who find them, and health to all their flesh. (Proverbs 4:20–22 NKJV)

DAY 150—KEEP ON KEEPING ON
By Brenda Pue—May 30, 2014 9:02 p.m.

Yesterday Carson took me to the hospital for another CT scan. This was a follow-up to the baseline CT scan that I had a few weeks ago. It was a contrast scan, which means they do a few scans, then inject dye intravenously and do a few more scans for contrast. The results from my scan yesterday will be compared to my baseline scan to see if there is any change. Or in other words, the results will show whether the chemo treatment I am on is effective. We will meet with our oncologist on June 9th, and she will confirm the results.

My body tells me there has been improvement. It's been gradual, but I sense a healing trend. I keep holding on to that when I am dealing with symptoms or chemo side effects. I admit that it is up and down for me, and thankfully, it's more up than down.

For those of you who pray, I continue to manage the pain in my lower right lung daily, occasional low grade headaches and nausea (this has improved a lot since January and February) and low energy, which has me sleeping 10–11 hours a day.

On the positive side, there is a long list of things I am grateful for, such as manageable headaches and nausea, being able to do my chemo treatments from home, growing energy, and a general trend towards wellness. I'm not sure I would be in this place without my loving and supportive family, friends and church, the wider Caring Bridge community and a God who is for me. I am experiencing the power of prayer, and that brings me such joy.

Amy Carmichael says that "Joys are always on their way to us. They are always traveling to us through the darkness of the night. There is never a night when they are not coming."

Whom have I in heaven but you? I desire you more than anything on earth. My health may fail, and my spirit may grow weak, but God remains the strength of my heart; he is mine forever. (Psalm 73:25–26 NLT)

DAY
151
TO
200

DAY 152—NO WONDER I'M SMILING

By Brenda Pue—June 1, 2014 10:09 p.m.

Here's something that made me smile the other day…As I was getting dressed, I pulled on my pants and then went to zip up the fly and do the button, only to discover that they were already done up. Apparently there is room for improvement in the weight gain department. :)

I have lots to smile about these days. I'm sleeping longer lately. I'm enjoying more variety in food again. I'm beginning to read for pleasure, in addition to my functional reading and research. My interest in cooking is starting to resurface. I'm taking interest in my garden again. I'm learning the best uses of my energy. I'm once again taking interest in life. My capacity for interest and caring had been at a low ebb for several months, even though I worked hard to care. I learned that it takes a lot of energy to be interested.

In my daily Bible reading, I recently came across "Jesus Christ is the same yesterday and today and forever" (Hebrews 13:8 NIV). As I read about what Jesus was like when He walked the earth, I see that He was pure love, He was deeply compassionate with people, He was incredibly wise, He miraculously healed everyone He encountered, He was sacrificial, He gave people a fresh start, He offered hope when there was none, and the list goes on. In addition to all this, I think He was fun to be with—otherwise I don't think His disciples would have stayed the course. That is what He was like yesterday. The verse says He is still like this today. And it is what He will always be like. No wonder I'm smiling—He is for me, not against me.

God is our refuge and strength, an ever-present help in trouble. (Psalm 46:1 NIV)

DAY 154—A PRICE TAG ON HOPE

By Brenda Pue—June 3, 2014 7:05 p.m.

I recently renewed my Nexus "Trusted Traveller" application. This may seem counterintuitive:

1. I don't hold a valid driver's licence.
2. I can't legally drive a vehicle.
3. I shouldn't leave the country, as I do not qualify for health insurance.
4. Even if the preceding three were doable, I don't have the energy to pull it off.

So renewing my Nexus card seems like an exercise in futility. Yet for me, renewing that card was important. I couldn't stop thinking about it. When I mentioned the idea to Carson a few months ago, he asked why I wanted to do it. I answered, "It would be a concrete way for me to hope." Carson smiled and replied, "Well, fifty dollars is a very reasonable price tag for hope."

So I did it! I walked around for two days with the biggest smile on my face. It's because one day I hope to get my driver's licence reinstated. I hope to have independence again. I hope that my health will improve to the point where buying health insurance is a non-issue. I hope to be able to travel again. I hope for renewed, restored energy. Renewing my Trusted Traveller card represents my belief that change and healing are possible.

I can't overstate the importance of hope in one's life. It impacts every moment of every day.

I pray that God, the source of hope, will fill you completely with joy and peace because you trust in him. Then you will overflow with confident hope through the power of the Holy Spirit. (Romans 15:13 NLT)

DAY 157—A SNEAK PREVIEW
By Brenda Pue—June 6, 2014 11:31 p.m.

This past Christmas, we gave our kids and grandkids a week's holiday in July together as a family up the BC coast at Pender Harbour. So today Carson and I decided to try a trial run. So our dear friends drove us up to Pender and showed us around. It was like a sneak preview of the place we are headed to later this summer.

What an wonderful day! What a beautiful place! What a warm welcome we received! We can hardly wait to get there for a whole week with the kids and grandkids.

Today was so hopeful for me. Being able to have a sneak preview prepared us well for what to expect.

I feel like God has given me small glimpses, or previews, to encourage me along in the healing journey. Every now and again I have a fairly good energy day, which feels like a sneak preview of things to come. There have been many other encouragements as well.

I am grateful for all these blessings along the way. Earlier this year, we weren't sure that I would be able to make it to July for our family holiday, so the family was keen to arrange time together in February and March. Now that June is here, it appears that our Christmas gift to our family may happen after all.

I am incredibly grateful for the encouragements of this day—for the gift of another sneak preview from the hand of God.

May our Lord Jesus Christ himself and God our Father, who loved us and by his grace gave us eternal encouragement and good hope, encourage your hearts and strengthen you in every good deed and word. (2 Thessalonians 2:16–17 NIV)

DAY 159—THROWN INTO THE MIDDLE
By Brenda Pue—June 8, 2014 10:24 p.m.

Some time ago I read a devotional about the story of Jesus' encounter with the disciples who had been fishing all night with no success. When Jesus came to them that day, he told them to take their boat to the middle of sea and try fishing again. I learned that the reason why fishermen usually fished at night is because the fish stayed near the rocks at the shoreline for protection.

Though against all the conventions and practices of the day, the disciples trusted Jesus and went fishing in daylight in the middle of the sea. When their net was so full of fish that it was beginning the break under the sheer weight of all the fish, the other boat went to help. God provided abundance His way, not their way.

So what has this story to do with me? Well, back in January when I received my cancer diagnosis, I was essentially thrown into the middle of the ocean of uncertainty. Tomorrow I will be at the cancer clinic for blood work and liver function tests and most importantly to meet with my oncologist about the latest CT scan results. Though I likely would have chosen a different healing path for this journey, God is doing this His way. I am trusting God. And as I trust, His abundance is overflowing in my life, so much that the nets of my gratitude are breaking.

C. H. Spurgeon expresses how I feel so well: "God is too good to be unkind. He is too wise to be confused. If I cannot trace His hand, I can always trust His heart."

"Do not fear, for I am with you; Do not anxiously look about you, for I am your God. I will strengthen you, surely I will help you, Surely I will uphold you with My righteous right hand." (Isaiah 41:10 NASB)

DAY 160—GOOD NEWS REPORT
By Brenda Pue—June 9, 2014 9:00 p.m.

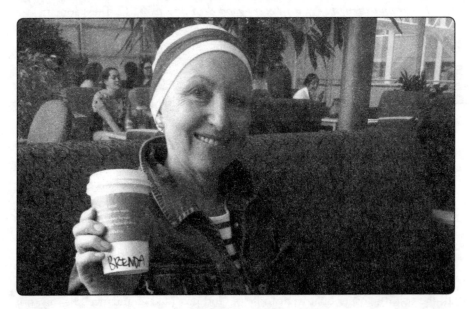

It's been five months since my cancer diagnosis. Today was a cancer clinic day, and we received the very good news that the tumour in my lung has shrunk by 26 percent. So it was the size of a golf ball, and it is now the size of a large grape.

While we realize that there is a long journey ahead, we are pausing to celebrate this news.

We want to savour this day...this moment...

A few times over the past few months I've dreamt of and prayed for an instantaneous miraculous healing. I've heard such stories that have amazed the medical community. But God has chosen a different path for me. Five months later, I see God's wisdom in a slow, steady approach to healing. My heart and soul need time and space to fully process the path I'm on. I travelled at a fast pace much of my life. I have much to learn, and God knows that I'll absorb it best by going S-L-O-W.

So much would have been lost on the fast road.

Thank you for literally being a caring bridge on this journey. For your prayers, love, support and encouragement. For carrying me in the moments when I couldn't carry myself.

A friend loves at all times, and is born, as is a brother, for adversity. (Proverbs 17:17 AMPC)

DAY 162—SOMETHING PRECIOUS LOST AND SOMETHING PRECIOUS FOUND
By Brenda Pue—June 11, 2014 11:18 p.m.

The other night, after dinner, Carson and I went for a walk around our neighbourhood. As we were on the final stretch towards our house, we came upon a Jack Russell terrier who seemed to be lost. We stopped to investigate. The dog was wearing a collar and tags but no leash. We could tell she was an older dog who needed some TLC, so we invited her to walk along with us. Neither of us had a cellphone [with us], so we brought her into the house.

I tried to contact the owners, but the phone number on both tags was for an animal shelter that was closed for the night. Momentary panic. I knew we couldn't put her back outside as by now it was dark. We had heard coyotes the night before. So we set about making her comfortable. She seemed to be hungry, [so] I sent Carson to buy a box of Milk Bones. I fed her while Carson made a makeshift leash, complete with a carabiner, which I thought was a lovely touch. :) I discovered that our new friend could do tricks. She was such a lovely old soul. Carson came in and said, "I hope you're not enjoying this too much." Too late...

Next we took her for another walk around the neighbourhood, a la leash, hoping we'd find a panicky dog owner. No such luck. So we brought her back home. I made [her] a little bed and got [her] a dish of water, and we settled in for the night.

I was almost asleep when I thought I heard whistling. I somehow materialized on the front porch and called out to the whistling man. We exchanged stories, and Ruby was reunited with her rightful owner. A precious Ruby was lost, and then that precious Ruby was found.

I don't think it was an accident that Ruby found me. I believe God had something for me in that little adventure. When I received the cancer diagnosis in January, I felt lost, alone and afraid. I wandered around, trying to figure it out the best way I could. I suppose it's what most of us do when life takes an unexpected turn.

I was given a reminder that in the same way that I welcomed Ruby into my heart and home, God is there for me, His arms wide open and eyes filled with such understanding. He continues to nourish me and soothe my fears on this journey. I know I am at my best when I don't wander too far from my Home.

And without faith it is impossible to please him, for whoever would draw near to God must believe that he exists and that he rewards those who seek him. (Hebrews 11:6 ESV)

DAY 166—COULDN'T LET THIS DAY PASS BY
By Brenda Pue—June 15, 2014 8:01 p.m.

Today I, along with many others, am thinking about fathers. As I see and experience my own boys as men, I admire who they have become, and I thought it would be worth thinking about how we all got here. I feel like their dad did some things really well. Things like (and these are in no particular order):

- Putting our marriage first, modelling the importance of that primary relationship to our boys.
- Making life fun; every day was an adventure to look forward to, from camping in the backyard to creative and personalized bedtime stories.
- Building wonderful memories on a budget.
- Engaging them at a feeling level regardless of their age; he knew when to be serious and when to break the tension with laughter (timing is everything, you know).
- Building trust; he is a man of his word.
- Modelling integrity and its importance, even when there were/are tough choices.
- He is a man of faith who is able to point our kids towards Someone beyond themselves when the road of life gets hard.
- When they were young, he somehow found the time to be physically very present.
- As they got older, he figured out how to be emotionally very connected to them.
- Whenever he built or fixed anything, he got them involved and taught them how to fix things.
- Saying yes to them as much as possible without betraying convictions.
- Teaching them to say, "I'm sorry…will you forgive me?"
- Not allowing the world to revolve around our kids; we as parents were the clear leaders in our family system, and our kids seemed to find security and peace in this.
- Letting God's values be the plumb line for all decisions.
- Placing value on church and connecting us and our kids to other people of faith.

Of course there is so much more than I can possibly write here, yet these are a few practices and values that come to mind. And yes, we have made a boatload of mistakes along the way. But for the most part as we bumbled along, we got a few things right.

And the proof for me has been watching our kids respond with authenticity, grace and faith when the road of life took a hairpin turn that none of us was prepared for. God's mercy has met us all.

So let us come boldly to the throne of our gracious God. There we will receive his mercy, and we will find grace to help us when we need it most. (Hebrews 4:16 NLT)

DAY 168—WISDOM IN THE NIGHT
By Brenda Pue—June 17, 2014 10:40 p.m.

The end of November last year, I was bothered by a pain in my side. About the middle of December I made a doctor's appointment. At the end of December I had a routine X-ray, which revealed a mass in my lung. The medical system went into action, and the news kept getting worse. The pain in my side became a non-issue…well, to everyone except me.

Diagnosing and treating the cancer is the right thing to focus on for now. This may not be the best time to get sidetracked, especially given that the bone scan, MRI, CT scans and X-rays all reveal nothing except some fluid in the lower right lung.

It is disquieting though. Pain of any sort is disquieting.

Carson and I were discussing my "disquiet" last week before bedtime. Before I went to sleep, I silently prayed, "Lord, I don't know how to *not* be afraid of this pain. Help me." I went right to sleep, only to wake up a few hours later from pain when I rolled onto that side. I lay there quietly for a while, and the thought came to me *Face into the pain.* As I pondered that, I realized that because I was afraid of pain, I had chosen to not breathe fully. Therefore facing into the pain could be as simple as breathing deeply again.

So every day I am intentionally breathing differently. It is my way of not being afraid or fearful. It is my way of trusting that God has my back. It is my way of choosing faith over fear. And one day, I hope to have this "disquieting" pain fully resolved.

"Behold, God is my salvation, I will trust and not be afraid; For the LORD GOD is my strength and song, And He has become my salvation." (Isaiah 12:2 NASB)

DAY 170—I THOUGHT I HAD CRIED ALL MY TEARS
By Brenda Pue—June 19, 2014 10:38 p.m.

Today I had a doctor's appointment, with a physiatrist. This is an expert who focuses on the development of a comprehensive program for putting the pieces of a person's life back together after injury or disease—without surgery. This appointment was a follow-up from a car accident that I had four years ago, and I had waited over a year for this appointment. Even though I have improved greatly in four years, I decided to keep the appointment.

As she was recording my case history, we of course ended up talking about cancer and my treatment. At one point there was a departure from the clinical history. She asked how I was feeling about the diagnosis and told me that two of the women on their team were cancer survivors. I told her that I was in a much better place compared to the early days of the diagnosis and that I was feeling okay about it now. I proceeded to tell her how blessed I feel by the support and encouragement of family and friends. She asked about my family, and I took great joy in briefly telling her about them.

And then I burst into tears. One second I was fine, and then next I could hardly talk. I told her that the hardest, most painful thing I have ever had to do in my lifetime was tell my family about my cancer diagnosis, knowing how much pain I would cause them. That is the greatest pain I've known.

I thought I had cried all my tears over this, but apparently not. I don't know why I let this stranger in, but it was beautiful, tender and sacred. It felt like a holy moment.

You will show me the path of life; In Your presence is fullness of joy; At Your right hand are pleasures forevermore. (Psalm 16:11 NKJV)

DAY 173—A PERFECT DAY…WELL, MOSTLY PERFECT
By Brenda Pue—June 22, 2014 9:58 p.m.

The day began over a lingering breakfast with friends. It was a wonderful time of catching up with each other. Good food. Pleasant atmosphere. Great company. Everything about it was pretty fine. When I got home, my mom and I took a long walk. The weather was pristine, and we felt blessed to be able to enjoy the beauty of it all.

After lunch, I had a great nap and then was gently awakened by my husband, who reminded me we were going to White Rock to walk the promenade along the ocean. I sleep so hard these days that it often takes me a few moments to recall who I am, where I am and what the plan for the day is.

We were walking along, taking in the incredible beauty of our walk, when we ran into our Jeremy and Shari and our two grandkids. So we visited awhile and then carried on. Our destination was Moby Dick's for fish 'n' chips. For some reason, I had a craving for fish 'n' chips, something I haven't felt in many, many months. I could barely remember what it felt like to crave something.

So we settled in to our table at Moby Dick's and enjoyed amazing fish 'n' chips.

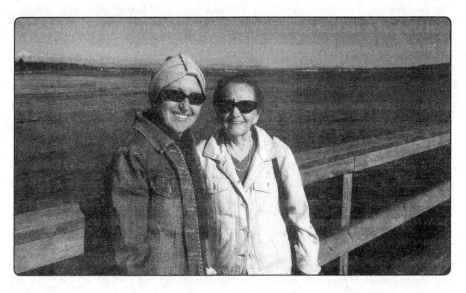

Then we began our hour-long walk along the promenade back to our car. This day reinforced for me the utter loveliness that exists in our world: in people, in food, in the natural beauty all around that God made for our enjoyment.

If you are wondering why it was a near-perfect rather than a perfect day, it's because I discovered that fish 'n' chips don't pair well with chemo pills. I put in a bit of a long night, but as I said to Carson, it was so worth it!

I feel so blessed to be alive.

The heavens declare the glory of God; the skies proclaim the work of his hands. Day after day they pour forth speech; night after night they reveal knowledge. They have no speech, they use no words; no sound is heard from them. Yet their voice goes out into all the earth, their words to the ends of the world. (Psalm 19:1–4 NIV)

DAY 175—I'M NOTICING...

By Brenda Pue—June 24, 2014 11:59 p.m.

Back in January, I was given a wonderful gift of hyperbaric sessions. Hyperbaric oxygen therapy is a treatment for increasing oxygen concentration in the blood and all organs by breathing pure oxygen at a pressure greater than normal from inside a hyperbaric chamber. Since cancer cells thrive in poorly oxygenated tissue, the expectation is that pure oxygen will inhibit growth of cancer cells. Due to medical concerns around my previous lung biopsies, I wasn't able to start using it until recently. This therapy is scheduled daily until July 10th. To be going for treatments, at long last, is an answered prayer.

Along with this treatment, I'm noticing other small signs of vitality lately and am journaling about these in what I call my Gratitude Journal. Here are a few items from my journal:

- I am not constantly chilled anymore. For several months, I have wrapped myself in blankets, layered my clothing and used a heating pad to keep warm.
- My appetite is returning slowly. I'm starting to care about food again.
- I'm sleeping well again—nine to ten hours a day.
- In my waking hours, I seem to have better energy than I've had in six months.

To be able to try hyperbaric therapy, along with my awareness of these changes that are happening, is symbolic for me. God is at work.

I am so grateful for many of you who have continued to pray and care for me over the past six months. I feel health returning in small ways.

But the godly will flourish like palm trees and grow strong like the cedars of Lebanon. (Psalm 92:12 NLT)

DAY 178—MY OLD, CROOKED TREE
By Brenda Pue—June 27, 2014 10:16 p.m.

We have a crooked pine tree in our front yard that is very old and very large. It leans out over the sidewalk and street, much to the chagrin of people out for a stroll or walking the dog. I routinely have to cut it back each spring.

One of the endearing qualities of this tree is its pinecones. The tree drops medium-sized pinecones every day, all spring, summer and fall. What makes this endearing rather than annoying is the interest our two oldest grandsons have taken in the pinecones. The boys have made it their mission to keep this area clean and safe. It helps that Grandpa times the boys to see how fast they can collect them, and then there is the drama of counting them all to see if they can beat their previous record.

Other trees on our street are also big, but for some reason they stand straight and tall. It seems that our tree leans towards the light. I'm sure there are other factors that an arborist would say contributes to my crooked tree's propensity for leaning. Light is an amazing thing. My tree got it right. It's leaning toward the light. Imagine what it would be like to live in darkness. That is not an existence I would want.

I confess that there were some dark times when we received news of the cancer diagnosis. There have been times when it has been a conscious choice and act of the will to turn aside from the darkness of critical illness and face into the light. God is my light. More and more, I want to be like my tree and lean into the light.

Let all that I am praise the LORD. O LORD my God, how great you are! You are robed with honor and majesty. You are dressed in a robe of light. You stretch out the starry curtain of the heavens. (Psalm 104:1–2 NLT)

DAY 181—TEN THOUSAND REASONS…
By Brenda Pue—June 30, 2014 10:47 p.m.

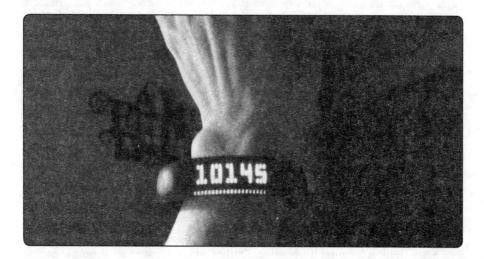

I n the past couple of weeks I've had a few people comment that I am looking better.

I feel better but don't necessarily "see" what others see. I'm still baldish, although the hair is making a heroic effort at a comeback. I think it's a solid one-quarter inch now. Nevertheless, it feels good to experience this sign of life. I'm still underweight, in spite of consuming large quantities of food. Nevertheless, I'm really starting to enjoy food again. It feels good to experience this sign of health too.

My husband mentioned again the other day that I was looking better. It finally dawned on me. I now know that in subtle ways I have changed. I responded to Carson by saying, "You know, just a couple of months ago I was on my way out of this world. I realize that now." There were all kinds of signs, though I didn't realize it fully at the time. I was fully focused on getting through a day at a time.

How does the change manifest itself? Well, here's one way. Carson gave me a Nike Plus bracelet for Christmas. I couldn't have known at the time how significant this gift would be. In the months following the cancer diagnosis, I began using it to track my fitness. It was a little depressing for many months as I struggled to achieve my daily goal of six thousand steps. But I stayed with it. Just a few days ago I more than met my target daily goal. It's taken six months, and it feels like a big accomplishment. I've posted photos that Carson took to celebrate the moment…ten thousand reasons to thank God.

A verse from one of my favourite worship songs, "10,000 Reasons (Bless the Lord)," by Matt Redman, has made me weep these past six months. The song says, "And on that day when my strength is failing/The end draws near and my time has come/Still my soul will sing Your praise unending." It echoes Psalm 103: "Bless the Lord, O my soul: and all that is within me, bless his holy name."

DAY 184—FEELING SAD AND SHAKEN
By Brenda Pue—July 3, 2014 11:19 p.m.

Life has been full this week with daily hyperbaric appointments. It's an incredible gift to be going, though a huge effort for me. I was in the bathroom upstairs as my friend arrived to drive me to my appointment. At the same time Carson walked into the bathroom to tell me the sad news that a friend, whom we will one day meet in heaven, died of lung cancer today.

Sean Trank is a young husband and father who was given an almost identical cancer diagnosis to mine: lung cancer that spread to the brain and the bone. We both received our cancer diagnosis on the same day. My heart has been sad and troubled all day. And, yes, there have been tears. I am praying today for Sean's family and friends.

This has hit hard. I have been fighting fear all day.

I only know one place to go when my spirit is shaken. That place where One is waiting for me with outstretched arms ready to hold me close and comfort me. God's love, grace and mercy will sustain me one day at a time.

> *Blessed be the God and Father of our Lord Jesus Christ, the Father of mercies and God of all comfort, who comforts us in all our affliction, so that we may be able to comfort those who are in any affliction, with the comfort with which we ourselves are comforted by God.* (2 Corinthians 1:3–4 ESV)

DAY 186—MORE THAN I DESERVE
By Brenda Pue—July 6, 2014 1:08 a.m.

What an encouraging day [in Penticton, BC]. It was well timed after the sadness of the previous two days. My spirit has been lifted by a series of conversations, kindnesses and prayers. God knows when my heart needs lifting.

It started with breakfast. Carson and I met with a friend [Mark Buchanan]—an incredible friend—whom I haven't seen since last year before the diagnosis. I loved everything about that breakfast. The laughter, the stories, the blessing, the sharing of pain and joy. It ended with our friend saying, "You look so good, so healthy. I didn't expect this. I've been a pastor for 24 years and have sat across from suffering [people]. I've seen a lot. But looking at you fills me with great hope."

Then my mom, my aunt, my sister and I hopped in the car and drove out in the country to a teahouse and gift shop high up on the hillside, called the Red Roost. The view was breathtaking, the grounds were beautiful, the ambience—serene! We sat on the deck drinking Earl Grey tea, enjoying each other's company and watching hummingbirds at the eight hanging feeders. Pure delight.

When Carson got home from today's session [at a denominational meeting], he shared stories and conversations from his time. All of them were so kind. One person mentioned that when he was praying for us he was given the word "faithful" and that God is the Faithful One carefully, tenderly watching over me. It took me back to the day after we received the devastating news of the cancer diagnosis. That morning, I was weeping and praying. Sad, beyond sad. I heard *very* clearly, "This isn't about you; it's about Me." That was all I needed to hear. There was some purpose to this. God has not ever let me down in my lifetime—He has proven Himself faithful in the good and the hard that have come my way.

I am so grateful for the encouragement of this day...a breakfast that filled me with great hope; a teatime that filled me with delight; and meaningful, caring

conversations and prayers that have reminded me of God's faithfulness. It is more than I deserve, yet gratefully received.

> *Understand, therefore, that the LORD your God is indeed God. He is the faithful God who keeps his covenant for a thousand generations and lavishes his unfailing love on those who love him and obey his commands.* (Deuteronomy 7:9 NLT)

DAY 189—MANAGING THE UNEXPECTED: SEIZURES, SLURRING AND SCANS
By Brenda Pue—July 9, 2014 1:52 a.m.

A lot can change in a day. Today started like any other day. Up at six to turn on the sprinkler system and water my little vegetable garden and grapevines. Next a great breakfast and out for a lovely walk with my long-time friend before my morning hyperbaric oxygen therapy appointment. I have been blessed to have a wonderful group of friends driving me back and forth between Langley and New Westminster for these appointments while Carson is at work.

But today the hyperbaric technician noticed that I wasn't quite responding like usual. She realized that my speech was slow and slurred and my mouth was slack on the left side (we all felt it was a seizure, although we didn't have an official diagnosis yet). The technician encouraged me to call my physician, which I did. My doctor ordered an emergency CT scan at Langley Hospital within five minutes. We left the hyperbaric clinic and drove to the hospital. I had another episode when we arrived at the hospital. I ended up with a blood test, a blood sugar test and an ECG, as well as the CT scan.

The family is, of course, concerned and came over tonight to hear about it first-hand. And, wouldn't you know—I had another episode with them all there. My doctor called back after consulting with the cardiologist and the neurologist over the results from today's CT scan. They feel I have had what is called a simple partial seizure, caused by one of the mets [metastases] (or scar tissue) in the brain, and I am starting on seizure medication tonight. In fact, I am writing this journal while I wait for the medication, courtesy of my dear husband.

I am at the cancer clinic tomorrow and meeting a new oncologist, and my doctor is trying to arrange for an emergency enhanced MRI tomorrow afternoon to figure out exactly what is going on inside of this brain of mine.

128

This was unexpected. I've never had a seizure before. I didn't know what one felt like until today.

I was fully conscious during all of these seizures, and it was perhaps the strangest sensation I've known, to sense my body not behaving right but not being able to do a thing about it. I felt completely powerless.

In spite of all this, I am at peace. God is with me. I trust that He is leading the way in this. I am grateful that it was today and not while I'm away on holidays. I'm grateful this is getting addressed sooner than later. I'm grateful for my dear friend who walked me through this scary day with faith and smiles. I'm grateful for my doctor, who is simply amazing (have you ever heard of getting a CT scan and results all in one day? He has done this routinely since this whole thing started); I'm grateful for the presence of God with me and the power of prayer. What more can I say? God's got my back!

He who dwells in the shelter of the Most High will abide in the shadow of the Almighty. I will say to the LORD, "My refuge and my fortress, my God, in whom I trust." (Psalm 91:1–2 ESV)

DAY 193—I MADE IT AND IT'S WONDERFUL
By Brenda Pue—July 12, 2014 10:46 p.m.

More than seven months ago, our family had planned a family holiday together, and [we] have continued to hope and plan for it in spite of the cancer diagnosis I received in January. Things were looking pretty bright for our family holiday, until this week when I unexpectedly started having seizures. Once again our plans seemed tenuous, for a few days. However…

We left early Friday morning for Pender Harbour via Horseshoe Bay Ferry Terminal. Earlier in the week, we wondered if our long-awaited family holiday would actually materialize due to the onset of unexpected seizures. I haven't had any further episodes but am managing side effects of the seizure medication, which include dizziness and drowsiness. I have the sense that these side effects will be less problematic as the week progresses. Just to be here with the whole family is such a gift!

This is our first full day. It is so beautiful here. Everywhere I look, there is such beauty that it makes my heart ache. I know that such natural beauty is good for my soul. One of the features of the place where we are staying is a prayer walk. Carson and I did about half of it this morning, the 23rd Psalm portion. It is divided into little stations with wooden houses that encase wooden books with Scriptures and meditations—very lovely.

As we walked back towards the house we could hear our grandchildren at the pool with lots of laughter and squeals of delight. One of the rich parts of this time for me is sharing all this with our precious grandchildren and our wonderful kids. We spent a few hours enjoying the incredibly perfect weather, reading and playing in pool.

I'm looking forward to our after-dinner devotional time, once the little ones are in bed, using my favourite devotional book, *Healing in His Wings*, by Anne Buchanan.

Did I mention how grateful I am to be here?

O give thanks to the LORD, for He is good; For His lovingkindness is everlasting. (1 Chronicles 16:34 NASB)

DAY 196—LESSONS FROM NATURE
By Brenda Pue—July 15, 2014 10:54 p.m.

Jonathan and I walked the prayer forest tonight after supper. This time, we brought phones so that we could take photos. The first time I walked it, I came across this story from the section called The Path of Perseverance. I haven't been able to get this particular story out of my mind, because it resonates with parts of my story…So I can't help sharing this lovely story with you…there is something here for all of us.

This tree is between 300 and 400 years old. The whole area was logged from 1900 to 1930, yet this tree remains. Perhaps there was something about it that would not have made good lumber. Perhaps it was forgotten—left behind. From the charred areas on its lower trunk we know it has survived one or more lightning strikes. Perhaps these occurred when it was left alone and exposed to the elements. It once had the company of a peer, as [can be seen] from the tree fallen beside it. But now it is alone in its old age. You could say that it is watching over its family, for the young firs in this forest probably came from its seeds. But whatever the [tree's] story, the one thing we can say for sure is that it has stood firm. It has persevered through all the challenges of its lifetime.

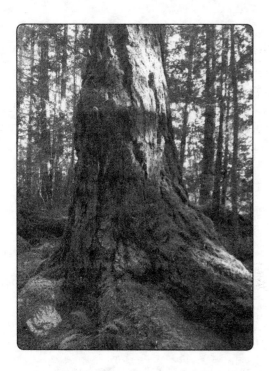

There are many times in our lives when it is hard to persevere. We are afraid, tired, lonely, confused, overwhelmed, sick, etc. Sometimes we don't think we are of much value to anyone. We may see ourselves as disabled, scarred, unable, disadvantaged, isolated, etc. But nature can encourage us—trees especially. Some of the most beautiful trees are the ones that grow in disadvantaged circumstances or in spite of great wounds. This tree is a case in point, continuing to grow in spite of extreme weather conditions. What is perseverance? The passage from Jeremiah below gives us one idea.

I aspire to take a lesson of perseverance from the story of this tree and from this wise passage of Scripture.

There are many untold stories of greatness in our world, often in people and sometimes in nature. My eyes are being opened to the wonders of perseverance lately.

> *"But blessed are those who trust in the LORD and have made the LORD their hope and confidence. They are like trees planted along a riverbank, with roots that reach deep into the water. Such trees are not bothered by the heat or worried by long months of drought. Their leaves stay green, and they never stop producing fruit."* (Jeremiah 17:7–8 NLT)

DAY
201
TO
250

DAY 201—UNSEEN STUFF

By Brenda Pue—July 20, 2014 6:01 p.m.

We packed up on Friday morning, and most of us were turning our thoughts towards home, except for the little ones, who want us all to live together forever. :) As we made our way to the Langdale ferry terminal, I began to realize how tired I was in spite of having such a relaxing week of resting, reading, swimming and playing with the kids and grandkids. Due to the seizure meds, the holiday ended up to be a bit of a slower week for me, as one of the side effects is drowsiness. I took my last dose on Friday and am thankful that there have been no further seizures this weekend.

As Carson and I have been unpacking my tiredness and the disappointment of this seeming setback, he commented on the impact of having a change of routine. I think he's right. I'm on a healing path that incorporates a fairly specific routine. I don't have the level of health and energy to deviate too much from my routine yet.

Tomorrow I have a follow-up doctor's appointment to further discuss the results of the brain CT scan and findings of the neurologist. On Wednesday, I have another bone scan to try to define the source of pain in my lower right side area that has been troubling me for the past eight months. I was praying about that scan this morning...do I really want to know? Not sure that I do. The test itself utilizes radioactive dye, among other things. And then there is the emotional toll of results.

This week of medical appointments is sandwiched between two weeks of holiday. That is a good thing for us. Carson is weary of trying to juggle work, medical appointments and the new realities that seizures bring. I understand completely. So I am grateful, more for Carson's sake, to be able to climb outside of the intensity of the past seven and a half months this summer.

Would you pray for us? This week is a bit of a low ebb for us on this journey. I still believe that faith is the substance of things hoped for, the evidence of things unseen (Hebrews 11:1). God is *really* good at unseen stuff like bringing joy out of nowhere when it is most needed.

I pray that God, the source of hope, will fill you completely with joy and peace because you trust in him. Then you will overflow with confident hope through the power of the Holy Spirit. (Romans 15:13 NLT)

DAY 202—ENCOURAGED TODAY

By Brenda Pue—July 21, 2014 11:26 p.m.

This will be short and sweet. Carson and I went to see our doctor this afternoon to follow up with him regarding the seizures and the medication and to ask questions.

Because of the nature of cancer and seizures, it's difficult to get a definitive explanation of what is going on in the brain. What we do know is that of all the kinds of seizures a person can have, mine is the best-case scenario.

He reported that the brain CT scan didn't show anything, which may mean a lot of things, but my personal favourite is that my treatment (including prayer) is working. So we will wait for an MRI, which will give more detailed info.

We also discussed the upcoming bone scan this Wednesday. When we asked our doctor about it, he said he didn't think it was related to the cancer (every medical person on my care team says the same thing—interesting, huh?). But here's the highlight of the appointment...Our doctor said, "You should be thankful for that pain, whatever it is. Because of that pain, we discovered the tumour. If you hadn't had that pain, you would not have come in to see me." Enough said.

Now I'm thanking God for *that* pain.

> *Do not be anxious about anything, but in everything, by prayer and petition, with thanksgiving, present your requests to God. And the peace of God, which transcends all understanding, will guard your hearts and your minds in Christ Jesus. Finally, brothers and sisters, whatever is true, whatever is noble, whatever is right, whatever is pure, whatever is lovely, whatever is admirable—if anything is excellent or praiseworthy—think about such things.* (Philippians 4:6–8 NIV)

DAY 208—PATIENCE THE HARD WAY

By Brenda Pue—July 27, 2014 11:48 p.m.

Patience has never come easily to me. I feel like most of my life I've been waiting for things. When I was young I couldn't wait to be a teenager, get my driver's licence, get married, have children, etc. Interestingly, I hit a few roadblocks along the way, and as hard as I tried, there was so much of life that

I couldn't control. I prayed and struggled. Sometimes resolution took years…a hard, but effective, way to learn patience.

I now know that God was fashioning His character in me through hurt, disappointment and waiting. Patience is a bit of a tough pill to swallow when in the middle of pain. I developed a few practices in response to challenges along the way that have stood the test of time.

1. I read the Bible.
2. I started to pray.
3. I attended church.
4. I invested in healthy friendships (Carson and I are enjoying our annual holiday with friends of 37 years this week).

These things helped me understand that even when life felt out of control, God still had a loving plan. I could trust Him. That has prepared me for what, arguably, may be the biggest challenge of my life.

My doctor must know that waiting is hard work for me because he sent a text before midnight on Wednesday, the same day of my bone scan, to let us know that the cancer has not spread to the rib area. We are feeling so relieved.

It was "kinda" nice to not have to wait until August to get those results.

In you, O LORD, do I put my trust and confidently take refuge; let me never be put to shame or confusion! (Psalm 71:1 AMPC)

DAY 213—DON'T GET LOST IN THE MORASS
By Brenda Pue—August 1, 2014 6:03 p.m.

We anchored today for a short while in a beautiful spot en route to our destination. The conditions were perfect for a swim…hot sun, no wind, and a sparkling ocean. So I ventured out for my first swim of our boat trip. I eased into the cold ocean water and sort of gasped. I say "sort of" because I couldn't quite get it out, as a gasp requires a deep breath. I am not able to breathe deeply these days due to pain. I instinctively knew that I couldn't stay in the water. I never expected that. I was disappointed, but I climbed out and got warmed up again. Maybe next year…

The incident caused me to reflect on my situation. I've come a long way in almost eight months, and I am full of gratitude for that. This unexpected event made me realize that I still have some travelling to do on this cancer journey. It was a good reminder of my complete dependency on God. I am still in need of a miracle.

Shortly after, I came across a paragraph that helped lift me out of my disappointment. I'm reading a book called *Pivotal Prayer* by Tim Elmore and John Hull. [It tells the story of a pastor, diagnosed with ALS, who was anointed with oil by a friend. It says,]

> His words of encouragement to Ed are for anyone praying for a miracle in his or her own life: "Ed, you need to get lost in the wonder of God. If you get lost in that wonder, who knows what He'll do for you."[14]

The book goes on to say that when we need a miracle, we usually get lost in the morass of the situation we're in or the overwhelming odds before us. But imagine being lost in the wonder of God. What a great place to be! When this happens, our prayers become focused on God, not on our problem, and we are truly able to pray, "God, whatever brings You glory, do it."

I am still praying for a miracle but have truly been lost in the wonder of God this week.

Many, LORD my God, are the wonders you have done, the things you planned for us. None can compare with you; were I to speak and tell of your deeds, they would be too many to declare. (Psalm 40:5 NIV)

DAY 215—LOST IN THE WONDER
By Brenda Pue—August 3, 2014 8:54 a.m.

Have you ever been invited to a private screening of a new movie? Well, last night God invited us and our friends to a private showing of sorts.

Yesterday afternoon, we tied the boat to a log boom. It wasn't the prettiest anchorage we've stayed in, but it was functional—giving us sun and privacy. As we settled in to our new location, we soon discovered that the log boom was a mecca of activity.

---

[14] Tim Elmore and John Hull, *Pivotal Prayer: Connecting with God in Times of Great Need* (Nashville: Thomas Nelson, 2002), 100.

As we were making supper, we watched a tugboat hauling a large load of logs towards our log boom. We watched the proceedings while we ate our dinner and gasped when one of the men fell in. Hopefully he was getting danger pay.

Even more fascinating than the tugboat activity was the display of wildlife around us. There were seals playing in the water beside us most of the afternoon and evening. We discovered a variety of birds, delighting in their chatter and antics. There were seagulls, crows, kingfishers, oyster catchers, a turkey vulture, a pair of red-breasted mergansers, a great blue heron and a crane of some sort. We had three pairs of binoculars on board and a bird book to aid us in this magnificent display. Our friend dubbed the evening a "three binocular event."

At one point, and very suddenly, all the birds alighted from the log boom in a frenzy as we watched a large bald eagle flying towards the log boom. It landed, and then its mate came for a visit. In all, there were three eagles who perched atop the highest point of the log boom, taking it all in.

In addition there were seals in the water and also one lying on top of a log. I thought it was sunning itself. After a couple of hours of being awed by the natural panorama spread before us, I noticed that the seal on the log seemed to be in a bad way. I voiced concern that something was wrong. We all wondered if the condition of this seal was the reason for the presence of all the carrion. Then suddenly, without warning, the seal gave birth to a seal pup. All these birds showed up, for different reasons, for the birth of the seal pup. (It was rewarding to see the mom and pup swimming together the next morning.)

We have been sailing with our friends for 36 years. Over all those years, we have seen some awesome natural sights. But I had not ever experienced an evening like that. Front row seats to a private showing for four. What an amazing gift! We were truly lost in the wonder of God.

O God, you have taught me from my earliest childhood, and I constantly tell others about the wonderful things you do. (Psalm 71:17 NLT)

DAY 219—IF THAT HAPPENS…IT'S A GOOD DAY
By Brenda Pue—August 8, 2014 1:05 a.m.

Since we arrived home from holidays four days ago we've enjoyed a wedding, a family birthday BBQ for Carson, a birthday dinner out at White Rock, and a day at the cancer centre for my usual oncology appointment and blood work. My mom and sister came with me to the clinic, and it was nice to introduce another member of the family to my oncologist. But…it's been a very full week.

I was talking about this with my mom—the age-old problem of fitting in what needs to be done in the hours that are available. For me a necessary part of the equation is finding a meaningful connection with God and our world every day. If that happens, it's a good day, regardless of circumstances.

At the cancer clinic we had an hour and a half between appointments. So rather than spend most of the day at the hospital, we found a nearby lake and park and had a picnic lunch in the beautiful outdoors in the shade of a tree. That was the highlight of my day.

All too soon it was over, and we were back at the hospital, meeting with my oncologist. I learned that the pain I have is caused by fluid that gets sloughed off by cancer cells and collects between my lung and chest wall. The best way to cure this is to treat the underlying cause—in my case, cancer. We discussed other treatments, but they are invasive, which can become a much bigger problem.

We also discussed my recent seizures, and she told me that a brain MRI will be scheduled in the next two weeks. All in all, it was a good appointment. With every step forward, I am intentional about living one day at a time. Otherwise, I lose focus and faith. I can get overwhelmed, wondering what the results of the MRI will show. It comes down to my desire to live with hope and trust rather than worry and fear, which paves the way for meaningful connection with God and others. As I've said before, if that happens in even a small way, it's a good day.

We love because he first loved us. (1 John 4:19 NIV)

DAY 221—CANCER: A LOSS OF INNOCENCE
By Brenda Pue—August 9, 2014 8:15 p.m.

Enjoyed a wonderful day today at the zoo with my mom, my daughter by marriage Shari and my precious granddaughter. There was something so precious about seeing the zoo through her eyes, watching her wander, point and climb fences. It was entirely wonderful. The thing that stood out to me was little Ellie's innocence and delight of life.

It saddens me that people lose these qualities as we grow older. Things happen. Insecurities take root. Fear becomes commonplace. Life gets complicated. We get hurt emotionally and physically.

I read an article today that quoted a person anonymously saying [that an experience like having] cancer is "a loss of innocence":

> "We go about our lives and we feel untouchable. But I know something now. I know something that someone who hasn't almost died doesn't know. And so everything I do is affected by it: The way I treat people, my priorities in a day, my priorities in a month, my priorities for my life. Everything is affected by the way this experience has made me feel."[15]

I don't think that God wants it to be like this. He wants so much more for us.

I so desire to reclaim all that God wants for me and know that the only way for that to happen is to spend time with Him.

All Scripture is breathed out by God and profitable for teaching, for reproof, for correction, and for training in righteousness, that the man of God may be complete, equipped for every good work. (2 Timothy 3:16–17 ESV)

DAY 224—MORE THAN I BARGAINED FOR
By Brenda Pue—August 12, 2014 10:43 p.m.

Yesterday started out with a beautiful walk with my mom. The freshness of the morning almost took my breath away. It was a perfect start to the day. After we got home, we worked through our little to-do list. One of the items on the list was stopping at the Service Canada office to pick up a CPP [Canada Pension Plan] disability form.

After dinner, I settled down to fill out the form. There was a section that asked me to describe *and* measure my limitations since my diagnosis. Things like sitting/standing, walking, lifting/carrying, reaching, bending, personal needs, bowel/bladder habits, household maintenance, seeing/hearing, speaking, remembering, concentrating, sleeping, breathing, driving a car and using public transportation. This ended up to be more difficult than I bargained for...I am so used to thinking about this illness in terms of what I *can* do, rather than what I *can't* do. It was a sobering perspective for me to think of this cancer diagnosis through the lens of limitation. A few tears rolled down my cheeks.

---

[15] "Tamara Taggart," *Forward* (Fall/Winter 2013), 12, http://digital.canadawide.com/i/237606-fall-winter-2013/11.

The final question:

Would I consent to vocational rehabilitation assessment?

Answer: No

Can you explain?

I've been told that my diagnosis is incurable.

Although the medical system tells me repeatedly that I cannot be cured, God tells me in hundreds of ways that He is for me and that He has plans and hope for me. Hope feels like such a better way to live than in despair.

I have felt in need of a miracle for a long time. Yet last night I felt the magnitude of my need in a new way. I had trouble getting to sleep over the pain of this, and today has been a day of being consoled by God and treasured friends.

I have another brain MRI tomorrow. Big sigh. I need to know, but I kinda don't wanna know, ya know? I'm praying…and trusting God with the results. I'm so grateful for your prayers too.

You keep track of all my sorrows. You have collected all my tears in your bottle. You have recorded each one in your book. (Psalm 56:8 NLT)

DAY 227—UNREMARKABLE
By Brenda Pue—August 15, 2014 10:15 p.m.

Since my last journal, I read a great story in the spring 2014 issue of *Forward* magazine about an active father with five sons whose athletic ventures have taken him around the globe. He blacked out on one of his bike rides (but finished the race) and upon seeing his doctor soon learned that he had cancer—stage four non-Hodgkin's lymphoma with an initial prognosis of two to four weeks to live. That was in 2011. He said, "At 55, I felt like I had done so much in my life, but my children still needed me." Throughout his cancer journey he chose to focus on things within his control. "As I tirelessly say to the irritation of my five boys, 'It is what it is, accept the fact, set a course, and attack it cheerfully!'"[16]

My mom read the article before I did and told me that I would resonate with this man's focus, determination and cheerfulness. So I continue to move forward…with God doing His best, my medical team doing their part, and me doing my part.

---

[16] Alex Blodgett, quoted in "A Journey Starts with a Single Step," *Forward* (Spring 2014), 21, http://digital.canadawide.com/i/284469-spring-2014.

Remarkably, I already have results from two brain MRIs, one on Wednesday and another enhanced MRI on Thursday. The results from the first MRI show a non-cancer related condition called a mastoid effusion on both the right and left sides of my head, which will need attention at some point. However, results from the enhanced MRI are better than I imagined. Of the six brain lesions that I was diagnosed with, the five small ones are *gone* and the larger one is shrinking.

Although I don't yet have a copy of the report, I've seen a portion of it and was fascinated by repeated use of the word "unremarkable" throughout various sections of the report detailing the technical measurements and diagnostics. In medical talk, "unremarkable" is a very good thing. And let me say how very much I am enjoying being "unremarkable"!

Yet in all these things we are more than conquerors through Him who loved us. For I am persuaded that neither death nor life, nor angels nor principalities nor powers, nor things present nor things to come, nor height nor depth, nor any other created thing, shall be able to separate us from the love of God which is in Christ Jesus our Lord. (Romans 8:37–39 NKJV)

DAY 232—BLESSINGS COME IN UNEXPECTED WAYS
By Brenda Pue—August 20, 2014 11:43 p.m.

Last fall our church participated in the Truth and Reconciliation meetings that were held in Vancouver as part of a nationwide effort to raise awareness of wrongs that were committed against native people. It was an eye-opener for me as I learned about some of the terrible things that happened years ago in our country. Our church invited two leaders, Chief Willy Littlechild and Chief Joe Dion (a long-standing member of First Baptist Church), from different Cree tribes to represent the Cree bands across Canada. On behalf of churches across Canada, we wanted to seek forgiveness publicly for past atrocities, even though very few people in our congregation were even aware of them. Forgiveness was granted. It was moving and powerful; true forgiveness always is.

Towards the end of the service, the Cree leaders bestowed the highest honour that can be given in their culture, an eagle's feather, to our pastor Darrell Johnson, on behalf of our church, as a thank you for making the effort to understand and to seek reconciliation.

This summer on a boating holiday with our long-time friends three of us decided to row to a little island and go for a hike. As we were climbing out of the tangled thicket towards a large rock, I found a beautiful eagle's feather. I brought it home with me for memory's sake.

It has turned out to be so much more than a fine memory. First Nation friends of ours who pastor a church plant in East Vancouver told us of the significance of my eagle's feather. "A person doesn't find an eagle's feather; it finds you," they said. It is a sign of God's blessing.

So God is showing me in a myriad of ways that He is watching out for me and that His great blessing is upon me, even through an eagle's feather. I have felt this since the beginning of this cancer journey, in spite of occasional fears and forgetful moments. Yet I am so very grateful for constant and unexpected reminders of God's care.

Taste and see that the LORD is good; blessed is the one who takes refuge in him. (Psalm 34:8 NIV)

DAY 233—MORE GOOD NEWS OF THE ENTIRELY FUN VARIETY

By Brenda Pue—August 22, 2014 12:57 a.m.

This summer, the health food store in our neighbourhood was sponsoring a free draw courtesy of a vitamin company called Prairie Naturals. Part of my regimen since I received the cancer diagnosis has been adding some supplements to my very healthy diet and chemo treatment. As a result, I spend a bit of time in that store these days. So all summer long I kept putting my name in for the draw for a gorgeous red bike.

Well, yesterday I got a call from the store telling me that I *won* the bike! I was told that they usually draw a first, second and third name, in case the first and second don't claim the prize. I had put so many entries into the draw that my name was drawn for all three! :) The salesperson said, "I think Someone wanted you to have that bike!"

When I told all my kids that I won *the* bicycle, one of them asked me, what kind of bike? My response: "Oh gosh. I don't know. It's red and super cute!"

Well today was the pickup of the bike and photos for their website. I learned that it is a CCM 21 speed mountain bicycle. Since I don't own a bike helmet, I had to walk it all the way home. Well, except when I reached the park near our house, I took it for a spin. It felt so good…the wind in my hair—oh, wait a minute…

It was an entirely fun day!

"So if you sinful people know how to give good gifts to your children, how much more will your heavenly Father give good gifts to those who ask him."
(Matthew 7:11 NLT)

DAY 239—MANAGING THE UNMANAGEABLE
By Brenda Pue—August 27, 2014

I awakened early this morning (it was still quite dark outside) due to discomfort. This drove me to prayer right away. Isn't that an interesting thing? Discomfort brings most of us to our knees…especially unresolvable discomfort. Having anything going on that is beyond my scope to manage puts me into a praying mood. Prayer is the best way for me to manage the unmanageable.

So here is how I am "managing" today—first, five blessings, then, my concerns:

1. *So* grateful to have a God in my life who knows me, who loves me, who cares for me and who gives me hope. Where would I be today without Him? Even my active imagination won't let me go there.
2. Where would I be without my family? My husband, who can't do enough for me; my mom, who packed up her life in Penticton to move in with me; my grown kids, who bring laughter and tenderness to my heart; my grandkids, who bring joy and remind me what it is to trust; my brother and sisters, who bring comfort and a sense of "normal" to this journey (in spite of their concern); and my extended family, who are so supportive and encouraging.
3. My "close-in" friends, who are there for me. They are a constant source of blessing—practical, emotional and spiritual. They inspire me.
4. My church. Even though I'm not there physically yet, I'm tracking activity, services and sermons, and I'm praying. I love and miss these people.
5. The natural beauty all around me that makes daily walks pure joy. Breathtaking!

Here's a list of the health-related things I'm praying about. It is my practice to voice my concerns, fears and tears once and thereafter to pray in faith and gratitude. I trust God is "on it.'

1. Pain in my right chest and lung area, which makes it challenging to find a comfortable sleeping position.
2. This pain limits some movement as well.
3. Low grade headaches and dizziness, which may be more related to mastoid effusion (fluid in the air pockets of bone behind the ears), which showed up on my last MRI.
4. My digestive system has improved but still suffers from time to time. This is an unfortunate side effect of my chemo treatment. It means I need to

think and plan carefully everything that I eat—my carefree eating days are long gone. :)

5. I have bursts of energy, but I deplete quickly. I know many people with cancer who work full- or part-time jobs and seem to carry on with life as usual. I am in awe. That simply is not my story but more of a longing.

My next oncology appointment is September 3rd, when all of the preceding will be discussed, and I know that God will lead the way. Thank you for praying with me. I hope I'm not taking this Scripture passage too much out of context, but it spoke to my soul:

I know what you are like! But I will heal you, lead you, and give you comfort, until those who are mourning start singing my praises. No matter where you are, I, the LORD, will heal you and give you peace. (Isaiah 57:18–19 CEV)

DAY 242—SO MUCH TO CELEBRATE
By Brenda Pue—August 30, 2014

Yesterday was my birthday. I woke up at the usual time to take my first prescription of the day. When I turned off the alarm on my phone, I saw that there were birthday messages. Tears of joy spilled out here and there as I read.

It was such a big day for me and my family, and another milestone on the cancer journey. Back in January, we weren't given any hope that I would see this birthday. So I was feeling joyful in a raw sort of way, as was Carson.

My family pulled out all the stops to celebrate this miracle birthday. My brother and nephew flew in from Alberta; my sister and [her] kids drove up from Portland; my other sister from Penticton Skyped in for the whole thing; and all my kids and grandkids were there. It was loud, and it was wonderful.

After a fantastic salmon BBQ meal hosted by my kids, my mom brought out a delicious gluten-free, dairy-free chocolate zucchini cake, which she made for the occasion. I generally don't eat GF bread, etc., due to the taste and texture, but this was amazing. The cake was also filled with little treasures—wax-paper-wrapped coins—just for some extra excitement for the little ones. My mom used to do that for us kids when we were growing up.

Of course, all three grandsons wanted to help me blow out the candles, which I agreed to as long as they didn't spit. Can you sense some history here? I encouraged them to practice blowing before the actual event. I quietly made my prayerful wish before God. I'm sure you know what my wish was. :) With four of us blowing we made short work of it. There was lively conversation and lots of excitement.

Liam: "Grammy I'm not going to tell you what we got you for your birthday present."

Me: "Okay. That's good."

Liam (with a stage whisper and sitting near me): "Auntie Kirstie, did you see the helmet yet?"

Me: Big smile.

There was a bit of a bicycle theme. The grandsons were priceless with the gifts. Of course they were so happy to open everything for me.

After gift opening, I had the thought to say a heartfelt and tearless thank you. *That* did not happen. It came out more like this:

"Could I say a few words?" Breakdown crying… "Well, I'm still here…" Long pause and tears… "And all of you are here…" More tears… "I can't imagine doing this journey with any other family. It's been the fight of my life for the past eight and a half months. And all of you are so worth fighting for. I thank you." Substantial nose blowing.

This was a celebration to remember.

P.S. The photo is one of the sweets gifts I received.

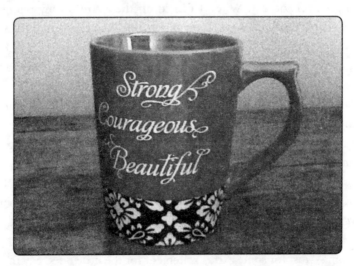

On the third day there was a wedding at Cana in Galilee, and the mother of Jesus was there. Jesus also was invited to the wedding with his disciples. (John 2:1–12 ESV)

DAY 246—BREATHING ROOM
By Brenda Pue—September 3, 2014

I am inspired by the story of King Hezekiah in the Bible. You may recall that he was a good king who revered God and who served his people well. Well into his reign he became deathly ill as a result of a boil gone very bad. God, speaking through the prophet Isaiah, told Hezekiah to get his affairs in order.

Not only was Hezekiah gravely ill but he was also heartbroken. He wasn't ready to wrap up his life on earth. So he prayed. The Bible says, "Hezekiah turned his face to the wall and prayed to the LORD, 'Remember, LORD, how I have walked before you faithfully and with wholehearted devotion and have done what is good in your eyes.' And Hezekiah wept bitterly" (Isaiah 38:2–3 NIV).

Amazingly, God's heart was deeply touched, and He sent his prophet with this message: "I have heard your prayer and seen your tears; I will add fifteen years to your life" (Isaiah 38:5 NIV). And so it was. Hezekiah was restored to health and lived another 15 years.

This is one of the Scriptures that is written on the mirror in my bathroom. I read it every time I brush my teeth. I am inspired and hopeful every time I read this verse. And this week I came across a devotional that focused on the second part of this story. The prophet went on to tell the king, "This is the LORD's sign to you that the LORD will do what he has promised. 'I will make the shadow cast by the sun go back the ten steps it has gone down on the stairway of Ahaz'" (Isaiah 38:7–8 NIV).

Sometimes when I am struggling and the road seems long, a sign is a great encouragement. God knows when we need a sign. Hezekiah wasn't asking for a sign, but God knew the king was deeply discouraged. This part of the story got me to wondering if I should ask for a sign. In the end, I didn't know what to ask for, so I let it go.

One day later, I lay down for a rest and took a big breath. At that moment, I sensed that I had slightly more lung capacity than I have had in a long time. It still hurts when I breathe, but I'm getting more air in my lungs. I smiled and thanked God for yet another sign to encourage me on this cancer journey…I was given some breathing room. And I didn't have to ask for a sign. God just knew.

DAY
251
TO
300

DAY 253—HOW DID I GET HERE?
By Brenda Pue—September 10, 2014

In February a good friend gave me a handmade journal. Later in the spring, when I began to have more energy, I started to record things that I am thankful for in the journal. I call it *My Thankful Journal*.

Over the months, I have also been researching ways to improve the immune system and ways to suppress and avoid cancer. All this reading has made me very reflective. I've been pondering my life choices and have started to add my reflections to *My Thankful Journal*.

Before I share my reflections, I should say the variables involved are as unique as every individual. No one really knows why some succumb to cancer and others do not. Someone once said to me, "I don't get it. You're so healthy. How can this be? Now, I can see me getting cancer. I'm a lifetime smoker, I drink a beer a day—whether I need it or not—I work in construction, where I suck more dirt into my lungs than most people would in three lifetimes. If anyone should have cancer, it's me, not you."

We all know that isn't how it works.

God in His wisdom knows what I need better than I do. I feel like I have learned more about life, and in particular my life, in the last nine months than I have in all the years leading up to this time. As I've scrutinized decisions, choices and experiences, I see things more clearly. It all falls into four main categories with subcategories:

1. Foods I consumed that were unhealthy.
2. Exercise I didn't do.
3. Not enough quality rest.
4. Stress—this one incorporates a number of areas:
     a. At home.
     b. At work.
     c. Travel.
     d. Perfectionism.
     e. Being a pleaser.

The combination of these things caused my immune system to become overwhelmed. Over the past decade I struggled with sinus infections, flus, colds, etc. I spent a lot of money on antibiotics. I now understand that my immune system was compromised. I'm a sloooooow learner.

I was sharing my journal entries around these categories with my mom early one morning. Each category has paragraphs of my thinking. My mom said, "This could be a book. A book to help people." I feel like she may be right.

But, suffice it to say, there are *many* contributing factors that play into how I got here. But probably the most important to me is that God in His wisdom wanted to show me some important things about myself—things that were needed—so that I can pass them along. I know that God has a plan here, and day by day I am paying attention to what God is showing me.

Someone once told me that the definition of a Christian is one beggar telling another beggar where to find food. It's in my heart to do what I can in the time that I have to bless others.

Do nothing from selfish ambition or conceit, but in humility count others more significant than yourselves. Let each of you look not only to his own interests, but also to the interests of others. (Philippians 2:3–4 ESV)

DAY 256—STARTING TO DREAM AGAIN
By Brenda Pue—September 13, 2014 6:46 p.m.

Fall is in the air. Our table grapes are turning to a pretty pale mauve colour and taste sweeter than candy. We have a few in our fruit bowl each morning. It's the time for pruning and planting. After what feels like a lifetime ago, I have the desire to get my yard and garden ready for fall.

So for an hour, sometimes two, in the mornings, my mom and I have been tackling projects that have needed attention for years. What a great feeling it is to have the energy to care! And almost as good is having a mom who loves gardening projects as much as I do. :)

So, with a lot of help, some things are coming together. Family and friends replaced all the broken lattice tops on our fence; my brother and nephew power-washed the main fence; and another friend restained it (I even got in on some of the action here and there).

To be honest, my re-engagement with life has been so gradual that it has been imperceptible. I'm starting to dream again. I know that flexibility is necessary in a cancer journey due to chemo reactions, medical appointments and pain. Yet, within this framework, I'm finding room to care again. My doctor says that cancer is episodic, not linear. This means that I have episodes that I can't plan for. It doesn't follow any pattern or cycle. That descriptor was very helpful for me.

So I find myself thinking about the future and asking, "I wonder if I could do that?"

The LORD your God is in your midst, a mighty one who will save; he will rejoice over you with gladness; he will quiet you by his love; he will exult over you with loud singing. (Zephaniah 3:17 ESV)

DAY 251—A LITTLE KINDNESS
By Brenda Pue—September 18, 2014

She walked up the stairs from her basement suite and introduced herself with a bright smile. I was staining the lattice of the fence between our yards but paused while we got acquainted. I told her about the cancer diagnosis and our family's journey. A sweet conversation followed. Finally, it occurred to me to ask her if all was looking good on her side of the lattice, which I couldn't see. She sweetly told me that there were a few drips. So I resolved that if it took me until Christmas, I would do my neighbour's side as well.

I learned that my new friend had recently married a school buddy of my boys and that they had moved into the suite of our neighbours' home the year before. She was going fruit picking for the afternoon, and after two sections of fence staining, I was more than ready for a rest.

I slept hard for an hour and a half, as I do most days, and was ready to stain the gate later that afternoon. As I started working on the gate, my new neighbour came around and offered me a bag of fresh-picked plums. Maybe it was the kindness of the gift, but no other plum has rivalled the sweetness of those plums.

I was already speechless over the plums when I thought I heard my new friend offer to stain their side of the lattice. I was stunned. It took a moment for me to absorb the offer. My time and energy have become such precious resources to me that I have trouble getting my head and heart around people who have given me hours of time and loads of effort to help me in this season of life.

The past eight months have been kindness upon kindness for me...for us. It's almost been too much for me to contain. Never before (and perhaps not again until I am in heaven) have I experienced such love, sweetness and kindness. It humbles me beyond words.

Kindness has always been overwhelming to me…God's kindness and mercy most of all.

For His lovingkindness is great toward us, and the truth of the LORD is everlasting. (Psalm 117:2 NASB)

DAY 264—WHY I LOVE CHURCH
By Brenda Pue—September 21, 2014

Today I went to church.

It's only the second time since the cancer diagnosis that I have been. The first time was Easter Sunday back in April. There were a few barriers for me. One is that I haven't been able to drive myself, due to the possibility of seizures. The other is that my immune system has been at an all-time low, and I've needed to exercise caution with large groups because of colds, flus, etc. And the other has to do with the amount of energy it would require for me to manage the drive in and back, plus two services (Carson leaves early and doesn't return until mid-afternoon).

I've missed being at church.

Here are some reflections on what I've been missing…

I've missed the people. Many are folks who, like me, reached a point somewhere along the road of life and acknowledged their need for God. It's good to be with people who have settled the "glory" issue. By that I mean, who is going to get the glory? Me? Or God? Now some are still working that out, and that's good too.

I've missed music. Sacred music. Truth put to a musical score. Music moves the soul differently than the written or spoken word. We sang some beautiful truth today. My soul connected with God this morning through the medium of music.

I've missed the spoken word of truth based on the Bible. Our pastor spends a lot of time delving into the original languages and historical background. I know he earnestly prays for the Spirit of God to help him help us. I love stepping outside of my small world into the bigness and beauty of God's perspective…a forty-minute gift each week.

Something powerful happens in my heart as I yield or, as the British would say, "give way" to God. It has been my joy to be in church weekly for most of my life. My parents took me when I was young, and I never stopped going…well, except for the extenuating circumstances of this past year.

God has used church to change me, enrich me, inspire me, challenge me and love me. I'm a better person thanks to church. God had a great plan when He founded His church.

That's why I love church!

You may wonder how I overcame the barriers to get there today. I've been trying to figure out a way for many weeks now but couldn't quite get there. A lovely couple who live in our area and who have the same church home offered to drive my mom and me there and back for the early service. How lovely is that?

> *For a day in Your courts is better than a thousand [anywhere else]; I would rather be a doorkeeper and stand at the threshold in the house of my God than to dwell [at ease] in the tents of wickedness.* (Psalm 84:10 AMPC)

DAY 271—SIGNS OF LIFE
By Brenda Pue—September 28, 2014

Much has changed for me since the beginning of 2014—spiritually, physically and emotionally. How does a person respond when looking death in the eye? Some face it with courage and faith and some with fear and anger. Having spent a lot of time at the cancer agency, I typically see these responses.

When I was presented with all the medical facts, I had to decide who would be in the driver's seat…me or God? I sensed that God would do a better job, and I made a conscious choice to let God drive…always a good idea when one's driving privileges have been removed. :)

The decision to let God drive was the second-best decision of my life (the first was responding to God's invitation when I was 12 years old). That has made the journey of the past 8.5 months more profound and beautiful than I could have ever imagined.

All the fluff of life has been stripped away for me. It's just me, it's raw, it's real, and sometimes it's not pretty. This has paved the way for meaningful conversations and moments. These would not have happened.

And now it's September. I've found myself lately reflecting on the signs of life that I am experiencing. So much is changing.

- I've gone from non-stop intense headaches and nausea (due to growth of lesions in the brain) to mild headaches and no nausea.
- Five of the six lesions in my brain are gone (two doctors say I'm in the miracle zone).
- My hair is starting to grow again.
- My energy level is slightly improved this month from last month, although midday rest is still needed.
- My appetite is returning.
- My interest and curiosity in the world around me are resurfacing.
- I seem to be tolerating my chemo drugs a little better.

There is so much more I could mention, but these are the main ones. I continue to pray about pain in my lung and chest wall and breathing pain, which awakens me during the night. In my heart I know that God continues to drive this thing. He is going at His pace and taking the route He knows best. And frankly, most of the time I am very content to be a passenger along for the ride.

You make known to me the path of life; in your presence there is fullness of joy; at your right hand are pleasures forevermore. (Psalm 16:11 ESV)

DAY 274—WHEN NEWS IS HARD
By Brenda Pue—October 1, 2014

Two weeks ago I had a CT chest scan, and today was my oncology appointment. I wish the news was better. In fact, it was hard to hear, as was looking at the picture she was drawing for us. Carson and I learned that the tumour in my lung is slightly larger than in my previous chest scan, which was in May. There are also two new, but small, tumours.

In my heart I was hoping to hear the exact opposite. I'm so disappointed that I can't quite get rid of the lump in my throat. I texted all the kids and emailed my mom to let them know. It was a fairly quiet drive home from the cancer clinic today.

So what does one do when hard, sad news comes around the corner?

For me, I need to feel the pain and emotion for a while. That is the mode I am in right now as I journal. And somewhere in the mess I'll find God in *this*. As I said in my text to our kids, "I wish the news was better…let's keep praying and trusting."

And then I'll keep on going. I'll stay true to the things that I believe God is showing me. First, prayer and reading my Bible. And I'll keep eating well, resting lots, exercising and researching.

And I'll resist the urge to panic. Instead, I'll put my hand in God's, and I'll learn all that He has for me from this new challenge. There's so much to learn. About myself. About God. About what it means to trust when I'm feeling overwhelmed.

And, as always, we are in great need of prayer.

Fear of the LORD is the foundation of true wisdom. All who obey his commandments will grow in wisdom. Praise him forever! (Psalm 111:10 NLT)

DAY 277—CREATING BEAUTY AND ORDER
By Brenda Pue—October 4, 2014 11:21 p.m.

Following my recent oncology appointment, I've noticed a pattern to my behaviour. My nights and early mornings are spent in reflection, reading and prayer. My mornings are characterized by mini bursts of energy…So [one day] I decorated my fireplace mantle for Thanksgiving, and the next day I painted my front door.

Upon reflection, I recognize that I am creating beauty and order at a time in my life that feels unlovely and chaotic. Today the peace of God has settled over me.

Although the news of the cancer growth brought me to my knees once again, it's a good thing. It's easy to get one degree off course without realizing it. So I am grateful for anything that realigns me with God. Early the morning after *the* disappointing news, I received an encouraging text from a wonderful Arrow leader (since there are hundreds of wonderful Arrow leaders, it might be tricky to figure out who) with this Scripture verse, which is what God used to get me back on my feet, so to speak:

> *His delight is not in the strength of the horse, nor his pleasure in the legs of a man, but the LORD takes pleasure in those who fear him, in those who hope in his steadfast love.* (Psalm 147:10–11 ESV)

In other words, my powerfulness does not please God, nor does my plan for where I want to go with these legs of mine. But humbling myself before God and hoping in His love are key to getting me on the right track. This was just what I needed to get reoriented. Thank you for continued prayers, care and love on this cancer journey.

DAY 282—FOR BETTER, FOR WORSE
By Brenda Pue—October 9, 2014

Thirty-eight years ago today, Carson and I stood at the front of First Baptist Church in Brandon and publicly declared our love for God and each other.

It was a beautiful fall day, not unlike this beautiful day that West Coasters are enjoying.

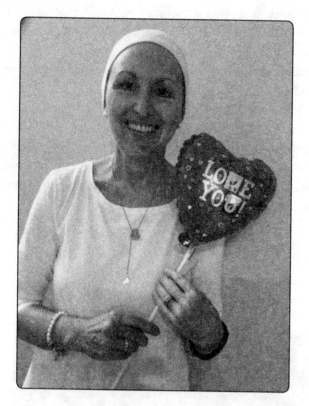

As we stood there looking at each other, our eyes sparkled with promise and hope. We've experienced a lifetime of joys and sorrows common to the human experience.

Raising our three sons was amazing, for the most part, with some tears and heartache along the way. I once heard it said that a parent is only as happy as their least happy child. That has proven true for me. When our kids suffered, we suffered with them. And their joy became our joy. These are the heights and depths that are shared between a husband and a wife.

And now our sons are married and having kids of their own. And there is something so right about that…At any time, if one of us had strayed from the vows we proclaimed so many years ago, our lives would have turned out so differently. Because, with God's help, we kept those vows, we have the joy of experiencing our grandchildren together. And you must know that we never tire of talking about them. Such joy!

And then came 2014. A cancer diagnosis, or any critical illness, puts tremendous strain on a marriage. We've had our work cut out for us trying to figure out how best to support each other. By God's grace, we have muddled through the past nine months. We didn't expect some of the sweet surprises along the way. We've talked deeply of things that we would rather not talk about but needed to. Tender prayers. The palpable presence of God. Deep love.

I can't think of anyone I would rather navigate the storms of cancer with than the man who has stood by me for better or worse for 38 years. This anniversary stands as a marker of God's goodness and faithfulness. We don't deserve such goodness, but we are so very thankful for it.

Be completely humble and gentle; be patient, bearing with one another in love. (Ephesians 4:2 NIV)

DAY 286—CANADIAN THANKSGIVING
By Brenda Pue—October 13, 2014

Family night was this past Friday, and we all liked the idea of celebrating Thanksgiving at the same time. So, with great anticipation, Mom and I started brining the turkey at 8:45 a.m. Something unusual happened this year though. As we filled the cooler with the brine solution, the water level was decreasing rather than increasing. It took me a few minutes to realize that the drain was open on the cooler....we had a good laugh over that. What a gift it was to laugh until my eyes watered. In fact, I laughed so hard that it really hurt.

I'm thankful for that moment.

Our dinner was second to none. All the Pue girls cooked, and we agreed to remember every detail of this dinner for a repeat performance this Christmas. I so enjoyed that meal—in fact, we all savoured it. I noticed a lot of appreciative moaning.

I'm thankful to enjoy food again.

Amidst the frivolity, animated conversation, smiling faces and joy, I found myself looking deeply at every person around that table. My heart was bursting with love and respect for each family member. What a wonderful night.

I'm thankful for a beautiful family.

Saturday morning we visited our long-time spiritual mentors and dear friends. We had tea and prayed together. There is something special about history, especially when it has spiritual foundations.

I'm thankful for people who are further along the road in the things of God than me.

On Sunday we attended our kids' church. As soon as I walked in the door, a woman I'd never met until that moment introduced herself and proceeded to bless and encourage me with such sincerity.

I'm thankful for the gift of kindness.

During the service they sang a favourite hymn, "Great Is Thy Faithfulness." I say "they" because I couldn't quite get it out. I was weeping. The words of that song expressed perfectly my cancer journey and God's faithfulness every step of the way.

I'm so thankful for the gifts of music and worship.

Then the pastor invited anyone who felt in the need of prayer to come forward. I couldn't get there fast enough, and some of my family came with me. It stirred my very soul.

I'm thankful for the opportunity to go forward for prayer.

And Sunday evening our wonderful in-laws brought dinner over to our house, and we shared a delicious meal and great conversation together. And before they left, we prayed together.

I'm thankful for the gift of conversation that is fun, yet deep.

And today, we went for a walk in the beautiful outdoors with friends who are very special to us. How wonderful to walk and talk while taking in the sights, sounds, and smells of nature.

I'm thankful for the beauty of the world around me.

What an amazing Thanksgiving weekend! It was another marker for me...I made it to Thanksgiving. I wouldn't change a thing about this holiday. God met me in profound ways all weekend long. It felt so good to set aside my troubles for a few days and stay firmly parked in a place of thankfulness.

Enter his gates with thanksgiving, and his courts with praise! Give thanks to him; bless his name! (Psalm 100:4 ESV)

DAY 292—ENCOUNTERS OF THE AMAZING KIND
By Brenda Pue—October 19, 2014

A few days ago Carson and I met for breakfast with a friend of many years from Ottawa, at our favourite little coffee shop. He is from out of town and went to a lot of time and trouble to meet with us. We hadn't seen each other for a year, and it was so good to reconnect and get caught up on each other's lives and families.

It was a restoring visit, and we were honoured that our friend would make the effort. It was a tender time, and there were a few tears and laughs as we talked. Our visit went by way too quickly, and it was time to get me home to rest. We explained this to our friend, and I started to put on my coat.

He said, "Wait, wait...I have something I want to say to you. In January when I got word about the cancer diagnosis, I was immobilized. I didn't know how to respond. So I wrote you a letter, and it would be the kind of thing that a person would say at a funeral, but I've been hoping to give it to you in person earlier rather than later."

So he handed it to me to read, but I hadn't brought my glasses and couldn't read his handwriting. I asked him if he would read it to me. So he did. It took my breath away. All three of us wept together right there in the coffee shop. It took us all a bit of time to recover from the holiness of that moment. In truth, I hope it will continue to stir in my soul for a very long time.

These kinds of encounters, gifts from the heart of God, bring such sweetness to this cancer journey. Isn't it an interesting thing that sorrow could bring such joy, that pain could bring such sweetness, that despair could bring such hope? Such is the nature of God.

They said to each other, "Did not our hearts burn within us while he [Jesus] talked to us on the road, while he opened to us the Scriptures?" (Luke 24:32 ESV)

Our breakfast time was a wonderful encounter, maybe a little like these friends' encounter with Jesus.

DAY 296—MUCH MORE TO LEARN
By Brenda Pue—October 23, 2014

My unfavourable oncology appointment at the beginning of this month has been a bit of a wake-up call for me...I think that's why the following quote impacted me, from the Salesian Missions in New Rochelle, NY. It helped to refocus me once again, and I wanted to share it.

- Take time to think...it is the source of power.
- Take time to play...it is the source of perpetual youth.
- Take time to read...it is the fountain of wisdom.
- Take time to pray...it is the greatest power on earth.
- Take time to love and be loved...it is a God-given privilege.
- Take time to be friendly...it is the road to happiness.
- Take time to laugh...it is the music of the soul.
- Take time to give...it is too short a day to be selfish.
- Take time to work...it is the price of success.
- Take time to do charity...it is the key to heaven.[17]

This is how I endeavour to live in the time that God has given me.

I am growing in my understanding of myself and God and the cancer situation I am facing. That is why I am pursuing [helping] my immune system in a more focused way. God has much more to teach me, and I am a willing learner.

Don't you realize that your body is the temple of the Holy Spirit, who lives in you and was given to you by God? You do not belong to yourself, for God bought you with a high price. So you must honor God with your body. (1 Corinthians 6:19–20 NLT)

---

[17] Unknown author.

DAY 297—PEACE THAT MAKES NO SENSE
By Brenda Pue—October 24, 2014

The past while, Carson and I have been talking and praying in earnest about how to manage the stress of an up-and-down cancer journey and his long hours.

The end result is that he is stepping down from his role of executive director at First Baptist Church. He announced it this past Sunday. I wasn't able to be there, but he said that he cried through most of it. His exact words were "Not my best pulpit moment." To which a long-time friend said, "Actually, it was your best pulpit moment."

Even though this seems fiscally irresponsible, we have tremendous peace about it. For me, having peace flood my soul is the sign I wait for from God when making difficult decisions. Carson and I know that we are heading down the right path, though it is filled with unknowns for us.

And so the decision has been made. Although many already know about this, here is the news release that went out recently:

Carson Pue Steps Down for a Promise

VANCOUVER, BRITISH COLUMBIA—October 22, 2014. At a crowded, historic, First Baptist Church in the heart of downtown Vancouver, the congregation showed their heart towards Rev. Dr. Carson Pue by gathering around him to pray at the end of both services.

Carson announced that due to his wife Brenda's cancer diagnosis, he had tendered his resignation as the Executive Director at the church effective the end of October. He has worked alongside senior pastor Darrell Johnson since January 2012 and during this time the church has experienced great favour and blessing.

Pue addressed the church amidst tears with Johnson beside him, saying, "Thirty-eight years ago I made a promise to Brenda to cherish and hold, in sickness and in health. Well, she needs me to hold her more right now and as result I have resigned as Executive Director..." Carson has cancelled all future speaking events at the present time so together they can focus on her health and their relationship. He and Brenda plan to continue some book projects, as they are able, but most of the time will be spent walking, talking and enjoying time with the family.

Carson and Brenda Pue are known globally for mentoring Christian leaders through the ministry of Arrow Leadership, which they led together since 1996. Brenda left Arrow unexpectedly this January after being diagnosed with stage four lung cancer. She decided to share her journey of faith while living with cancer on a Caring Bridge journal. With over 70,000 visits, many have been blessed by her authenticity and faith inspiring lessons.

Looking ahead, First Baptist Church has invited Carson to stay on staff in a part-time role as the Executive Advisor for the church's "Heart for the City Project." This is an ambitious building initiative in the downtown of Vancouver that will allow the church to enhance ministries of affordable housing, serving the homeless, venue for conferences, coffee shop, a full service counselling center, older adults programs, bookstore library, daycare and family resources in the downtown.

Lilac Hawkey, moderator of First, states, "Our church leadership completely supports Carson in this decision, and we are very grateful that he will be continuing to serve our congregation still even in a limited capacity. We continue to lift both Carson, Brenda, and their whole family up in prayer during this very challenging time."

DAY
301
TO
350

DAY 302—INCREMENTAL AND ALMOST IMPERCEPTIBLE
By Brenda Pue—October 29, 2014

I have the most wonderful friends! The six of us have been meeting together for about 20 years to pray. We first connected through our church and have stayed committed to each other in spite of inevitable moves, etc.

This past weekend, we met together in Whistler, BC. This is the first time I have left the "nest" without my family since being diagnosed with cancer almost nine months ago. I seem to function best when I am at home. So I wondered how I would manage…

Turns out, I needn't have given it a second thought.

I ended up with five mothers who cared for me beyond expectation. I was able to sleep, exercise and eat as well or better than at home. These days, I eat for nutrition rather than entertainment. That means no sugar, including limiting the amount of fruit I consume each day. It also means an abundance of fresh veggies every day, in addition to being gluten free and dairy free. This regimen requires a lot of effort, but my talented and loving friends rose to the challenge, and it was nothing short of amazing. I was pleased and a bit surprised with how well I did. It felt like another milestone and was a weekend to remember.

And our prayer times were beyond sweet.

As I look back on all the times that I've been away this past year, I've seen measurable improvement. Our family weekend trips were all I could have managed earlier this year. And as the months went by, my health improved, allowing me longer times away this summer.

Even though we know that the targeted chemo treatment may be close to finishing its course (that is, the cancer cells are figuring out a work-around the chemotherapy, rendering it ineffective), this weekend prayer retreat was once again an improvement over the summer. It's been helpful to look back on these times away from home this past year to see how far I have come and that God is at work…in incremental and almost imperceptible ways.

Fact is, I really do believe that prayer is the most powerful force on earth. I know that I am greatly in need of prayer to sustain me from day to day. Without prayer, I may not be writing this journal.

At my oncology appointment today, the tone was one of waiting for my next CT chest scan in three weeks to see how it measures up against the previous one. This waiting game can be nerve-wracking at times, and I find myself looking heavenward a lot these days.

God has sustained me far beyond my expectations. And I know that He is working day and night on my behalf.

I lift up my eyes to the hills. From where does my help come? My help comes from the LORD, who made heaven and earth. He will not let your foot be moved; he who keeps you will not slumber. Behold, he who keeps Israel will neither slumber nor sleep. The LORD is your keeper… The LORD will keep your going out and your coming in from this time forth and forevermore. (Psalm 121:1–5,8 ESV)

Reverence for the Lord is the foundation of true wisdom. The rewards of wisdom come to all who obey Him. Praise His name forever!

DAY 313—CHINA CAME TO ME
By Brenda Pue—November 9, 2014

Over the past few years, Carson and I have had the privilege of getting to know some of the leaders of the urban house church movement in China. Carson also has had the opportunity to minister in China over the past couple of years.

When their churches grow too big, it catches the attention of the authorities, and they are eventually shut down. The leaders are sometimes imprisoned—they and the church members, including their children, endure much intimidation. These people love and serve God at great cost.

When we received news of the cancer diagnosis, it wasn't long until we received word that the urban house church [movement in China] had been mobilized to pray. They function under the radar here on earth, but heaven is moved by these wonderful saints.

Since January there have been three visits by urban house church pastors to Vancouver, and we have jumped at the chance to get together. Recently, a good friend brought one of these pastoral couples to our home and also acted as our interpreter.

Our visit together was very sweet and tender, and towards the end our Chinese friend asked if he might pray over me. It was very special to experience prayer through an interpreter. He prayed for a miracle and believes that we will come to his home city one day and testify of God's miracle. He also said, "In China there are many walking miracles…why not here in Canada?" It was amazing.

It is encouraging to know that prayers in China are added to those around the world. God hears the longings of those who pour out their hearts to Him.

All the nations you have made will come and worship before you, Lord; they will bring glory to your name. (Psalm 86:9 NIV)

And we are confident that he hears us whenever we ask for anything that pleases him. (1 John 5:14 NLT)

DAY 315—LAUGHTER IS COMING BACK
By Brenda Pue—November 11, 2014

I'm laughing again. Any exertion on my right lung is terribly painful, so laughing until I cry comes easy to me these days. Nonetheless, this kind of joyful abandon is welcome after ten months of a somewhat intense and sober cancer journey. It feels good to be laughing like I used to…hard and long.

Perhaps I have more fully released this cancer thing into God's hands. I'm not as anxious or tense about it anymore. I know this sounds counterintuitive, and I am at a loss to describe why my hope quotient should be so high when I haven't had good medical news since September.

My family is such a great source of joy. While we were away together recently, we went out for dinner (all 12 of us), and after all the grandbabies were in bed the adults settled into playing some games. Here's a good example of life with our kids.

The game of choice was Bananagrams, which is a version of individualized speed Scrabble. At the end of each round, we all critique and admire the word choices of the winner. On this particular round Kirstie won. So we began the usual post-mortem to ensure that all the words were actual words.

Me: "What's a crawnail?"

Kirstie: "It's c-r-a-n-i-a-l!" (She is a nurse so defaults to medical terms these days.)

Me: "Ohhh…" (In my defence I was at the opposite end of the table, not wearing my glasses. And I think this is as good a time as any to pull out the brain cancer card.)

Jon: "Doc, I've had a crawnail stuck in my leg for the past three weeks…"

Jer: "Jon, that could be a line right out of *Duck Dynasty.*"

You might have had to be there, but I am still laughing and hurting…

This is typical fare around our table and is exactly what I need in my life. A little laughter goes a long way. God truly gives good gifts.

With joy you will drink deeply from the fountain of salvation! (Isaiah 12:3 NLT)

DAY 320—FEELING RIGHT AT HOME
By Brenda Pue—November 16, 2014

We spent time away in Whistler, BC (a world-class ski resort two hours north of Vancouver), last week with our family, thanks to the generosity of good friends. I felt right at home there. It was a wonderful time for many reasons.

For starters, I fit right in with the crowd. Almost everyone there wears hats or toques. Nobody gave me a second look, and I liked that. Nice just to fit in with the crowd for a change.

Another wonderful thing was huddling together with the family. It's been such an intense year for all of us. Being able to talk, laugh and make memories is so important for us. The little ones called this "our mountain house."

Another thing that made this week great was that it seemed so normal. By that I mean I had no medical appointments, and I did my best to focus on fun.

It was maybe the closest I've come to leaning towards carefree since this cancer journey began.

After all the kids left, Carson and I had two days to ourselves. It was just what we needed. We did lots of walking, reading, talking and planning. One big change that has evolved out of the past year is that we used to plan two years ahead and have always counselled younger leaders and couples to do likewise. It's generally a busy leader's best chance of maintaining balance with priorities. However, we realized we only feel comfortable planning a month out, two at the most. And for now, that's okay.

More and more we realize that we are utterly dependant on God. And that's okay too. Somehow God has arranged for us to feel "at home" with all that we are going through. This is our life for now, and we embrace it.

> *I give you thanks, O LORD, with all my heart…I praise your name for your unfailing love and faithfulness; for your promises are backed by all the honor of your name…Though the LORD is great, he cares for the humble, but he keeps his distance from the proud…The LORD will work out his plans for my life—for your faithful love, O LORD, endures forever.* (Psalm 138:1–2,6,8 NLT)

DAY 324—A NIGHT I'LL ALWAYS REMEMBER
By Brenda Pue—November 20, 2014

Although my last day of work was January 2nd of this year, it was official this week. As soon as I received the cancer diagnosis, it became apparent that my 19 years of service at Arrow Leadership had ended rather abruptly. Retirement is often a time of travel, plans and dreams. As you can imagine, my retirement has been a little different.

It has taken me this long to feel "ready" for a celebration night.

My friends and colleagues at Arrow Leadership hosted a heart-warming retirement party for me with 55 guests. The room was filled with goodness, blessing, encouragement and love. The venue was my most favourite coffee shop, Porter's Bistro Coffee and Tea House, which had been transformed from the usual quaint red-and-white checkered tablecloths. It was filled with fresh flowers, table runners and candles. Guests were being served delicious appetizers throughout the evening.

There was a table set up for guests to write messages for me to take home, and I was given a beautiful personalized photo-and-message book as well.

In typical Arrow fashion, not a detail was missed. There were two gifted Arrow leaders singing songs they had written while a video feed with photos of Arrow leaders and their words of encouragement scrolled. There were a few speeches, and my son Jeremy sang a song that Carson and I have loved since the day we were engaged. It's called "Renaissance," by Valdy. My sister happened to record it on her phone, and even though it's not professional quality, it captures the essence of Carson and Brenda. When we can figure out how to link it, I'll post it for you to listen to.

As this beautiful evening was winding down, Arrow's president, Dr. Steve Brown, gave the last speech of the night. This amazing night filled with laughter and tears wasn't quite over. During Steve's speech, he announced that the Arrow board has created a ten-year fund in my honour for an Arrow spouse in financial need to attend the final Arrow week spouse portion of the program. This a dream come true for me, and I am deeply touched.

I spoke at the very end, to express my gratitude to my Arrow colleagues, the loving and caring community inside and outside that room, my supportive family, my mom, who has been my primary caregiver this past year, and my wonderful husband, who has brought such sweetness to an intense year.

Of course, my ultimate thanks go to my Maker and Sustainer. He has given me hope where there was none. He is truly the Lifter of my head.

My friend posted her perspective on the evening on her blog entitled *Pix n Prose* if you'd like to hear more about this wonderful evening.

But you, O LORD, are a shield about me, my glory, and the lifter of my head. I cried aloud to the LORD, and he answered me from his holy hill...I lay down and slept; I woke again, for the LORD sustained me. (Psalm 3:3–5 ESV)

DAY 330—ALMOST BACK WHERE WE STARTED
By Brenda Pue—November 26, 2014

Today, Carson and I met with a new oncologist. We both really liked her, and she gave us the straight goods from my last chest/abdomen CT scan. We appreciated that she took time to answer our many questions.

The straight goods: The cancer is slowly progressing, but it's "not galloping," as she phrased it. The main tumour in my lung is about the same size as it was back in January, but new smaller tumours have appeared, and there is notable pleural fluid. We discussed my options at length, which are two different IV chemos combined every three weeks; just going with one of the IV chemo drugs instead of both; and radiation of the main tumour and surgery to drain the pleural fluid.

The oncologist wants us to take time to think about future treatment. It's a big decision. The discouraging part of all this for me is that I would start all over again. The proposed chemo has difficult side effects—my current chemo treatment pales in comparison. And I would lose my hair again.

Although this is quite sobering news, I'm not feeling as wrecked as I thought I would, nor am I in denial. I still trust God. I still believe that He has something for me in this. There are always blessings.

So on this American Thanksgiving day, here is my list of things that I am thankful for:
- God's heartbeat in my life.
- The gifts of prayer and Scripture.
- My loving family.
- Encouraging friends.
- A roaring appetite.
- Pretty good energy.
- The hope of Christmas, now just weeks away.
- So much love and goodwill at every turn.
- Hope.
- Laughter.

171

There is more, of course. Always so much more to be thankful for. But this is a good start.

O give thanks to the Lord, call on His name; make known His doings among the peoples! (1 Chronicles 16:8 AMPC)

DAY 335- SETTING UP CHRISTMAS IN MY HEART
By Brenda Pue—December 1, 2014

We usually set up our Christmas decorations at the beginning of December. And so Carson brought the bins of decorations from the garage, and thus began our annual tradition. Only this year feels a little different for me. For starters, I underestimated the emotional impact of these traditions. As I pulled things out of the boxes, a part of me [could] hardly believe that I get to do this once again. And yes, there have been a few tears here and there.

My last oncology appointment for 2014 is on Christmas Eve. How fitting. The timing feels so good, so right. In spite of being told back in January that I would not see another Christmas, I sensed that God had other plans for me. And so I have been setting up Christmas in my heart all year long.

After last week's oncology visit, when my December 24th appointment was set up, it became very clear to us that the only thing the cancer agency can offer me is treating my symptoms and reducing pain. We are hoping for so much.

After almost a year of radiation and chemo, plus reading and researching, we have decided to explore other options.

I was given 30 more days on my current chemo drug, mostly to give us time to think and talk about the treatment options that the cancer agency has proposed. In essence, we have a thirty-day window to try some other protocols.

We have decided on a multi-faceted approach for the next month to try to "de-bulk" the main tumour. Tomorrow I will begin a three-day-per-week regimen for about three hours per session for the month of December, with a break for Christmas and Boxing Day.

That kind of schedule in December would not be optimal for most people, but for me it feels like the best possible use of my time. And if this is successful it will be the finest Christmas gift that I could give to my family this year.

Since I know prayer to be the most powerful force on earth, would you join us this month in praying for my chemo treatment and this new protocol to be effective?

This is the confidence we have in approaching God: that if we ask anything according to his will, he hears us. (1 John 5:14 NIV)

DAY 341—LIVING IN DAYS OF GRACE
By Brenda Pue—December 7, 2014

The countdown to Christmas is well underway. It feels wonderful and a little surreal to me. So far my December has been focused on medical appointments—three down and fourteen more to go.

So far my appointments at the Integrated Health Clinic are going well. We are taking a dual approach that is focused on strengthening my immune system and de-bulking the tumour. We are using several approaches to achieve this, utilizing both old and new technology. And so far there are no side effects.

After my first three treatments I have noticed some good things, such as sleeping better, slightly reduced lung pain, slightly better breathing capacity, my weight is maintaining nicely, better energy, and the best sign is that I had a full-on sneeze for the first time in almost a year. Although I had what I call a demi-sneeze in the spring, the one today was actually satisfying. Even though it hurt, it somehow was able to get enough momentum to succeed. It just happened, and I can't stop smiling. This feels like a great accomplishment at a few levels:

- It's a wonderful sign of physical improvement.
- I feel like God is enjoying this more than I am…I sense His smile and joy.
- I have tangible signs of hope that make me feel like I am living in days of grace.

My beautiful sneeze is a sign that the current treatment regimen seems to be working. Thank you for praying with me this month. God knows that I have a ways to go to turn the tide of stage four cancer. God is hearing and acting.

Let us then with confidence draw near to the throne of grace, that we may receive mercy and find grace to help in time of need. (Hebrews 4:16 ESV)

DAY 344—MESSAGE FROM THE FAMILY: A WAY TO HELP
By Jason Pue—December 10, 2014

In the midst of the busy Christmas season we wanted to take a quick moment to pause and reflect on what this Christmas means to our family. Almost a year ago our entire family crammed into a small doctor's office, and we were given very little hope that we would be celebrating this Christmas with our mom. However, here we are almost a year later, full of hope and joy as we prepare to celebrate Christmas.

As we anticipate this Christmas with our family we wanted to just take a moment to thank you for your support of Mom, Dad and our family over this past year. You may or may not know this, but all of our family members have been encouraged and blessed by the comments and interactions on this site. Simply logging on and seeing a community of people viewing Mom's site almost 80,000 times over the past 11 months is encouraging.

Over the past year many of you have come to us kids and asked us to let you know if there were ways that you could help Mom and Dad in a practical way during this time. As you know, Mom recently started some new medical treatments that are not being covered under a medical plan and are quite expensive. With the help of some close friends, we have set up a website where our community can bless Mom and Dad in a practical way, removing the financial burden of these treatments. Please feel free to visit the website for more details on how you can help: www.youcaring.com/brendapue.

Thank you for your continued love and support. From our family to yours, we hope that you have a blessed Christmas season.—Jason, on behalf of Kristin, Jeremy, Shari, Jon and Kirstie

DAY 349—WAITING AND WAITING MORE
By Brenda Pue—December 15, 2014

Yesterday was the third Sunday of Advent. As I sat in church absorbing the Scriptures, the music and the spoken Word, I was deeply touched by the theme of waiting. Advent is one of my favourite times of the year...it's all about waiting for the arrival of Christ, the one who would save us from our suffering.

How amazing that the God of the universe is concerned about people's suffering! I feel God's concern about my situation. And as I read the Bible, I see over and over that He actually does something about it.

And so I wait on God. I am hopeful that God will use the nutrition, the supplements, the heat therapy, etc., to turn the tide towards health for me. At my appointment last Wednesday, the doctor explained that cancer has overwhelmed my immune system, and all these treatments are designed to get my immune system to, once again, overwhelm the cancer.

Tomorrow I go for my seventh treatment of twelve this month, plus ongoing lab and oncology appointments. And so I continue the protocols that are set out for me, trusting God each day. I wait and pray.

The LORD said, "I have indeed seen the misery of my people in Egypt. I have heard them crying out because of their slave drivers, and I am concerned about their suffering." (Exodus 3:7 NIV)

Since ancient times no one has heard, no ear has perceived, no eye has seen any God besides you, who acts on behalf of those who wait for him. (Isaiah 64:4 NIV)

These are the Scriptures we read and heard at church yesterday.

DAY
351
TO
400

DAY 354—EPIC BATTLE
By Brenda Pue—December 20, 2014

Yesterday was a "day off" between treatments. I usually have a bit more energy the day after each treatment. It began with my third grandson's preschool Christmas party, which was pure delight to this grandma's heart. He was the cutest innkeeper I've ever seen. That lasted about an hour and was followed by Starbucks coffee time with the girls: Shari, Ellie and my mom. There is something special about being in the presence of a child.

Then when Carson got home from work, we went on a movie date…the final episode of the Hobbit trilogy. The last time we went out to a movie, I didn't do so well. It was too much for me, and it took me a couple of days to recover. Although slightly hesitant, I wanted to give it a try again. I'm happy to report that I survived the outing intact, except managing pain here and there (which is the case whatever I do or don't do). I so enjoyed being with Carson, and it was very good to take our minds off cancer for a while.

The Hobbit: The Battle of the Five Armies is the story of four armies joining forces to battle against the Orcs, who were overwhelming the allied forces. There were great moments of leadership, courage, kindness, sadness and even humour.

Today I've been reflecting on the story, which I first read as a teenager. What was happening on the big screen reminded me of what is going on inside of me. My practices of nutrition, exercise, hyperthermia and a clinical trial drug are joining forces to do battle against cancer cells that are wreaking havoc in my body.

At my last appointment with my doctor, I was told that there is an epic battle going on inside of me. Cancer cells are attacking my immune system, and my armies (as listed) are battling the cancer fiercely. I was told that at a molecular and cellular level, my immune system is working the hardest it has ever worked in my lifetime.

I am so very thankful that God has sustained me to the place where I am able to wage war on the enemy at every level: physically, spiritually and emotionally. I sense that all the resources of heaven are engaged in this battle. And I'm joyful to be celebrating the wonders of the Christmas season, whilst my immune system battles on. :)

Stand therefore, and fasten the belt of truth around your waist, and put on the breastplate of righteousness. As shoes for your feet put on whatever will make you ready to proclaim the gospel of peace. With all of these, take the shield of faith, with which you will be able to quench all the flaming arrows of the evil one. Take the helmet of salvation, and the sword of the Spirit, which is the word of God. (Ephesians 6:14–17 NRSV)

My paraphrase: To do battle I need truth, righteousness, the gospel, faith, salvation and God's Word. I think I'm ready, with God's help!

DAY 362—SIGHTS AND SOUNDS OF CHRISTMAS
By Brenda Pue—December 28, 2014 1:45 p.m.

I will never forget this year. In one 15-minute conversation my life was altered beyond anything that I thought possible. Then came a flurry of tests that confirmed the initial suspicions of my doctor. There were phone calls, tears, fear and prayers.

With months for me to live, we began to try strategizing how we might best spend those numbered days. I quit work. I cancelled our Israel trip with our church. I stopped driving. Carson, along with caregivers, are with me 24 hours a day, should I suddenly have side effects from the cancerous tumours in my brain. Of course, moments with family and friends took on new meaning.

To accomplish this, we began a series of retreats, most with family and one with my prayer group. The first family retreat at Barnabas is etched in my memory. Applegate was filled with flowers, beautiful meals prepared with love, talking time with our kids after the grandkids were settled for the night, and sharing and prayer times with the Barnabas staff. It was a wonderful weekend. However, the icing on the cake was a children's Christmas book entitled *An Angel's Christmas*. The inside cover was inscribed with the words "This book is to read to your grandchildren at Christmas." Prior to that moment, I had not dared to think past June. It was a faith-stretching moment for me.

Really, Lord? Is that in Your plans for me? Could it be? I dared to believe...

We celebrated our family Christmas on December 26th this year. We did a potluck turkey dinner that was ummm good. After dinner the grandkids and I settled onto the couch to read *An Angel's Christmas*. Sheer joy. After the story was finished, I sat there taking in all the sights and sounds of Christmas. Landon and Marielle delivered the gifts, with soft Christmas music playing in the background (although there was so much excitement, I'm not sure it was noticed). So much love and goodwill filled that room, I was overwhelmed. Tears spilled out here and there as I watched it all in wonder.

Thank You, Lord! Christmas this year was immeasurably more than I hoped for.

Now to him who is able to do immeasurably more than all we ask or imagine, according to his power that is at work within us. (Ephesians 3:20 NIV)

DAY 365—OUR CHRISTMAS CARD
By Brenda Pue—December 31, 2014

Christmas Blessings...from our Home to Yours

Charles Dickens wrote, "It was the best of times, it was the worst of times."[18] The year 2014 has proven to be such a year for us. On January 2nd a routine X-ray revealed a tumour in Brenda's right lung that was confirmed as stage four lung cancer. We agree that this is the worst news we as a family have ever received in our collective lifetime.

Within ten days Brenda's mom moved in to care for us all, and, gratefully, she is still with us. Brenda was told to get her affairs in order and was given about six months to live (June). Family and close friends became even more important. Time with God was and is essential. People around the globe began praying for

[18] Charles Dickens, *A Tale of Two Cities* (London: James Nisbet & Company, Limited, 1902), 3.

us. This has been a year marked by prayer, listening, learning and seeing God in the ordinary.

Photo credit: Jane Omelaniec

It has been a year of family retreats. All 12 of us gathered together on four different occasions—grandparents, parents and grandchildren. These times away, plus family nights twice per month, have brought tenderness to an otherwise intense year.

In August, we boated up the coast with life friends, and Brenda celebrated the birthday that we didn't think we would see.

In October our hearts filled with gratitude for the gift of another Thanksgiving, which also marked our 38th anniversary. On the 31st Carson stepped down from his role as ED at First so that we could have more time together. He continues to work part-time on the church's building project.

In November Arrow Leadership hosted a retirement celebration for Brenda that was deeply moving. As well we enjoyed three grandkids' birthdays. All these celebrations held something deeper for us.

The best of times?

Well, we didn't know that such goodness was possible in a cancer journey. But we do know that with God all things are possible.

Love,

Carson and Brenda

P.S. This letter is the inside of our card, and the photo is the front cover of the card.

P.P.S. Thank you for loving, caring and praying us through this past year!

DAY 368—TURNING THE PAGE ON THE YEAR PAST
By Brenda Pue—January 3, 2015

We brought in the new year very quietly this year. My family ordered Thai food, while I opted to make myself something with no sugar. After dinner, we played games. I was in bed by 9 p.m., something that has never happened before…It was glorious! I had a great sleep and greeted the new year in a refreshed frame of mind.

For about 30 years, we have celebrated New Year's Eve with long-time family friends. It has always been a fun-filled yet meaningful occasion because we typically end with a sharing time that is often profound. As our children have grown and have started having children of their own, we have realized that it was getting more and more challenging to keep up this wonderful tradition. So we revamped it in favour of a New Year's Day brunch. We started last January 1st and did it again this year…yet another wonderful celebration.

If I think about my life as a book, in one-year chapters, I confess that I was relieved to turn the page on this past year. Although I was the recipient of miracles, love, kindness, mercy, grace and much prayer, it was difficult. In many ways the year was beyond all that I could've imagined, and my gratitude is simply too deep for words. And I know that such beauty is born out of great sorrow and pain. As I floundered at times in a sea of tears, fear and uncertainty, God buoyed me up with mercy and hope. It's been a beautiful and hard chapter in the book of my life. And the most wondrous part about that chapter is that I have no wish to do a rewrite.

And now a new chapter has begun. I'm writing it as I go. I'm off to a good start. At our New Year's Day brunch, our large group talked about memorable blessings from the past year and a single focus word for the year to come. My word is "health"—emotional, spiritual and physical. It will keep me challenged all year long, and I look forward to it.

Weeping may stay for the night, but rejoicing comes in the morning. (Psalm 30:5 NIV)

DAY 374—MIRACLES, HEALING AND ME
By Brenda Pue—January 9, 2015

This past Sunday, we were able to be at church. I have been mulling over the sermon about healing ever since. It was likely the finest sermon I've ever heard on the subject of miracles, which has stimulated thoughts about healing. As you can imagine, every word gripped me in a way that likely wouldn't have impacted me in the same way prior to the beginning of 2014. But God has my rapt attention these days.

There were many things that captured me from the message on Sunday, and I could journal pages from that message, but for the sake of brevity I'll focus on one aspect that I desire to be a part of my spiritual health rhythm in the coming year. I learned about the importance of invitation. That is, the necessity of inviting God in…into my circumstances, into my feelings, into my fears, into my joys, into everything. God doesn't force Himself into my life: He always waits to be invited.

In other words, miracles and healing don't happen apart from invitation and desire on my part. Story after story in the New Testament show Jesus clarifying by asking something like "What do you want Me to do for you?" Invitation and desire.

This year, I want to take every opportunity possible to invite God in…

And so, my next chest CT is scheduled on Monday morning, and I am inviting God into all the feelings around that scan and the upcoming results the following week. I know that many miracles have graced my life this past year.

Whenever I find food in my fridge that is past its expiry date, I cringe. But I have to say I'm pretty excited about passing my original medical expiry date! I'm looking forward to the unfolding of God's plan in this new year. I'm inviting God into my upcoming scan and beyond.

I now believe that God's view of miracles and healings is different from my view, and I suspect that I will spend the rest of my days sorting that out.

"Whatever He [Jesus] says to you, do it." (John 2:5 NKJV)

Note: I hesitated to pull one verse out of this chapter, as the whole chapter is a fascinating read.

DAY 381—I NEED A MOMENT
By Brenda Pue—January 17, 2015 12:03 a.m.

The past week of medical appointments rivals the same week in January one year ago. I started on Monday with a chest/brain contrast CT scan. When I was being set up for the scan, it took seven tries to finally get the IV line in. Ouch! After a year of medical appointments, blood tests and IVs, maybe I'm starting to get picky.

On Wednesday, we met with my naturopathic doctor, who is also anxious about getting the CT scan results. In the meantime, he walked through current symptoms and suggested an adjusted treatment plan, pending CT scan results.

Thursday's appointment was with a pain specialist that I was referred to many months ago. I felt hopeful as we left her office armed with stretching exercises, a prescription and an arsenal of helpful suggestions going forward for managing lung-related pain.

Today we met with my oncologist, who just returned from a working sabbatical. We learned today that my cancer is advancing slightly. You may recall that this was similar to my November CT scan. However, this week's scan revealed the addition of slight progression in the brain and lower back. Not good. It was hard news to hear, but it's not the first time we've faced disappointment this past year or at other times over the years.

My oncologist shared today that I may qualify for a clinical trial that is being conducted out of the cancer agency in Vancouver. We have an appointment on

Monday with a new oncologist. In order to find out whether I qualify for this trial, I would need to have a fourth lung biopsy. It's a blind trial, which means I have a 50 percent chance of actually getting the new generation drug, which isn't even named yet (identified by numbers and letters currently). Or, I could end up on IV chemotherapy and start an even more intense year than last year.

I delayed communicating this news because I needed a moment. A moment to feel the depth of sadness and disappointment. A moment to share this new round of information with the family…time for prayer and time to get a sense of next steps. It feels like my boat took a big wave from the side and it's going to take a bit to get steady again. Just talking and praying with our family was a good step in stabilizing things. How amazing to have three generations sharing this burden together. It was a good ending to a hard day.

After this big medical week, we are looking to God once again.

Those who know your name trust in you, for you, LORD, have never forsaken those who seek you. (Psalm 9:10 NIV)

DAY 388—DECISIONS, DECISIONS
By Brenda Pue—January 23, 2015 9:54 p.m.

We are processing a big decision that will dramatically impact the rest of 2015 for me, for us and for our family. We met with a research oncologist regarding a clinical trial that is starting that I may qualify for. I would need to have a fourth lung biopsy in order to determine whether the lung tumour has mutated from its original mutation (a specific genetic coding of lung tumour for never smokers).

It was a very good 90-minute meeting, *but* we learned some things about clinical trials that made us realize this is a big decision. We can count on three or four times the number of CT scans, MRIs, blood work, and such. This would have us at the hospital and cancer agency a lot. The trial is conducted out of Vancouver, which means we also add commuting to the equation. The trial is expected to last a year, and it is not inconceivable that we would spend two or three days per week in Vancouver at randomized appointments whenever machines, doctors and oncologists can be scheduled.

So the burning question is, assuming my days are numbered, is this the best use of the time that God has given me? There are many layers to this question, even though it may appear to be simplistic. Such as the value of research, time with family and friends, the matter of energy for a regimen such as this, etc.

This is how we are working through our decision thus far:

1. Scripture—always my go-to place for hope and wisdom.
2. Prayer—to invite God to speak, move, and act and, of course, to listen.
3. Wise Counsel—in our case, our kids, trusted friends, doctors and several oncologists.
4. Gathering Data—to be as informed as possible.

Due to the complexities of the decision that must be made, we are seeking not advice but rather prayer over the next week in particular...as we continue with appointments and consultations and of course direction from above.

Oh, the depth of the riches and wisdom and knowledge of God! How unsearchable are his judgments and how inscrutable his ways! (Romans 11:33 ESV)

DAY 392—GLIMPSES OF GLORY
By Brenda Pue—January 27, 2015

It's true. I have received many glimpses of glory over the past year. Here are a few that come to mind. You may recognize many of these, since all of them have been shared previously in my Caring Bridge journal at some point:

A hummingbird that hovered and looked me in the eye much longer than expected—a sign that God "sees" me.

A lost dog who was welcomed in our home briefly one night—reminding me of the loving welcome I have from God when I feel "lost" and overwhelmed by cancer occasionally.

An eagle's feather that "found" me—a sign of God's blessing in native culture.

An angelic moment in a restaurant with a miraculously healed cancer survivor.

The old crooked tree in our front yard, which unashamedly leans towards the light.

And then there are the deeply tender moments with people, letters, prayers and cards that have revealed something new about God.

I am profoundly grateful for these glimpses of God's glory that have been gifted to me over the past year. I can hardly take it all in. Such kindness. Such mercy. Yet God beckons me on into depths of this journey. There is more glory.

I've had a wonderful Scripture on my bathroom mirror for the past year. It has lifted my heart many times.

> *His disciples asked him, "Rabbi, who sinned, this man or his parents, that he was born blind?" "Neither this man nor his parents sinned," said Jesus, "but this happened so that works of God [or the glory of God] might be displayed in him."* (John 9:2–3 NIV)

This week I have a new take on this story in the Bible, as I think about the decisions that we are currently facing. I've come to realize that all decisions I make are about either giving God glory or satisfying me—and sometimes I am fortunate enough to have the two coincide. :) Perhaps this perspective will bring more clarity around our decision-making in the coming weeks.

DAY 396—MAKING MEMORIES WITH FAMILY
By Brenda Pue—February 1, 2015 12:49 a.m.

It's been a great week for family connections, made all the more important as I monitored symptoms during the past two weeks of information gathering. Some things that I notice are pain that is spreading a little into my right arm, less energy and strength, mild weight loss, and decreasing lung capacity due to increasing pleural fluid…there just isn't as much room for my lung to move. As alarming as all this might sound, I am not alarmed. But I have an increased desire to make memories. We made some good progress this past week gathering information and have two more consultations next week. We welcome your continued prayers.

So on Tuesday, Carson and I took our third grandson, Mac, who is four years old, on his first "Big Adventure." We went to Metrotown, where there is a small, colourful train that kids and adults can ride from one end of the mall to the other and back again. It reminds me of something one would see at Disneyland. Of course, the train ends up at the Disney store, so we included that in the Big Adventure, as well as lunch. It was such a great time.

Then on Thursday afternoon, we took the two older grandsons to see *Paddington Bear*, complete with popcorn, candy and water. It is one of the most precious children's movies I have seen in years. Two thumbs up from this grandma.

On Friday morning was Mac's preschool party. It is a monthly event on our calendar and is always such a fun time. The kids sing wonderful songs with actions to demonstrate to all the parents and grandparents (and in our case also Mac's great-grandmother).

Do you ever have those moments when something catches you by surprise? That happened to me as Mac was singing his little heart out. The words of the song reached into my soul. I didn't expect that! The refrain went something like this:

Our God is a great big God
Our God is a great big God
Our God is a great big God
And He holds us in His hands
He's higher than a skyscraper
He's deeper than a submarine
He's wider than the universe
And beyond my wildest dreams
He's known me and He's loved me
Since before the world began
How wonderful to be a part of God's amazing plan[19]

It was a perfectly timed reminder.

My week was completed with a Starbucks coffee date with my one and only granddaughter and her mom, Shari. This week was a true gift to me, especially as we consider the regimen that we may be facing in the coming months!

---

[19] Jo Hemming and Nigel Hemming, "Great Big God," © 2001 Vineyard Songs (UK/Eire). Used with permission.

Your eyes saw my unformed body; all the days ordained for me were written in your book before one of them came to be. (Psalm 139:16 NIV)

DAY 399—REASONS TO SMILE
By Brenda Pue—February 3, 2015

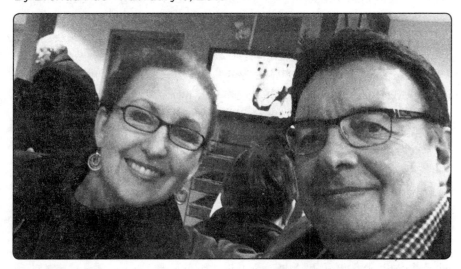

My heart is full. I have so many good reasons to smile. However, I'll focus on three to respect your time. :)

Yesterday afternoon, Carson and I met with a new, to us, oncologist (I know…that sounds like a used car). He has been in the cancer business for about 35 years, and it was very clear to us that he is brilliant, despite his old-school style. He got right down to business.

After hearing my history, he physically examined me. My personal highlight moment was when he listened to my breathing with his bare ear on my back. After all this, he said, "It's clear to me why you are having difficulty knowing how to move forward. You don't have facts. The only way to get the facts is to have a PET scan and a brain MRI immediately. Then we will know how to proceed with treatment."

Our long-time friend and mentor Bobb Biehl told us many years ago that when you have all the facts, the decision jumps out at you. It is for this reason that we are hoping to have another consultation with another research oncologist, who specializes in my particular diagnosis, this week.

In the meantime, we have made the decision to do the needed scans privately in order to expedite the results. I learned that as soon as the scans are completed, we will be shown the actual images immediately, with written results following shortly after. He is also in favour of removing the tumour in my brain, through either directed radiation or what he called "easy brain surgery" due to the location of the tumour. I confess that I have never thought that brain surgery could be easy. He would like this all settled within two weeks, because, as this oncologist says, "Time matters, right?" We walked away from this appointment strangely encouraged. We like this guy. A lot. We are smiling because it feels like God is answering your and our prayers.

After that appointment, Carson and I went on a date. We went to a lovely restaurant that features vegetarian, vegan and fusion food. The meal was truly wonderful, but the highlight for me was the wonderful man I got to share it with. To celebrate, we shared the first dessert I've had since my birthday cake five months ago. It was a brownie topped with chocolate sauce, pumpkin ice cream and fresh pomegranate. *And*…bonus…it was gluten free and dairy free. Did I mention it was delicious? I told Carson that he is a rock star for handling the past year plus with such grace, wisdom and kindness. Amazing! I like this guy. A lot. Yet another reason to smile.

And finally, it is my mom's birthday today. I get a big lump in my throat when I think about my mom. She is full of such amazing, sacrificial love. Mom has lived and served selflessly with us for over a year now. I don't know how I deserved to have someone this wonderful in my life. I thank God for putting this all together. Mom, of course, does not want one shred of glory. She would say that God gets *all* the glory. But I know that she is likely God's favourite. We are looking forward to celebrating her today. I have to say, I like her. A lot. And I can't stop smiling.

Of course, there are so many reasons for me to smile. God is good. So very good.

For the LORD is good. His unfailing love continues forever, and his faithfulness continues to each generation. (Psalm 100:5 NLT)

DAY
401
TO
450

DAY 403—WHEN A CHILD ASKS A QUESTION
By Brenda Pue—February 7, 2015

This moment was bound to come. And so, when our oldest grandson, Landon, was six years old, I took the time to sit down with him to explain my diagnosis without using the "c" word. I didn't want to scare him, so I tried to keep it simple and factual, yet hopeful. I explained about the "dots" in my brain and how the doctor was trying to make them go away. I thought it went fairly well. That was last March.

Fast-forward to this past Thursday…Kristin brought the two oldest grandsons for a visit. Landon is working on a school project about Ireland, and his grandpa was helping him. So Landon and Grandpa headed upstairs to Carson's office, while the rest of us stayed downstairs, making dinner and playing games.

As soon as Landon got to Grandpa's office, he closed the door. The first words out of his mouth were "Grandpa, does Grammy have cancer?"

Carson was taken aback but answered, "Well, yes, she does."

Landon: "Because we learned about a guy who ran across Canada and he had cancer and he died."

Grandpa: "You mean Terry Fox?"

Landon: "Yeah, Terry Fox. Is Grammy going to die?"

Grandpa: "Well, you know, Landy, the doctor thought that Grammy might die before we went to Pender Harbour last summer, but she is still here."

Landon: "Oh. That was a long time ago."

Grandpa: "She has a lot of people praying for her, and we need to keep praying."

Landon seemed satisfied with that and was ready to move on to his Ireland project. At supper, however, he quizzed me about all my supplements, so I explained which were vitamins and which pill was medicine, not knowing about the conversation that had taken place upstairs.

I have always believed that when a child has the maturity to formulate a question, he or she is ready for an honest answer (using age-appropriate terminology, of course). It's so easy to respond dismissively when a child asks a direct or uncomfortable question. Yet I have found that these awkward moments are often the teachable moments in life. These moments are the building blocks of trust, which pave the way for relational depth later on in life.

There may be similar conversations with the other grandchildren as well, and I pray that God will give us the courage and wisdom to respond graciously and authentically when each teachable moment arrives.

But Jesus said, "Let the children come to me. Don't stop them! For the Kingdom of Heaven belongs to those who are like these children." (Matthew 19:14 NLT)

DAY 410—BE STILL
By Brenda Pue—February 14, 2015

This week Carson and I received cards and letters from long-time family friends—actually long-time friends of Carson's parents long before either of us appeared on the scene. There is something about generational friendship. What a breath of fresh air.

One of the cards had the following words on the front: "When we are unsure which path to take…" followed by this thought on the inside of the card: "God says to stay in the place where we are until He shows us the next step."

It's so easy for me to run ahead and make quick decisions in the moment. But with the decision for my future treatment plan, I am content to wait until we hear back from various oncologists and doctors. Our last appointment is this coming Monday, when we hope to receive definitive results from my recent PET scan. This will be followed by a brain MRI the following week.

Sometimes when I read medical reports, I am tempted to worry. Yet there is something deep in my soul telling me to breathe deeply and slowly and wait on this, though it runs counter to my desire to take control. I sense that God has wisdom for me in the waiting.

In the meantime, I continue with my current protocol, which is made possible by many who gave financial support on the YouCaring site that our family and friends set up. Thank you for prayer, cards, flowers, financial support and so many expressions of love. I am overwhelmed by such generosity. I have written a thank you letter with more details on the YouCaring site.

Be still before the LORD and wait patiently for him. (Psalm 37:7 NIV)

DAY 413—JOY IN THE ROOM
By Brenda Pue—February 17, 2015

We are celebrating. We all have been praying for clarity for my health journey, and God answered our many prayers in tangible ways yesterday. The day began with a beautiful breakfast and a heartfelt prayer time with my prayer group. Six of us gals have been praying together for over 20 years. It was a beautiful, sacred time.

Shortly after our prayer time, Carson picked me up, and we met with my new oncologist. When we got there I saw that he had the report from my PET scan from last Monday. This is the scan that measures cancer activity in the body through a tracer (radioactive dye) and glucose injected into my veins. It took about an hour for it to be absorbed. Since cancer cells love sugar, the PET machine is able to take a video of cancer activity in the body.

My oncologist said, "This PET scan is good news. There is cancer activity, but it is not alarming. Most of the activity is around the main tumour, and I suggest we use directed radiation to kill that tumour. Then after we get the results of your brain MRI next week, I propose scheduling you for brain surgery to remove that tumour, if results show that is necessary."

He told me to continue with my current naturopathic regimen since "You seem to be responding to it favourably." There was more discussion, but the upshot of this is that I am treatable!

My oncologist was genuinely happy. There was joy in the room as the preceding truth registered in our hearts and minds. It has been many months since we have felt such clarity and hope. Thank you for your fervent prayers. God is listening. God is caring. God loves. God is working. Be encouraged, as we are, that God has heard every word that has been in prayer.

Like with King Hezekiah of old, God has heard our prayers, seen my tears and given me more time. I am filled with hope and joy, even though there are so many hurdles still to jump on this journey.

Our path forward is clear:

• Continue with my current protocol, including my chemotherapy regimen of the past year.

• Directed radiation for the main tumour.

• Possible brain surgery to eliminate the metastatic tumour.

• Pray, pray, pray (not in that order).

Thank you for travelling this long, sometimes chaotic, yet often beautiful road with us.

Whether you turn to the right or to the left, your ears will hear a voice behind you, saying, "This is the way; walk in it." (Isaiah 30:21 NIV)

DAY 419—BRAIN MRI
By Brenda Pue—February 23, 2015

Tomorrow afternoon (Tuesday) I am scheduled to have a brain MRI. This test will determine whether or not I need to have brain surgery in the near future.

Up until tonight, I've taken all this in stride. But tonight, while Carson and I were out walking, I realized that this test is bothering me more than I realized. We have an appointment to receive the results on Friday.

And so, I am writing to ask for prayer. Thank you for caring and praying.

"Peace I leave with you; my peace I give you. I do not give to you as the world gives. Do not let your hearts be troubled and do not be afraid." (John 14:27 NIV)

DAY 422—TATTOOS AND SUCH
By Brenda Pue—February 26, 2015

I don't get excited about tattoos. Nor have I ever had any inclination to get a tattoo. Good signage has its place—just not on me. This has been a great source of disappointment to two of my three sons, who are fairly decked out in the tattoo department. To this day, they still try to talk me into getting a tattoo.

Last year, when I was having full brain radiation, the technician put permanent ink dots on my face and neck using a series of CT scans, so that the radiation wouldn't damage my eyesight and other necessary brain functions. That is the closest I have ever come to having a tattoo. There is little that compels me to get a tattoo. That is, until this past week.

After the brain MRI this past Tuesday I began and finished reading a new book entitled *Fight Back with Joy* by Margaret Feinberg. When I am waiting for test results, I like to keep my head and heart focused in good ways, and this book did just that for me. In the book, Margaret talks about seeing a man in a coffee shop with a tattoo that said "But if not..." Intrigued, she asked the man about it, and he told her it came from a story in the Bible.[20]

This story takes place after King Nebuchadnezzar of Babylon overthrew the nation of Israel in 586 B.C. Those who survived the siege were taken as slaves to Babylonia. Of note were four Israeli nobles who rose to notoriety in the king's service, namely Daniel, who was chosen as governor, and his three friends Shadrach, Meshach and Abednego, who served alongside him. You may recall that the king built a nine-storey gold statue of himself and commanded all the people to bow down and worship the statue at the sound of the trumpet. The penalty for not doing so was execution in a large furnace. Of course the three young men refused to worship the statue and were brought before the furious king. Here is what they said:

> "O Nebuchadnezzar, we have no need to present a defence to you in this matter. If our God whom we serve is able to deliver us from the furnace of blazing fire and out of your hand, O king, let him deliver us. But if not, be it known to you, O king, that we will not serve your gods and we will not worship the golden statue that you have set up." (Daniel 3:16–18 NRSV)

These courageous young men survive the ordeal with not so much as a singed hair.

As I think about this story and my cancer journey, I know that God is able and willing to heal me miraculously, *but if not*, I want you to know that He has a better plan. I wouldn't venture to guess at God's plans and ways, but I do know they are filled with goodness. At last, I have found three words that are actually worthy of a tattoo.

Read Daniel 3 for the full version of this wonderful story.

---

[20] Margaret Feinberg, *Fight Back with Joy: Celebrate More. Regret Less. Stare Down Your Greatest Fears* (Brentwood: Worthy Publishing, 2015).

DAY 424—STILL WAITING
By Brenda Pue—February 28, 2015

Hi all,
A quick note. The MRI report was not ready for yesterday's oncology appointment. We expect it middle of next week and will update then.

We took the time to ask questions about brain surgery and learned that, if it is deemed necessary, it will be scheduled within two weeks of getting the MRI results.

We also discussed treating the lung tumour. He used the following humour to help us remember the options:

Zap—Radiation to reduce the size of the tumour.

Cook—Radiofrequency ablation: a probe inserted into the tumour, then heated.

Cut—Surgically remove dead tissue, if possible.

More news next week. Thank you for waiting and praying with us.

Every blessing,

Brenda, for us both

DAY 427—IF YOU PRAYED
By Brenda Pue—March 3, 2015

If you prayed for me, God heard. And I am grateful. I received great news regarding my brain MRI tonight. The last and largest lesion in my brain is no longer evident. Although I don't actually have the MRI report in hand, it would appear that there isn't even any scar tissue. Therefore *no brain surgery is required*, even though there is a small "freckle" in the frontal lobe—the plan is to keep an eye on it.

To not have to undergo surgery at this time is a huge relief. It means that we can begin to focus on the primary tumour, which is the source of my biggest concern due to continual pain. The thought of being pain free is frankly unimaginable to me since it has been my constant companion since December 2013.

I have no idea what the road ahead will bring, but I am *very* motivated to move forward as soon as possible. I can hardly wait to talk with my oncologist about next steps. God has been hearing our prayers, and my sense is that this hard-fought battle has been waged on our knees.

It's been one year and two months of what feels like hard work at so many levels. Although I know there may be difficult days still to come, I am filled with joy. Thank you for sticking with me. This is your joy too!

> *"It shall come to pass that before they call, I will answer; and while they are still speaking, I will hear."* (Isaiah 65:24 NKJV)

DAY 434—NO THEATRICS OR DRAMA
By Brenda Pue—March 10, 2015

He sat calmly with his legs crossed and hands gently folded on his lap, talking quietly. No theatrics or drama, just substance. This is my beloved oncologist and this is how my oncology appointment went…

We discussed my latest brain MRI at length. The last brain lesion in the cerebellum, that I've had for more than a year, is gone. There is a new "something" in the frontal lobe, and he is going to keep an eye on it since they don't know what "it" is.

Next on my agenda was how to manage the increasing pain that I am experiencing. He asked lots of questions, examined me, sent me to the lab next to his office for X-rays and then ran over, upon completion, to have a look. Satisfied that there are no new lesions on my spine, we made our way back to his office.

He sat quietly and then shared that he believes the best way forward is five to ten sessions of directed radiation treatments to the actual tumour to kill it, which should solve most of the things troubling me. Once the tumour is dead:

- It will no longer produce pleural fluid, which is crowding my lung, causing breathing challenges.
- It should remedy the pain caused by pleural fluid, since it will have an opportunity to dry up.
- It should stop nerve- and referred-pain, since it will no longer press on nerve corridors.

I can't tell you how good it was to sit there and begin to think about what it might be like to be pain free with every breath and movement on the right side. That was yesterday's appointment.

Today I got a call from the cancer agency, telling me that I have an appointment with my new radiation oncologist next Thursday, March 19th. So in nine more days I'll know a lot more about this than I know now.

In the meantime, I will continue on with all the good practices that have become a part of my routine the past six months, with the addition of one more: bicycle riding. Carson and I try to get out on our bikes every day, and it is wonderful. And yes, I'm referencing my shiny red bike that I won last summer. For now they are short, easy rides that I can manage with limited lung space.

It feels good to have direction. It feels good to have promise. God is so gracious to me...to us.

The LORD says, "I will guide you along the best pathway for your life. I will advise you and watch over you"...unfailing love surrounds those who trust the LORD. (Psalm 32:8,10 NLT)

DAY 443—SO I'M GETTING A TATTOO
By Brenda Pue—March 19, 2015

Today I met my newest oncologist—the radiation oncologist. He's young. I judge he is married with no kids. He's very down to earth, soft-spoken and likeable. And did I mention smart? This doctor will likely forget more than I know. The tone of our appointment was very encouraging and hopeful, except for one sentence: "I need to tell you that this treatment is to make you comfortable. It is not a cure." Every time I hear this (and I've heard it many times), it takes the wind out of my sails. This was the low point of the appointment for me.

He took an hour with us, explaining what to expect before, during and after my radiation treatments. Here's what I can expect:

1. Initially, more pain than I am presently experiencing. Gulp.
2. Tiredness for several weeks.
3. Scar tissue around the deadened tumour and surrounding tissue forever.
4. Reduced breathing capacity—the lost lung tissue cannot be recovered.
5. Reduction of pleural fluid production, and pain, with the hope and prayer that my body will eventually absorb the existing fluid without surgical intervention.

He sweetly asked me if I would like to wait for the end of spring break when my original radiation oncologist returns to work. I responded, without hesitation, that I'd like to "git 'er done."

Tomorrow is tattoo day for me. At 10 a.m. I have a CT-guided appointment to get set up for radiation treatments. I'll be getting permanent markings on my chest and back so that the directed radiation goes to the right place each day. He decided on a five-day course of treatments commencing this Monday and finishing on Friday. I have to discontinue my daily chemotherapy during radiation, and he doesn't want me to be off the chemo for very long. Then we'll wait and see. I am ready to move forward into this next stage of the cancer journey.

I have dubbed 2014 the Year of My Brain, and this year is the Year of My Lung. I have no idea what the future will bring, but I'm content with what God has given me to manage for today. One day at a time.

Trust in the LORD, and do good; dwell in the land and befriend faithfulness. Delight yourself in the LORD, and he will give you the desires of your heart. Commit your way to the LORD; trust in him, and he will act. (Psalm 37:3–5 ESV)

DAY 446—AND YET I KNOW
By Brenda Pue—March 22, 2015

It is the evening before I begin my second round of radiation treatments, one year later. It's beginning to dawn on me that this may be a longer journey than I ever imagined.

So much has happened in the past year. I am not the person I was 14 months ago. There was a time when I could "flex" with life. There was a time when I had options. All that has narrowed significantly for me. I've always been a fairly responsible sort of person…I've never been one who lived on the wild side of excess. In some ways life feels more narrow now.

Yet now I need to care, more than I ever have, about what I eat or don't eat, about getting enough sleep—I technically don't have a lot of control about that :)—about exercising the best I can, and about reading and researching. And I pray and seek help from above day and night. I think it's good to care that much because God does.

The thing is, I'm in this situation that often feels so far out my control that I am constantly brought to my knees. I never imagined that I would ever in my life experience the depths of fear, emotions, and physical pain that have been my portion over the past year plus.

In the past, when I've contended with physical pain, I've always had the sense or at least the knowledge that the pain was productive…that with time the situation would improve. Cancer is not the same thing. Somehow, at the physical level, it feels like unproductive pain. It's hard to articulate how senseless it feels.

And yet I know…

There is a God in heaven.

He deeply loves and cares for me.

Life is immeasurably better because He values me.

He isn't finished pouring out His love on me.

Although I don't understand the depth and mystery of what I've been called to, bit by bit it is unfolding. The song entitled "Oceans" by Hillsong United was shared with me a few days ago, and it does a good job of capturing where my heart is lately.

P.S. My radiation tattoo ended up to be much ado about nothing. It's the size of a tiny freckle.

DAY 449—CAUTIOUSLY OPTIMISTIC
By Brenda Pue—March 25, 2015

The bunker, that is where we go every day this week for radiation treatments. There is something depressing about the bunker. Perhaps that's why we call it the bunker. In reality, it is the basement floor of the Abbotsford Cancer Clinic. The people waiting in the bunker look sad and tense, [giving off] a sense of hopelessness. I get so caught up in the sights, sounds and smells of the bunker that I forget to pray.

The upper three floors of the cancer agency are different. There is more light, and, somehow, that translates to hope. It is palpable. It's easier to be on these floors…and there is even a Starbucks in the lobby.

But for this week, I am doing time in the bunker. I am halfway through my week of nine medical appointments, totalling approximately 19 hours.

Yesterday, a receptionist said to me, "You must feel like your life is all cancer appointments."

My instant response was "Yes; I feel so blessed to be able to have the time and energy to work at this."

There was a long pause…and then she said, "Wow. I've never heard anybody say that before."

Somehow in all of this craziness, God is lifting my chin and allowing me to find joy. The past few weeks, when pain has been more impacting, I realize how much worse this could be. But today, day three, finds me cautiously optimistic. The pain is slightly de-escalating. Last week, I could find no comfortable position—sitting, standing or lying down. It seemed the only way to distract my brain from pain was walking and cycling. Today the pain feels more tolerable.

Thank you for continued prayers. I often wonder where I would be without the prayers, care and love of so many. This week and next week, friends are providing meals and grocery shopping to practically help us. I can't tell you how great it is at the end of a big day not to have to put energy into meal planning and execution. Thank you for hanging in there with me…with us…we are blessed beyond measure.

Some specific things that we seem to circle around lately:
• That the radiation treatments will actually work.
• That I can manage pain and that it will resolve soon.
• That I can tolerate the side effects of the anti-inflammatory drug, which include insomnia and indigestion.
• That nausea from radiation will be held at bay in the coming days and weeks.

Take delight in the LORD, and he will give you your heart's desires. Commit everything you do to the LORD. Trust him, and he will help you. (Psalm 37:4–5 NLT)

DAY
451
TO
500

DAY 453—GOODNESS IN STRANGE PLACES
By Brenda Pue—March 29, 2015

My oldest grandson, who is seven, and his dad accompanied us to my last radiation treatment on Friday. He was all curiosity and questions, having learned about Terry Fox at school…he has an insatiable desire to understand.

We headed straight to "the bunker" and checked in. I changed into my men's XXXL hospital gown (there is no way to look fashionable in those things), and I was immediately summoned for my treatment. I introduced Landon and asked if we could show him around the unit. The technicians were delighted and enthusiastic and engaged with him right away.

One of them asked him if he did the annual Terry Fox run, and our mini tour of the cancer agency got off to a great start. As we entered the room, I showed Landy the eight-inch-thick steel door. Once inside the room I lay on the narrow bed, and they let Landon move the bed to its highest position. Then the techs showed him how to aim the laser lights onto the markings on either side of my rib cage. Next was watching the radiation machine move to underneath the bed, where they would shortly radiate the tumour through my back.

Everyone stepped out of the room, and Landon got to press the all-clear button, which is for the last person leaving the room. My entourage watched me on the computer screens while Landon peppered them with questions way beyond his years.

Landon: "Does the radiation go everywhere on Grammy or just where it is aimed?"

Technician: "What a great question! How old are you?"

They went on to explain exactly the area they were targeting and showed him the X-ray of the tumour. He definitely got the full tour.

His bright eyes, laughter and polite demeanour brought such goodness and delight to us all. I suspect Landon's visit may have been the best thing that has happened there in a very long time.

We also had an oncology appointment, where I was told that often the pain gets worse for a few weeks before it gets better, due to swelling of the tumour and resulting nerve pain. He gave me a prescription for narcotics, just in case. I've also been warned about a kind of exhaustion that is hard to describe. By Friday, after five consecutive days of radiation treatments, these warnings became my experience. So I've laid low the past few days, even missing family night, which may be a first for me.

It is precious to have a grandchild so engaged with this journey and joining so many others in praying for my healing.

Something that I didn't know before is that it takes about a year to fully recover from radiation. What an amazing thing the human body is! It is designed for healing and recovery. It works hard, day in and day out, to heal.

So although I haven't felt skookum the past several days, I've set my heart on healing and better days ahead.

If you do these things, God will shed his own glorious light upon you. He will heal you; your godliness will lead you forward, goodness will be a shield before you, and the glory of the Lord will protect you from behind. (Isaiah 58:8 TLB)

DAY 458—A PERSONAL PSALM
By Brenda Pue—April 3, 2015

It is Good Friday. I am still in the aftermath of radiation—moving a bit slow, dealing with pain, tired from radiation and also the narcotics I am on.

I got up early today for quiet time, thinking about life. For me, Good Friday is about suffering, powerfully exemplified by the crucifixion of Christ (Luke 22–

24). I see the cross as a place where great suffering and great love meet. I wonder where I'd be right now without the cross? Fifteen months into a cancer diagnosis that has turned my world upside down, I have joy, hope and gratitude *because* of that cross.

This week I reread the book entitled *When God Interrupts* by M. Craig Barnes. Often when we suffer, we experience what some call the silence of God. Barnes says, "God is often silent when we prefer that he speak, and he interrupts us when we prefer that he stay silent. His ways are not our ways."[21]

So I wrote a personal psalm today. It is based on Psalm 40 and brings together my journey and reflections on Good Friday.

BRENDA'S PERSONAL GOOD FRIDAY PSALM

I wait patiently for Your help, Lord.
You lift me out of despair.
You set my feet on solid ground and You steady me as I walk.
As I trust You, there is joy.
Oh Lord, You have done many miracles for me.
You have all kinds of great plans for me.
If I tried to recite all Your wonderful deeds, I would never come to the end of them.
I take joy in living for You, my God, for Your words are written on my heart.
I have told everyone I know about Your grace.
I have not been embarrassed to tell the world about You.
I have not kept this good news to myself.
I have talked openly about Your faithfulness and saving power.
I have shared with many of Your unfailing love and good intentions.
Lord, don't hold back Your tender mercies from me.
My only hope is in Your unfailing love and faithfulness.
Come quickly to me and rescue me.
May all who search for You be filled with joy and gladness.
May those who love Your salvation proclaim Your goodness.
As for me, I need You and I know that You are thinking about me right now.
You are my helper and saviour.
Do not delay, O my God.

[21] M. Craig Barnes, *When God Interrupts: Finding New Life Through Unwanted Change* (Downers Grove: InterVarsity Press, 1996), 135.

DAY 465—FOR A SEASON
By Brenda Pue—April 10, 2015

I have been blessed with my mom's genetic code for energy. At age 81, her energy level is remarkable. This capacity for energy and getting things done has accompanied me all the days of my life…that is, until cancer.

In the past 15 months, my energy capacity has changed. And yet I have continued to live with the same expectations that I've always had of myself. I'm learning that this is counterproductive at this stage in my journey…trying to create, or force, myself to be something I was.

Every day, people ask me how I'm doing. Hmmm. That's a tough question to answer sometimes. My standard response is "Good." It's a good response because it's true…I'm blessed…I'm loved…I'm grateful. It's also true that I don't have the energy to explain all that I am going through, learning and experiencing to every person who asks the question. It's a deeper conversation that I reserve for certain people at certain times.

As well, trying to quantify how I am doing on a daily basis is challenging since the path I am on is constantly changing, hourly and daily. So I've started measuring my recovery by weeks. I find it easier to compare weeks rather than days. And this week I received a little gem of wisdom from a friend who has travelled the cancer road ahead of me. It is helping me untangle the web of low energy, personal expectations and trying to please everyone around me.

Wait for it… "OTAD" or "One Thing A Day" that requires energy. [I only have the capacity to do one thing a day if it requires energy], at least during this stage in my healing. I am told there will come a time when I can manage two things a day, but not now. I can't tell you how freeing this has been for me. It has clarified and simplified life for me. I'm better able to prioritize. It's not forever; it's for a season.

Today's OTAD is family night, and I am excited. I missed the previous one due to side effects of radiation treatments. I'm managing the side effects a little better this week.

For everything there is a season, and a time for every matter under heaven.
(Ecclesiastes 3:1 ESV)

DAY 468—DADDY'S GOT YOU

By Brenda Pue—April 13, 2015

"Family night" is always a collection of treasured moments with all 12 of us sharing a meal and sharing our lives together. This past family night was no exception.

A typical family night goes something like this...

Before I get too involved with the dinner effort, I usually take time to watch the grandkids and talk with them or play a game. (Have you ever noticed how penetrating the gaze of a child is? Kids look right into the soul somehow.)

After talking and playing with each of the little ones, I make my way back to the kitchen to help with the food and connect with our adult kids. We get caught up with each other.

Then we eat. We all contribute to the meal, and it is always yummy.

The visiting continues while we eat. As soon as the little ones finish, they go play with each other, and we adults take that opportunity to share on a deeper level and pray together amidst peals of laughter, the inevitable arguments and the general excitement of cousins being together. Did I mention it's loud?

This past Friday, something happened that captured me.

The kids were playing upstairs, and little Ellie, two years old, accidentally turned on a clock radio. The "white noise" frightened her badly, and she started wailing. The moms ran upstairs to help and brought her down into the family room, and she instantly ran to Daddy and climbed up to cry it out and cuddle. Jeremy held her close and said, "It's okay. Daddy's got you."

She lingered and calmed.

I have often felt like Ellie. Frightened by the "white noise" of a cancer journey. Not understanding it fully and sometimes being reduced to tears.

There isn't anything more comforting than being held close by my Heavenly Father and hearing Him say, "It's okay. Daddy's got you."

He heals the brokenhearted and binds up their wounds. (Psalm 147:3 ESV)

For You have been my help, And in the shadow of Your wings I sing for joy. My soul clings to You; Your right hand upholds me. (Psalm 63:7–8 NASB)

DAY 479—A REALLY GOOD PRAYER
By Brenda Pue—April 24, 2015

Cancer and pain go hand in hand. Like salt and pepper. Like black and white. Like Batman and Robin. It was pain that drove me to the doctor 1 1/2 years ago when I eventually learned about the stage four lung cancer diagnosis. There have been many ups and downs in the pain journey since then. It has crescendoed the past few months, especially post radiation treatments. This has driven me to my knees in prayer and to seek help.

I am relieved to report some improvement, although I am still on a daily regimen of narcotics to alleviate pain. However, as I was getting dressed for the day yesterday, some new pain developed. My back seized up, which made walking and getting dressed a challenge. As I made my way to the top of the stairs, I stood there trying to figure out the best way to navigate my way down to breakfast. Be assured that missing breakfast was not an option. :)

I was able to get in to see my physiotherapist, who felt that my body had succumbed to the tension of a month of intense pain, causing severe muscle spasms and a locked spine. It feels good to get some relief. But that's not the best part.

Carson was talking on the phone to a church friend of ours yesterday morning, and out of the blue, she said, "Tell Brenda not to think about the pain. I'm going to pray that Brenda won't think about the pain."

It was another message from heaven…So each moment of yesterday and today became an opportunity to focus on good things, rather than the pain. I felt like I was able to practice the following Scripture in a new way:

Finally, brothers and sisters, whatever is true, whatever is noble, whatever is right, whatever is pure, whatever is lovely, whatever is admirable—if anything is excellent or praiseworthy—think about such things. (Philippians 4:8 NIV)

DAY 486—AGAINST ALL ODDS
By Brenda Pue—May 1, 2015

There is a wonderful story in the Bible of how to respond or react when the odds are not favourable. It is long, so I'll do an executive summary. It is taken from 2 Kings 18–19.

The opening scene depicts the nation of Assyria laying siege to Jerusalem, which is under the leadership of King Hezekiah. The representative of the Assyrians threatens and denounces the nation of Israel and their God. The Jewish people remain silent, by order of their king. The odds are against Israel. Israel is outnumbered and seemingly beyond hope.

King Hezekiah's response to this attack is a model for anyone who is facing a hopeless situation:

He makes no direct response to the threats but instead turns to God for help and direction. In other words, he puts a pause between stimulus and response.

This is the message that God gives to him through the prophet Isaiah: "Do not be disturbed by this blasphemous speech against me from the Assyrian king's messengers. Listen! I myself will move against him" (2 Kings 19:6–7 NLT).

Sometimes I feel like cancer is "laying siege" against me. I've been told that the odds are against me...that there is no hope. However, today marks the fifth week since my radiation treatments finished, and my pain levels are incrementally less with each passing week. Thank you for prayers. This morning my heart is encouraged by God's mercy and strength.

I've been told over and over that the odds are against me, but I also know that with God there is no contest.

DAY 492—RESTORING THE BALANCE
By Brenda Pue—May 7, 2015

This week started out quite relaxed by my standards—only two medical appointments! That is almost a record for me. However, by Monday afternoon my week rounded out with a total of six medical appointments. It played out like this:

Monday—cancer-related appointment at Integrated Health.

Tuesday—physiotherapy appointment re muscle spasm due to cancer pain.

Wednesday—IV Vitamin C treatment in the a.m. and medical oncologist in the late afternoon.

Thursday—family physician re viral infection on my arm and fungal infection on my toe.

Friday—cancer-related appointment at Integrated Health.

Everyone agrees that the extraneous appointments are likely cancer related due to a compromised immune system. The challenge is how to treat them [the complications due to the cancer] when my body is already on so many meds. Lots of room for prayer in all of this, I think. :)

Although I didn't expect my week to end up like this, the past 492 days of this cancer journey are teaching me to expect the unexpected. Although I have occasional moments of distress around all of this, for the most part I am learning to take it in stride.

I quite like the expression "When life gives you lemons, make lemonade." This week my lemonade was sweetened by

- An organic moose dinner at our friends' home.
- Amazing homemade chicken vegetable soup.
- A beautiful gourmet dinner and evening with dear friends in our home.
- A fabulous dinner with Carson at a restaurant en route home from my oncology appointment.
- Enjoying ten minutes of wonder watching two hummingbirds' antics on an early morning walk.
- Taking our three grandsons to see Disney's movie *Monkey Kingdom*.

Our "lemonade," though not expected, was like healing balm to our souls. We have been deeply and richly blessed this week. God seems to have a way of restoring the balance. Next week, we anticipate a follow-up appointment with my radiation oncologist, blood tests, a PET scan (to measure cancer activity post radiation), plus four other appointments of the cancer and non-cancer variety.

That's the expected list…the unexpected blessings have yet to unfold.

Worship the LORD your God, and his blessing will be on your food and water. [He] I will take away sickness from among you. (Exodus 23:25 NIV)

DAY 497—CIRCLE OF LIFE
By Brenda Pue—May 12, 2015

I awakened early Sunday morning to my alarm, reminding me that it was time to begin my daily pill regimen.

Except that when I picked up my phone to turn off the alarm, I saw there was a message from JP2 (short for Jeremy Pue, second son).

The message said that Shari was in labour and had been admitted to the hospital. I quickly dressed, told Carson the news, and waited for Shari's mom, Anne, to pick me up for a very special delivery room moment.

Shari was having regular contractions, and it wasn't long until she was in transition. Tears quietly rolled down my face as I watched the miracle unfolding before me. My second granddaughter, and fifth grandchild, was entering the world. And I am here to behold this blessed event. She arrived at 9:59 a.m., weighed 6 pounds 1 ounce, and was 19.5" long. And her name is Georgia Anne Susan (named after both grandmothers). (My middle name is Susan.)

She is so tiny and so beautiful. What a wonderful Mother's Day! Everything has come full circle, as God would have it. I am blessed beyond measure.

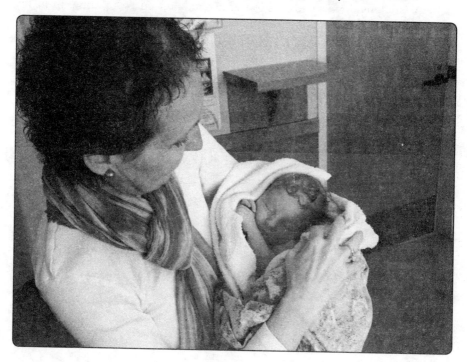

He called a little child, and placed the child among them. And he said: "Truly I tell you, unless you change and become like little children, you will never enter the kingdom of heaven. Therefore, whoever takes the lowly position of this child is the greatest in the kingdom of heaven. And whoever welcomes one such child in my name welcomes me." (Matthew 18:2–5 NIV)

DAY
501
TO
550

DAY 501—500 DAYS AND COUNTING
By Brenda Pue—May 16, 2015

Five hundred days have passed since [we first were made aware that I may have cancer, and then] the cancer diagnosis was confirmed on January 11, 2014: stage four non-small cell lung cancer. I was told to get my affairs in order, since I only had approximately 150 days left on this earth. Since I am long past my expiry date, we are celebrating this milestone.

I believe that all of our days are numbered. Some of us just happen to be more aware of it than others. So each day that I awaken to greet a new day is a true gift.

I admit that not all the days have been stellar. There have been times of deep grief and sadness. Yet I've noticed that the pain of low moments adds depth to life that is hard to articulate. This is one of life's great mysteries. I could not have imagined the multiple medical appointments each week that I've been through or the side effects of radiation, chemotherapy and other drugs. This is my new life, for however long God calls me to it. And wherever possible, every day, I embrace all the goodness that He sends my way.

- An amazing husband who can't find enough ways to express his love for me.
- Getting to share daily life with my beloved mom.
- Sharing life with sons and daughters who make me laugh until I cry and then pray for me from the depths of their souls.
- Five precious grandchildren who take my breath away.
- Being on the receiving end of cards, letters, books, emails, texts and phone calls that have stirred my heart and given me hope.
- Getting to know God even better.
- Friends…oh my wonderful friends.
- Practical gifts like meals, gift baskets, blankets and supplements.
- Not-so-practical things, like jewellery, makeup, movie coupons, restaurant gift cards, that have been a delight when delight was needed.
- Beholding God's beautiful world as I've walked the neighbourhood in all the seasons.
- Flowers…every kind you could imagine.
- Every imaginable prayer that could be uttered from every corner of the world.

Oh I am a blessed one!

It seemed so right to share this moment of celebration with my bigger family. Thank you for hanging in there with us. Thank you for not giving up.

I will be giving a medical update next week…just not today!

"The LORD bless you and keep you; the LORD make his face shine on you and be gracious to you; the LORD turn his face toward you and give you peace." (Numbers 6:24–26 NIV)

DAY 505—THE REPRIEVE IS OVER
By Brenda Pue—May 20, 2015

It was nice while it lasted. Four whole days with no medical *stuff*. We laid low, went for walks, went out for dinner one night, watched a couple of movies; and I read a book. It was such a nice change from the usual intensity of medical appointments and deadlines.

The only thing I didn't get a break from was…pain. By the end of the long weekend, I knew that I wasn't handling my pain levels very well. So I contacted my family doctor to talk through my options. In the end, we decided that the narcotic I am on is actually a good drug. I just wasn't getting enough of it.

Earlier last week, my oncologist was concerned about my breathing, or, perhaps better stated, my lack of breathing. So he ordered a chest X-ray. The results showed two to three litres of pleural fluid, which won't allow my lungs to function properly. The end result of all this is a procedure called thoracocentesis. A tube is placed between the ribs into the pleural cavity, and pleural fluid is drained out for two to three hours. If done slowly enough, the lung should not collapse. It is a fairly common procedure, and I'm told there is nothing to fear.

I think this might be one of those "Easy for you to say" scenarios. :)

We will get a call from the hospital tomorrow morning, and, though I would rather not walk this road, it seems to be my only viable option. This is another one of those "jumping into the arms of Jesus" moments. One would think I would be used to this after 500-plus days, but no. Rather, I find myself much in need of prayer.

A few days later, on Monday, I am scheduled for a PET scan, which will measure cancer activity in my chest cavity eight weeks post chest radiation treatments. So we are fully back into the medical stuff that has been my full-time job over the past year and a half.

You may be wondering what I am grateful for. I am so thankful for the medical team of people who have come alongside me on this journey. They have knowledge and skill that far exceed my capacity. I so appreciate these gifted people and thank God for each one's part. I realize that such knowledge and expertise is a fraction of the mind of God. As I head into this next phase of treatment, I take great comfort that God's got this.

> *Great is the LORD and most worthy of praise; his greatness no one can fathom.* (Psalm 145:3 NIV)

DAY 511—ON THIS SIDE OF STRANGE
By Brenda Pue—May 26, 2015

My previous journal entry chronicled my pleural fluid removal. It seemed to go quite well. At least I thought so, until I started hearing talk of being admitted onto the medical ward. And so it came to be—me and three burly guys sharing a room.

The next day I was moved into a room with a nice lady—just the two of us. It seemed as each day passed, the accommodations just kept getting better. On Thursday night, an ambulance transfer delivered me to a completely different hospital with a private room, so that I could have access to a thoracic surgeon.

However, that's where the fun ended and the serious side of this procedure surfaced. After approximately three litres of fluid were drained, X-rays showed that 50 percent of my lung had collapsed. So now I am faced with excessive pain and surgical decisions to be made.

As I write, Carson and I are waiting to meet with the thoracic surgeon.

This just in…We met with my surgeon and are hoping to have the surgery done this week. These are our prayers:
- For full healing.
- For pain to resolve.
- For strength, in every way, to get through this.

This whole cancer journey just seems to get more unusual as we go. These are strange times indeed! *Where is God when strange becomes the norm?* I wonder. The only place I can find an answer is in God's Word.

Who comforts us in all our affliction so that we will be able to comfort those who are in any affliction with the comfort with which we ourselves are comforted by God. (2 Corinthians 1:4 NASB)

DAY 517—A SONG FOR THE SOUL
By Brenda Pue—June 1, 2015

My dear friend J. John in the UK recently passed along a song for me. It was written by Dan Pringle, an award-winning songwriter and producer, and he wrote this song for me. I was so deeply touched that I asked Dan if I might share it on Caring Bridge. I got an enthusiastic yes. I hope you enjoy it too.

Here is the link, so that you can follow along: https://carsonpue.net/brenda-pue/hallelujah-by-dan-pringle/.

HALLELUJAH
by Dan Pringle 2015

No I won't let my lips be silent
I will praise You through my falling tears
No I won't let my heart stop fighting
I'll speak Your name until the darkness clears
I won't give up
I won't give up
I'll sing for You
Hallelujah!
Hallelujah!
Hallelujah!
Our God be praised!
In the middle of the fire
In the middle of the desert
In the middle of the fight
I'll sing Your praise
Hallelujah!
Hallelujah!
Hallelujah!
Our God be praised!

DAY 522—GOOD TO BE HOME
By Brenda Pue—June 6, 2015

This past Monday, after almost two weeks in the hospital, I was finally at home sweet home. Even our moderately busy household is peaceful by hospital standards. In fact, two nurses from Langley Home Health came on Wednesday to drain pleural fluid via my pleurastat. This little unit was surgically installed about a week ago, and, after draining over three litres of pleural fluid in two hospitals, we drained another 75 ml on Wednesday and another 100 ml today.

Since I've been home, I have rebooked a PET scan and a follow-up medical oncology appointment. The idea is to sort out cancer activity in my body, and a PET scan is the best way to do that.

I have been going for short walks twice each day, increasing the length of each walk slightly in an effort to build muscle strength in my body. It may take the better part of the summer to accomplish that. And I suspect there will be all sorts of twists and turns along the way.

Still…it's good to be at home and sleeping in my own bed. Perhaps that is what heaven is partly about. Feeling entirely "at home."

I've found myself wondering if this is a foretaste of my great homecoming to heaven someday.

The Bible has a lot to say about heaven. Randy Alcorn spent about 30 years writing his masterpiece entitled *Heaven*. I started reading it in 2013 and was close to halfway finished when I received the cancer diagnosis. Some good reading awaits me this summer…

> And I heard a loud voice from the throne saying, "Look! God's dwelling place is now among the people, and he will dwell with them. They will be his people, and God himself will be with them and be their God. 'He will wipe every tear from their eyes. There will be no more death' or mourning or crying or pain, for the old order of things has passed away." (Revelation 21:3–4 NIV)

DAY 541—THE UPS AND DOWNS OF CANCER
By Brenda Pue—June 25, 2015

Sorry it has been a while since my last post. Let me explain.

On June 10, Carson and I made our way to West Vancouver to meet with my wonderful medical oncologist. He read to us his copy of the PET scan report, and we were pleasantly surprised. We were pleased that the tumour markers were slightly down in all areas.

We now have a home care nurse coming each week to drain the pleural fluid from my lung area. The nurse is going to help Kirstie (daughter number three) learn how to drain the pleural lining plug, so that we can get this all sorted out. She is getting fitted in and out with [training in] all things "pleural." So nice my son married a nurse!

However, things escalated this past Friday in a way I had not expected. I began throwing up and was unable to speak for several hours. Kirstie and my friend Faye got me to Emergency, where our family physician helped us figure out how to navigate all this. It turns out that there are new metastases in the brain causing swelling—hence the throwing up and the speech difficulties. It sure gave me insight into how difficult it is to want to communicate and be unable to. I wonder if my grandbabies struggle with that before they can talk.

Saturday, in the middle of the night, I suddenly started speaking in full sentences again as the swelling in the brain subsided. Carson and I were smiling over this sudden noise coming from my mouth after several hours of nothing. The doctor kept me in the hospital until Sunday late afternoon to make sure I was okay…

Was I glad to get home! What a great feeling!

As you can imagine—this is a lot for me to process, but we have processed a lot on this journey. This week is all about trying to figure out a new normal. For now I'm taking it easy and figuring out how to manage all the nuances of pain.

My nurse is coming to drain the pleural area this Saturday and to remove the cord that holds the valve intact—it was installed in my right back area, then the little tube was brought around the front under the skin and secured with a little cord. At least I don't have to go anywhere!

Here are a few things that we are praying about this week:
• Reduction of pain, especially along my right side.
• Weight gain…I am at 99 lbs.
• We'd like to make a short trip to Victoria next week.
• Staying close to God.
• Praying for the whole family.

I am confident of this: I will see the goodness of the LORD in the land of the living. Wait for the LORD; be strong and take heart and wait for the LORD. (Psalm 27:13–14 NIV)

DAY
551
TO
588

DAY 551—PRAYER AND MEDICAL ADVENTURES
By Brenda Pue—July 5, 2015

As I reflect on a medical update this week, I am mindful of the prayer requests [I made in] my Caring Bridge journal on June 25th, most of which were medically focused. So I'd like to take a few minutes to focus on each one.

Reduction of pain, especially along my right side—it is gradual but improved. I feel like I have got the medications figured out and am resting better as a result.

Weight gain—I am gradually putting on a few pounds. It is challenging to keep these calories following surgery, etc., and yet it is worth the great effort to try. After the previous pleural drain, I was in pain and hoping for some relief. This occurred, and I am so grateful.

Taking my mom on a short trip to Victoria, BC, to bless her—It had been so many years since she had been to Vancouver Island. We calculated approximately 30 years! We did it and stayed at our in-law's timeshare right on the harbour. We took Mom to Spinnakers Restaurant and Pub, one of our spots that is "Brenda-friendly." After lunch, we took her to another favourite stop—Capitol Iron—a great kitchen, furniture, marine antique, camping and clothing store. The next morning, we got up early and went for a leisurely breakfast before heading to Butchart Gardens for a few hours of delight. The highlight for us was watching Mom take it all in. It was a great time away.

Staying close to God—We built time into this trip to just be quiet and watch the sights and scenes of Victoria's Inner Harbour, which was so good for the soul.

Praying for our whole family—Although we were sorry to leave the beauty of Victoria, we got back home in time for "family night" and to spend time with the whole Pue clan. I wish you could see us all together. I was tired, but it is always so good to support one another. Although I feel my own great need for God, I also see my kids' need and Carson's need too.

We somehow managed to get a quick photo op with all the grandkids and me. It's definitely not professional quality, but it will give you an idea of "a day on the life of…"

All your prayers mean so much to us. I feel like God has blessed us beyond measure. Thank you for caring enough to pray.

Train up a child in the way he should go; even when he is old he will not depart from it. (Proverbs 22:6 ESV)

DAY 561—GOOD TO HELP
By Brenda Pue—Monday July 15, 2015

We are up at Pender Harbour enjoying our family holiday with not 12 but 13 Pue family members. The first few days were a bit overcast and rainy, and we enjoyed the change from the heat wave that has been our portion for many weeks.

It's been a treat for me to observe the sights and sounds of grandparents, parents and grandkids. The Lord has been very kind, gracious and loving to me (and to our whole family)…I am eating, sleeping and enjoying this week away from home in spite of all the physical stress during the month of June.

Having time for reflection up here, I can't help but feel that we are put on this earth to make a difference for other people. I recently read a short story about a little girl, named Opal, who lived her life so. She went about helping her mom and others, [making] their way lighter in the world. When her mom would lie down for a rest, Opal would gently rub her mom's head to ease the lines of worry.

This story is from a book entitled *A Tree Full of Angels* by Macrina Wiederkehr. She writes, "Ask Jesus to rub the forehead of the world so that our worry lines go away and trust lines will come upon us. For Jesus, too, does think it is nice to help folks have what they do have longings for."[22]

---

[22] Macrina Wiederkehr, *A Tree Full of Angels: Seeing the Holy in the Ordinary* (New York: HarperCollins, 1988), 104.

That is my mission, although it hasn't always been so. There is a myriad of ways…

- Children need attention.
- Families…so much love is needed.
- Spouses need tenderness.
- Babies are dependant for their very lives.
- Mothers need so much love.
- Fathers need touches of kindness as well.
- Sisters are special.
- Brothers are one of a kind.
- Friends make the world a more beautiful place.
- Strangers bring insight.

There is much to be noticed and attended to. This is how Jesus lived His days. He loves to rub away our worry lines…[and] all of us need this.

> *Don't worry about anything; instead, pray about everything. Tell God what you need, and thank him for all he has done.* (Philippians 4:6 NLT)

DAY 566—HOW TO PLAN FOR THE FUTURE…QUICKLY!
By Brenda Pue—July 20, 2015

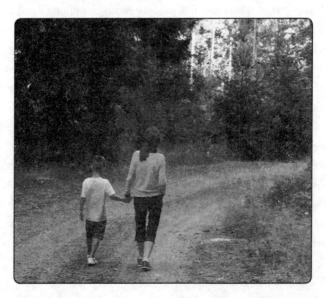

My heartfelt thanks to you for your love and prayers.

We have just returned from the most amazing week as a family. It quickly picked up the hashtag #puecation from Kirstie, and if you are on social media you have probably been inundated with our photos already. We stayed at Rosewoods Retreat at Pender Harbour. To get there we drove to Horseshoe Bay Ferry Terminal and caught a ferry to Langdale. From there we drove about an hour and a half north to our beautiful, peaceful setting.

On the ferry my sweet "Biam" (his real name is Liam, but this nickname his older brother concocted has stuck since he was just "baby Liam") realized we were going right past Barnabas, and he asked, "Grandpa, can you phone Kathy [Bentall] and let her know we are going by and get her to wave at us?" Liam then hauled us all outside, and we stood there waving at our favourite place on the planet. It is at Barnabas that Arrow Leadership still holds many of their residentials. Hundreds of leaders have been impacted there, and it has been a big part of life for the Pue family. All three boys have worked there in the summer months, and we as a family have attended their summer family camps and hope to do so again.

Our family holiday week was amazing. Rosewoods has created a lovely prayer walk in the forest across the road from our cabin that we made use of. A highlight of the week was a worship and prayer time in their chapel with all of our grandkids participating. Jeremy brought his guitar and led some beautiful worship while all the grandkids played their homemade instruments. At the end Carson gave a three-minute message about the Celtic cross that stands in the chapel and also the symbolism of the "tree of life" engraved on it. When he finished, our dear little Ellie came up beside him and repeated the message to all of us with hand gestures and sincerity. It was so sweet and amazing. I think Jer and Shari are raising a strong, gifted woman leader—and Carson adds "like her Grammy."

The #puecation week [our hashtag created for social media] was made up of many components. We had deep talks, hilarious laughter, fun games, walks, swimming, prayer and many one-on-one conversations.

Our holiday actually started on Friday, July 10th. [That week] Carson was teaching at Regent College in the mornings and was unable to attend a meeting with my radiation oncologist at Abbotsford Cancer Centre. My close friend Penny came to take notes for Carson and me. The essence of the meeting was to discuss candidly where things are at with my cancer—especially focused on five brain tumours that have returned.

On the Wednesday of our holiday week, we had a follow-up meeting by phone with the oncologist to ask a number of clarifying questions we had, along with some [questions] from our kids.

As a result of these appointments, and the news, we prayed together as a family, and we ask you to join with us in prayer. The doctor confirmed that there is nothing more medically that can be done to halt the progression of the cancer in the brain—without [the] treatment efforts themselves causing significant side effects for little gain.

The primary concern has always been the cancer in my brain, even though cancer is still present in my lungs and bones. The brain makes it nearly impossible to forecast what will happen, or when it will happen. The doctors told me that I have defied all of the odds and they are very hesitant to be firm on timelines concerning end of life, saying it is possible that I might defy the odds again. However, they did share that in my current state the general range is one to two months.

I continue to be in pain, and, even though I am on hydromorphone, there are still times when the pain can be extreme…not always, but sometimes. Despite this, I had an amazing week at Pender Harbour with my beloved family.

The oncologist mentioned that this might be my last good week. So imagine that! We booked this last holiday as a family a year ago—thinking that perhaps I might not be here but that it would be a great way for us to be together as a family and support one another regardless. By God's grace we [have] made memories that will never depreciate.

Emotionally and spiritually, Carson and I are actually doing quite well. Our family is united and fully supportive. The doctors have also been supportive of my wish to stay at home, and we are pleased they are working to make this happen. We have a team in place and are thinking about some changes to the home to make it as comfortable and convenient as possible.

So what now? Well, as odd as it seems writing this—we are not doing much differently:

- Taking one day at a time.
- Savouring every moment together.
- Praying.
- Planning.
- Helping our family and friends, as you have been walking this journey with us.

I am really guarding my energy now. I get exhausted easily and am not often able to visit. So, for now, I am reserving my energy for family. Carson and I have some very specific things to deal with, including working together to plan an amazing Celebration of Life (memorial) service. Our communications to you…Inner Circle [a small group of our closest friends and prayer supporters] and Caring Bridge…will be less frequent at this time, with the exception of specific prayer needs.

The week prior to our family holiday, Carson was teaching a course called "Aging Matters" at Regent with his friend of more than 30 years, who uses the phrase "passing through" instead of "dying." We like this because it accurately describes our faith in what is eventually about to happen. Our Christian faith assures us that death is the experience of transition (a passing through) to a far better place where there is no pain, no crying, no cancer and no death. The fact that Jesus has gone before and taken the lead in facing death straight on is our inspiration and hope.

My friend yesterday called me a "warrior teacher," as some feel that I am courageous in teaching how to do this well…not my words. :)

Thanks again for your love and support throughout this journey.

"Fear not, I [Jesus] am the first and the last, and the living one. I died, and behold I am alive forevermore." (Revelation 1:17–18 ESV)

DAY 587—DWELLER ON THE THRESHOLD
By Carson Pue—August 11, 2015

This is Carson writing now to share that Brenda has taken a downward turn physically the last few days. She is incredibly peaceful and continues to teach us all how to do this well.

I wrote this brief update on my blog, and we will share more of the blessing of these days when we can. Presently our family just needs this time together with her. I know you will understand.

Blog: carsonpue.net

When the doctor told me it would be good to gather the family, my knees began to wobble. While I have had more than a year and a half to absorb my Brenda's living with cancer, this brought a solemn view of time for me.

My father before his death used the phrase "dweller on the threshold" to describe his understanding of where he stood—between this world and heaven.

This aural poetry from Northern Ireland is a vivid image of end-of-life days. Brenda is there now, standing on that threshold with the door open awaiting her to step across at the appointed time. Knowing how much my dad loved her, he will likely be fighting to be right behind Jesus, greeting her entry into heaven.

Our family is all together now in one big sleepover. The love, prayers and care are beyond description. It is Brenda's desire that she be able to die at home, and our doctor and incredible medical team are helping make that wish reality. Shifts between all our sons and daughters ensure that Mom is never alone. There is nothing left to be said—just love to be felt, actually felt. It is an amazing privilege.

There is only One who numbers our days, and that is the Lord. Brenda knows this and has taught us this by exceeding all of the medical predictions and giving us so many new memories to cherish. Memories we will collect even today, and they will never diminish.

More reflections, and more of the story, will follow, but presently we want to be left alone to savour the hours—remembering this actually is how we should live life every day.

DAY 588
By Kristin Pue—August 12, 2015

Shortly after 12:30 this morning, Mom "slipped into heaven" to be in the arms of Jesus. [On Brenda's last boat cruise with Carson and life friends David and Alison, she shared with a smile that she would like to just slip into heaven.]

She was peacefully surrounded by Carson, her sons and her daughters. We know we are covered in prayer and thank you all for your support. We know Mom now has no more pain, no more disease. She is fully whole in the arms of her Saviour.

The Celebration of Life for Brenda will be on August 22nd at 1:30 p.m. Pacific Time, and we invite everyone to join us for the testimony of a life well lived. The service may be viewed online worldwide, because that is how far and wide Mom's impact has been.

Christian Life Assembly will host the service, and there is plenty of parking and the audiovisual capability.

Even in the last 24 hours we have been amazed at seeing the impact Mom had on so many lives. She walked this road with grace, and we're grateful for the shared journey.

Kristin, on behalf of the entire family

(A link to Brenda's Celebration of Life can be found at www.carsonpue.net.)

BRENDA'S PASSING THROUGH
By Carson Pue—August 12, 2015 2:43 a.m.

Just after midnight this morning, surrounded by love from her entire family, Brenda answered the call and slipped into heaven. Our loving warrior teacher has gone ahead of us, and we look forward to joining her in glory one day.

The celebration of her life will be held August 22nd, 1:30 p.m., at "CLA" Christian Life Assembly, 21277 56 Ave. Langley. All are welcome (typical of Brenda).

Come be inspired by the life of an amazing leader in life, family and faith. You will leave a better person as a result.

AUGUST 15TH—THE OBITUARY
By Bob Kuhn and David Bentall

PUE, Brenda Susan—Aug. 29, 1955 – Aug. 12, 2015.

A spunky, fun-loving leader of leaders, Brenda Susan Pue made a lasting impact through her work with Arrow Leadership, where she mentored and encouraged leaders from around the world to "Lead More Like Jesus."

On August 12, Brenda passed over the threshold peacefully while at home. She was 59 years of age. Surrounded by her loving family, and after courageously living with cancer for 588 days, she quietly "slipped into heaven."

Throughout her life, and especially as she faced cancer, Brenda was a woman of courage and faith. Writing authentically about her journey, she impacted many readers who followed her blog (www.caringbridge.org/visit/brendapue). A charismatic woman, Brenda was known for her contagious laughter and winsome smile. Just being around this remarkable Vancouver resident made God seem closer at hand and easier to know and trust.

She will be lovingly remembered by Carson, her husband of 38 years; their three boys, Jason (Kristin Paterson), Jeremy (Shari Boileau), Jonathan (Kirstie White) as well as their five beloved grandchildren, Landon, Liam, Mac, Ellie and Georgia.

The immediate family is profoundly grateful for all the love and support they have enjoyed over the past 20 months from Brenda's mom, siblings, friends, and medical professionals.

Come join an inspiring Celebration of Life and Hope that will be held on Saturday, August 22, 2015 at 1:30 p.m. at Christian Life Assembly, 21277 56 Ave, Langley. In lieu of flowers, donations will be gratefully received for two of the ministries about which Brenda was most passionate: Arrow Leadership and Barnabas Family Ministries.

Brenda Pue—too well loved to ever be forgotten.

(Published in *Vancouver Sun* and/or *The Province* from Aug. 15 to Aug. 16, 2015.)

So thanks for reading and loving my dear wife,
Carson

VIDEO LINK
By Kristin Pue—August 16, 2015

If you cannot attend the Celebration of Life in person on Saturday, we will have the video link available by 5 p.m. PST on Saturday, August 22. Please feel free to share this.

https://carsonpue.net/brenda-pue/brenda-pue-celebration-of-life/

Photo credit: Tania Di Meglio, RedHanded Photography

EPILOGUE

TONIGHT MY MOM DIED
By Jon Pue—August 12, 2015 10:24 p.m.

Tonight my mom died.

We were getting ready for the evening, about to take turns by Mom's bedside throughout the night. Jer and I were going to have a glass of wine but then opted for something a bit stronger. We poured our glasses as Kristin came downstairs and said that Kirstie was crying. There had been a lot of tears over these last couple of days, but somehow I knew that this was different. We all gathered quickly around Mom to be with her. Her breathing was different, struggling more so than before.

The doctor had joined us and assured us that she didn't feel any pain as we watched her breathe. Each breath was full of anticipation and wonder; *Is this the last breath?* Minutes turned into hours and the hours felt like moments suspended in time.

We cried. We laughed at memories. But mostly we waited and were not sure what to do. My family and I were just content to be present. Everything had been said; love from each of us was well known to her. We held her hand, her arm, stroked her head in comfort—for ourselves and for her. Her breaths were shallow, and short, and the space long in between. The small breaths lingered like watching a bubble slowly climb into the air until it eventually burst.

On what was her last breath, the doctor listened for a heartbeat, searching and waiting for any sign. But there was nothing to be heard, and he turned to us and said, "She's passed."

For all the days I had to get ready, nothing really prepares you for that moment. She was gone. And in an instant, in one moment, she moved from a living and breathing saint to someone who dwells not just in heaven but also in all of us. She remains now in our memories, in our minds and actions, and in pictures that hang suspended from the walls.

Grief and sorrow take over. A sudden realization that life is no longer the same. Everything is altered. I said goodbye with a kiss on the forehead, which was unexpectedly cold for someone whose love was so warm.

Already, as a family, we had leaned on each other greatly. Now, more so than ever. What's ahead? Conversations that come far too early with precious nieces and nephews, and for me the fear of now trying to live without an anchor that has grounded me for years. Seems overwhelming…and it is.

I take comfort in knowing that Mom died exactly how she would have wanted to—at home peacefully, with loved ones close at hand.

It still seems so surreal, like having a bad dream and waiting to be scared awake to reality.

Already, I long for Mom to know my sons and daughters. That they could know the woman she was. I wish she could love them and guide them through this life as she did with me. I rue the times when I will go to call her while I drive, simply to see how her day was, just as I have done for years. I must tell myself that I did the best I could with the time that was given to us. And to not fall into guilt over how I used my time. Did I work too much? Should I have called or visited one more time? Rather, I can trust that she knows the deep and unrelenting love I have for her. The moments we have had will never be replaced and never lost.

I thought I was ready. But I was not.

Today marks the beginning of learning how to live again.

MOM IN THE NEIGHBOURHOOD

By Kristin Pue—August 18, 2015 9:01 p.m.

Since Mom "slipped into heaven" the days have felt so long…and the roller coaster of emotions, so overwhelming. Mom had prepared so well. She took time to plan the details of her Celebration of Life and Hope Service. There were details for the family, gifts for people she loved. She left us lists, all sorts of lists, and every day as I look through them, they make me smile.

Photo credit: Tania Di Meglio, RedHanded Photography

One of the first things we found was her "communication plan." On this plan she had written who she wanted us to let know of her passing, and the memorial details. So Kirstie and I printed some pictures of Mom with her Celebration of Life details and headed out one afternoon to fulfill her wish. As well as the neighbours around Mom and Dad's house, the list started with Porters, her favourite coffee shop. Then the dry cleaners she went to and the Subway next door, owned by a high school classmate of Jeremy's. It seemed a bit strange doing this, but it soon became very clear to us what an impact Mom had on the people around her, in every area of her life.

Just before we had left the house the home nurse came by to pick up supplies and told Dad how she loved getting to know Mom and that nurses in her office had been reading her Caring Bridge entries and want to attend the service if they can.

At the dry cleaners, the owner started crying and hugging us, saying how sorry she was and how much she loved Mom. At Subway, the owner was brought to tears. He thanked us for coming in and letting him know and told us that he'd be at the service without a doubt. I can't say that the guy at our Subway would know who I am, but I am definitely inspired to live my everyday life a bit differently.

Kirstie and I got back to the car and just sat there for a minute. Kirstie then said, "So many people loved Mom. She even touched the lives of these people who only knew a small part of her. And we get to be a part of her family!"

Mom was the first person I went to for advice on raising my boys…she had so much wisdom to share. I will always be thankful for the times she allowed me to call in tears and how she'd help me walk through any situation with grace. She taught me so much, and I pray that I can raise my boys to be godly men as she did hers.

THOSE LAST DAYS

By Kirstie Pue

I had the incredible honour of caring for Mom in the last week of her life. As a nurse, it was the only thing I had to offer to her as a gift, to fulfill her wish to die at home, and it was the greatest privilege of my life. Yet, even now, it seems so small in comparison to all of the gifts she gave me in the five years I've been a part of her family.

That last week was hard for everyone. Realizing how quickly everything had changed was a huge shock, but we were yet again blessed with extra time with Mom. Her strength still astounds us all. In those last days we all had individual time with her—time I think we will all hold on to dearly because of the real moments of connection with her. Moments we never thought we would have again when we first gathered as a family around her bed. But Mom continued to amaze us by opening her eyes, smiling and even speaking small sentences to us. The five days passed both too quickly and so slowly at the same time. Those days all blend together now.

The most amazing thing I witnessed during that last week, however, was the love between Carson and Brenda. Their tenderness toward one another was beautiful. How Dad would do anything for her, assisting me in caring for her in a way that no one else could. Helping me change and wash her; lifting her gently to reposition her on the bed; putting her favourite lip chap on so her lips wouldn't dry out (even though he went too far down her lips, making Mom wave him off). The way he whispered in her ear in her final moments, selflessly encouraging her to go meet her Lord, was both amazing and heartbreaking. I can only begin to imagine how hard that must have been, to let go of your life's great love. It was so beautiful, the way he served her until her final breath.

Even in those last days, Mom served Dad too, giving him gifts better than presents. Gifts like opening her eyes when we didn't think she would again. Doing things for him that were better than an "Oh wow," which she gave to others when she woke up and recognized them, but not to him. The gifts she gave him were things that seemed so simple, like pulling Dad in by his shirt so he was closer to her. The way she would spend so much of her precious energy just to reach up and touch his cheek. How she would turn her head to lean in and kiss him, and then how Mom spent an entire day's worth of her energy moving over to Dad's side of the bed because, after 39 years, her side just wasn't close enough to him anymore. She loved him so deeply.

Mom served Dad by giving him the moments of confidence that allowed him to let go. Being able to witness those intimate moments meant everything to me. It was just another gift that Mom gave me, sharing glimpses of their love with me, showing how even in the final moments, love is more than enough. I learned so much about marriage in those days, that it is about carrying each other to the finish, even if just one of you crosses the line. Theirs was, theirs is, a great love.

Love is what Mom emanated. It's been more evident to me than ever since she passed. She shone in every room she entered, and she brought people into that light by loving each person. The fact that people who, to most of us, may seem insignificant in the grand scheme of our lives cried when they heard of her passing speaks to how Mom touched their lives. It demonstrates how important people were to her and how much love was a part of her life. I learned so much about godly love from Mom. I learned that love cannot be confined to just a marriage or a friendship, but it is meant to be given equally to every relationship that we enter. She has inspired and challenged me to love differently.

MOM STILL GOT TO BE A GRAMMY IN HER LAST DAYS
By Shari Pue

I first met Mom, or Mrs. Pue as I called her back then, when I was in grade 10. I remember noticing then how forgiving, sweet and welcoming she was. I know about the forgiving part because I had an accident, bumping into her car. <Big smile>

Mom invested in me spiritually. She had a few teenage girls over to her home weekly and created a safe place for us to share and pray with each other. Her love and her faith are so significant to me. Just having an older adult who was not my parent listening to me and giving me her undivided attention modeled something I want to be.

I then had the privilege of working alongside "Mrs. Pue" at Arrow Leadership so had the chance to observe her at work long before becoming engaged to Jeremy. As soon as we got engaged I immediately started calling her Mom; it just seemed so right. Mom was always inclusive. She always made me feel like I was a part of her life, and later her family. These traits remained until her very last breath.

Mom got all her daughters through our marrying her sons, so she loved spending time with us doing girly things like shopping and having coffee or tea times. I so miss those times, just Mom, her beloved granddaughter Ellie and I. Mom would encourage me, saying things like "You are such a good mom."

Photo credit: Tania Di Meglio, RedHanded Photography

Mom had an encouraging presence. It was hard to come away from hanging out with Mom and not be happy. She always had her ways of making me feel better about what was going on. I appreciate her never-ending faith in me; she never doubted my abilities to be something or do something with God at the centre.

Watching Mom and Dad also taught me a lot about marriage. It's hard to pick out individual things, as their whole marriage is one to strive for. Not many people are still that in love with each other after 39 years and genuinely that happy together. I think I learned that all the hard work is worth it.

I also learned much about parenting from Mom, hearing her stories about raising "Pue boys" and watching how Mom continued to interact with her sons, treating them all as unique, special individuals—Mom's characteristics I want to emulate with my kids.

With Mac, she just got him! I loved to see them snuggling up together. Mom realized that he has a different temperament, and "Grammy" was often just what he needed in the middle of the chaos that is often our family gatherings. LOL. She never said no when the kids wanted to play. With Ellie they would have teatimes and go for walks, and she was always quick to hold them and assure them of her love.

It was after Mom's cancer diagnosis when I found out Jeremy and I were going to have our third child. I could hardly wait to tell Mom I was pregnant with her fifth grandchild, knowing that it would bring real joy in the midst of her prognosis. At the same time, I began praying earnestly that God would give Mom the days needed so she could meet this new baby.

God answered that prayer, and we had no idea how special it would be. I'd invited Mom into the delivery room with me for the birth of Marielle, and I really wanted her there, along with my mom, Kristin, Kirstie, Jer and me, for the birth of Georgia.

It all worked out so well. There will never be another moment in life that's more significant, special and amazing than meeting your child for the first time, and to think that Mom actually saw Georgia before I did is very special. The picture on Day 497 says it all.

Well, during Mom's last days, all of us moved into Mom and Dad's house. We wanted to be together with Mom and Dad and to also support each other. At this time Mom was unable to talk and it would take all her energy to do the slightest thing. So imagine our surprise when Mom started trying to "skootch" over on her bed (a term Mom loved to use). Kirstie as the nurse asked if she was in pain or wanted to roll on her side. Mom shook her head back and forth, indicating that wasn't it. We were puzzled.

"Where are you trying to move, Mom?"

She tilted her head up and said, "Georgia!"

Amidst my tears, I clarified that she wanted me to bring Georgia. Mom tried to smile and nodded, so I ran and brought Georgia and laid her beside Mom. There was a special bond between those two. Grammy gently touched Georgia and studied her face carefully.

The sacredness of this moment did not pass me by. Mom was present for Georgia's birth, and now here was Georgia, present for Grammy's rebirth. It almost seemed like they were communicating through this. There was a special connectedness.

Having Georgia there with Mom in her last few hours was very special for me. It will also be special for Georgia in time, although her memories of Grammy will be from stories and photos. But Georgia will have one of the best stories because we will never forget Mom specifically asking for her. She wanted Georgia to lie with her.

Georgia brought joy to Mom in those moments, and Mom still got to be Grammy even on her last day.

"IT WAS THE BEST OF TIMES, IT WAS THE WORST OF TIMES..."

By Jason Pue

This famous opening of Charles Dickens' *A Tale of Two Cities* has been at the forefront of my mind lately. There is something that connects with me about the tension between two extreme opposites, the best and the worst, coexisting in one moment or in one situation. Not only do "the best of times and the worst of times" coexist, they seem strengthened through their equality. For me, this tension of equally matched opposites has defined the past two years as my mom graciously led me through her journey with cancer.

Photo credit: Tania Di Meglio, RedHanded Photography

No single person made a deeper impact in my life than my mom. Mom had a way of getting through to me and often didn't even need to say a word to do it. Mom had a way about her; she could look you in the eye and in that one glance bless you with love and acceptance. Other times she would engage in conversation that somehow always ended up with me floating away into the clouds affirmed, encouraged, challenged and loved.

One such conversation happened when Mom first sat down with us to tell us that she had been diagnosed with cancer. I could tell that she was scared. However, it was always hard to tell what exactly she was scared about, the cancer itself or the pain she was potentially going to cause her family. I realized in that moment that it was my turn to give back to Mom a small portion of what she had given me throughout my lifetime. Unsure of whether or not I was up to the task, I put my arms around Mom, held her and whispered, "Don't be scared; you can do this." Much to my surprise, Mom perked up, looked me in the eyes and confidently said, "I know I can. Everything I have gone through in my life has led up to this moment. God has equipped me with everything I need to do this. The Lord promises that He will not give us more than we can handle." You see, right from the very first moment of my mom's cancer journey I could tell that she was confident that God would draw near to her, walk hand in hand with her and at times carry her when needed. For me, this was the beginning of Mom's incredible journey. It started with her following her heart, which was entwined with God's, and not her mind, which was scared.

What a gift it was to journey through this with my mom. Despite all the pain and hardship, she found a way to love me, care for me, encourage me and teach me. One moment that stands out for me came on our family trip to Pender Harbour just one month before she crossed the threshold into heaven. Dinner was being prepared, and I was asked to drive down to the grocery store to pick up a few ingredients. I found myself slightly agitated, as I had already been to the store once for this very purpose. However, on this trip Mom asked if she could join me. We drove down to the store and grabbed what we needed, and then Mom asked if I could take her to get a treat from the café. Of course I agreed, and as I went to get back in the car Mom said, "Let's walk up there!" This made no practical sense, but I went along. As we walked Mom grabbed my hand, and we walked hand in hand. Despite our walk already seeming impractical, we decided to take the long way up to the store.

I could sense that this was a special moment with the woman who had raised me. We didn't say much but rather just enjoyed being connected and together. I knew that I would never forget this walk and tried to savour every moment. It was the best of times. Just weeks later as Mom was in her final moments here on earth I struggled to find many words but managed to spend most of the time sitting beside her holding her hand, just as we had on our walk. I tried my best to communicate how much I loved her, but the words I could muster up paled in comparison to the connection of holding her hand one last time.

I was holding her hand as she took her last breath. It was hard to let go. Normally, this moment would forever be remembered as one of the worst times of my life. However, what a gift it was that as I held her hand that one last time it wasn't her lifeless grip that I felt but rather the hand that had held me so tightly and swung through the air with so much life just weeks before. It was the best of times; it was the worst of times.

Looking back, I could never have asked for a better model of how to face life's toughest challenges than Mom. I learned so much watching her journey with grace and joy. Don't get me wrong; it wasn't without pain and sorrow, but what was remarkable was Mom's ability to create so many moments that felt like the best of times when really her journey with cancer could have just settled for being the worst of times. What a gift it has been and still is to struggle with the tension of the best and worst of this life. Mom, you set the bar high yet graciously gave us the secrets to true happiness.

A LETTER TO MOM
By Jeremy Pue

Dearest Mom,
It was days ago that you went to be with our Jesus. I know that you are more alive now than you ever were here on earth, and the thought brings joy to me in knowing that you have no more pain or suffering. You are with our King, and everyone knows that was the desire of your heart.

Adjusting to life since you passed through hasn't been easy—not that I expected it to be. There are many great and significant things about you that many people miss.

You were an amazing leader and mentor. Your influence has spread to hundreds of leaders across the globe. You played a part in these leaders becoming stronger. You pointed to Jesus so chains could be broken in their lives. Churches are better for it, their marriages are better for it, and the Kingdom of God is better for it. God used you in such a massive way here while you let Him lead you the whole way.

You had a way of making everyone you encountered feel loved. This was evident everywhere you went as you were greeted with smiles and hugs—from the dry cleaners to the grocery store. In little conversations you were so invested in people's lives and truly cared for their well-being. All of these people miss you.

Photo credit: Tania Di Meglio, RedHanded Photography

I love these things about you. A son could not be more proud.

Life is not the same. Of the many large and significant things that people miss about having you here, I personally find the little things the hardest. It's these little things that bring tears to my eyes and make my heart ache with longing to talk to you, hug you and kiss your forehead.

Like how you would phone me just to hear about my day and get updates on Shari and the kids. I was always greeted with a "Hi, sweetie!" in your loving voice. We would chat about our day, and you would encourage me as a man of God, husband and father. It seems you always knew what to say…

Like the way we would laugh together. Discussing *The Far Side*, reciting stand-up comedy routines and making up fictional real-life scenarios that only a select few would find funny.

Like the way I would pop in to see you if I was ever driving past the house for work. You would ask me to sing worship songs to you, and you would sit with your eyes closed and your head back in your chair. These were moments I will treasure for the rest of my days.

I love you, Mom. Every day is filled with these little things that break my heart for selfish reasons. Some days I just want you to be back with us all. Some days I want my phone to ring just so we can catch up and I can hear your voice. Some days I long to laugh with you.

But now you are in the presence of Jesus. As much as I miss you, He has been longing to bring you home because of His love for you—which is greater than anyone can imagine.

Thank you for teaching me about that love and pointing me to Jesus. One day we will be together in His Kingdom. Until that day comes, I find peace in these words from Psalm 84: "For a day in your courts is better than a thousand elsewhere" (Psalm 84:10 ESV).

I love you, Mom. I miss you every day.

Jeremy